K.I.S.S.

DK

Th... s
Yo... !

THIS SERIES I ... stages and situat ... f life's care for your ne ... or connoisseur or a ... ne pick up a K.I.S.S ... ust

Expert authors w ... finish, using simp ... to step at a time. Bu ... one of the book, you'l ... nd with the topic but ... ar pick up where yo...

The K.I.S.S. Guid ... to all the information you'll need on one subject. Other titles you might want to check out include: Caring for Your Horse, Dreams, Digital Photography, and many more to come.

K·I·S·S

GUIDE TO

Planning a Wedding

STEPHANIE PEDERSEN

Foreword by Mama Gena
Author of *Mama Gena's School of Womanly Arts*

DK Publishing

LONDON, NEW YORK,
MUNICH, MELBOURNE, DELHI

DK Publishing, Inc.
Project Editor Anja Schmidt
Project Director Sharon Lucas
Publisher Chuck Lang

Dorling Kindersley Limited
Project Editor Angela Wilkes
Project Art Editor Kelly Meyer

Managing Editor Julie Oughton
Managing Art Editor Heather McCarry

Production Sarah Coltman
Category Publisher Jackie Douglas

Produced for Dorling Kindersley by

studio cactus

13 SOUTHGATE STREET WINCHESTER HAMPSHIRE SO23 9DZ

Project Editors Kate Hayward, Aaron Brown
Project Art Editor Sharon Rudd
Design Assistance Laura Watson

First American Edition, 2004
02 03 04 05 10 9 8 7 6 5 4 3 2 1

Published in the United States by DK Publishing, Inc.
375 Hudson Street, New York, NY 10014

Library of Congress Cataloging-in-Publication data

Pedersen, Stephanie
KISS guide to planning a wedding / Stephanie Pedersen.
p. cm.
Includes index.
ISBN 0-7894-9695-X (alk. paper)
1. Weddings - Planning. I. Title: Guide to Planning a wedding. II. Title.
HQ745.P375 2004
395.2'2--dc21

2003057281

Color reproduction by Colourscan, Singapore
Printed and bound by MOHN Media and Mohndruck GmbH, Germany

Discover more at

www.dk.com

Contents at a Glance

Part One

Creating Your Wedding

First Things First: Engagement 13
Envisaging Your Dream Wedding 29
Creating a Budget 53

Part Two

Looking Good on the Day

Deciding What to Wear: The Bride 67
Deciding What to Wear: The Groom 87
Outfitting the Wedding Party 103

Part Three

Getting Organized

Invitation Basics 117
Giving and Receiving Gifts 129
Eat, Drink, and Be Married 139
Setting the Stage 163
A Picture's Worth a Thousand Words 173
Sweet Melodies 183
Coming and Going in Style 193

Part Four

You're Nearly There!

Official Details 203
Pre-wedding Soirees 215
Pre-wedding Freakouts 227

Part Five

Your Wedding Day

The Actual Ceremony 239
Party Time: The Reception 247
We're Married! Now What? 257

Appendices

Glossary 274
Appendices 278
Index 282
Acknowledgments 288

Foreword

AHHH, WOMEN. We work hard, we serve, we plan meetings, we exercise, we network, we make deals, we take care of our families, we nourish, we nurture, we get the job done. We rock, basically.

And then there is this marvelous, ancient tradition, called a wedding, where we are celebrated, not for our hard work, but for our innate ability to attract a great guy and inspire him to ask us to marry him. Weddings are a piece of poetry, a fragrant flower, which bind us to a part of ourselves that, perhaps, we don't celebrate or honor enough in our daily lives.

Darlings, your wedding is your day to lavish yourself with the attention, the celebration, and the honor that you, as a woman, deserve, for just being you. This is your day to have it your way, to treat yourself as the Goddess that you are, in honor of the woman you have become, and the woman you are growing into.

Mama wants you to take advantage of every juicy drop of research that Sister Goddess Stephanie has done in writing the K.I.S.S. Guide to Planning A Wedding. *Think of this book as a menu, designed to stimulate your appetite, your desires, your pleasure, so that you can create a wedding day that truly gratifies you. Choose exactly the experience that will make you feel the most gorgeous and loved. Why? The most fun, memorable, joyous weddings are the ones where the bride has everything she wants.*

Why? When the bride is happy, everyone is happy. Her groom is proud, her family is thrilled, and his family is dazzled by their new daughter-in-law. Having your way on your wedding day is the most generous thing you can do for everyone.

So use K.I.S.S. Guide to Planning a Wedding *as a way to explore every nook and cranny of what's pleasurable for you on this special day. It is your obligation to your husband-to-be, and your guests, to make sure you receive this pleasure. In fact you might even say that it is your obligation, as a bride, to serve your joy and happiness to the people you love, guaranteeing the pleasure of everyone around you. Not only today, but every day.*

Perhaps that is what the ancient tradition of a wedding day is all about. A wedding is a reminder to celebrate our beauty, our womanhood, and our capacity to receive and give love. And with this very special book as your guide, you will be able to create a dream-come-true experience – not only for yourself, but also for everyone you love!

MAMA GENA

AUTHOR OF *MAMA GENA'S SCHOOL OF WOMANLY ARTS*

Introduction

CONGRATULATIONS – YOU'RE ENGAGED! As you've probably already discovered, being engaged is hard work. You've got a wedding to plan, legal details to attend to, a honeymoon to arrange. Sounds daunting, doesn't it? Fortunately, getting married can be great fun if you follow your desires. Your wedding day will be one of the most special days of your life, and it's important that it is the day you want it to be. After all, the most entertaining and memorable weddings are usually the most personal occasions.

Planning a wedding offers a terrific opportunity to weave in treasured cultural traditions, revisit a beloved locale, decorate with your favorite colors, flowers, and themes, wear gorgeous clothes, enjoy luscious foods and music, and welcome friends and family members. In short, a wedding is a fabulous opportunity to have fun! Yet all too often a wedding becomes a power struggle between "shoulds" and "wants." Your mother demands you wear white; you want to wear red. Your father-in-law wants to invite all his business associates and 20 of his old college buddies; you'd like an intimate ceremony. Your grandparents want a traditional church ceremony; you want to write your own vows and get hitched at midnight in your friend's penthouse. Or perhaps you've read some ideas in a bridal magazine suggesting you do x, y, and z when all you've ever longed to do was a, b, and c. It can be a frustrating business, getting married.

The K.I.S.S. Guide to Planning a Wedding *helps you weed through the "shoulds" and incorporate the "wants," so you can have the nuptials of your dreams. Whether it's a picnic ceremony atop a daisy-covered hill, a traditional church wedding, a low-key elopement, or something else entirely, this book shows you how to create a wedding that is as unique as your love. It doesn't matter if this is your first marriage or your fifth, whether your engagement is long or you want to get married next week, or if your budget is tiny or unlimited – the* K.I.S.S. Guide to Planning a Wedding *offers practical, how-to advice on every aspect of getting married, starting with your engagement and then covering every other matrimonial topic.*

You'll learn the ins and outs of announcements, invitations, parties, and presents. I'll explain the importance of having a wedding timeline. I'll also reveal why it is essential that both the bride and groom be involved in planning, how to settle on a date and venue, how to create a guest list, find a caterer, choose attendants, hire a photographer, and more. I'll also teach you how to avoid financial debt before and after you are married. In short, I'll ensure you plan for the wedding of your dreams. Heaven forbid you should suddenly change your mind about marrying, but the K.I.S.S. Guide to Planning a Wedding *also addresses pre-ceremony jitters and how to handle an unexpected case of "cold feet."*

There's no denying that looking fabulous can add to the enjoyment of your fun day. To help you and your partner look your best, the K.I.S.S. Guide to Planning a Wedding *offers grooming timelines designed to get both bride and groom looking picture perfect. Also included is information on finding professional beauty help, how to coordinate dress, hair, and makeup, and the importance of packing bride's and groom's kit for quick touchups. For further guidance, you'll find numerous wedding resources, from must-read books to must-visit websites. It's my hope that by the time you've finished reading the* K.I.S.S. Guide to Planning a Wedding, *you'll not only have a strong idea of what kind of wedding it is that you'd like, but you'll also have the know-how to create that wedding. Ready to marry? Relax and enjoy the book.*

Happy nuptials.

Stephanie Pedersen

STEPHANIE PEDERSEN
NEW YORK CITY

What's Inside?

THE INFORMATION in the K.I.S.S. Guide to Planning a Wedding *is arranged so that you will learn how to announce your marriage, plan a wedding you'll love, pay for the occasion, create a memorable honeymoon, and more.*

Part One

You're engaged. Part One addresses what you need to do next depending on your personality, budget, and desires. Learn how to announce your upcoming wedding, choose rings and attendants, draw up a guest list, and decide when, where, and how you want to get married. Equally important is budgeting, which we'll also investigate.

Part Two

Who doesn't want to look amazing on his or her big day? Part Two ensures you'll shine by helping you choose wedding-day attire that works for you and reflects your personality. There's also advice – along with some practical timelines – for getting your body, hair, skin, and more in shape, ready for your walk down the aisle.

Part Three

Getting everything done is the theme for Part Three. I'll go through item-by-item those small but necessary chores that must be addressed to make your wedding and reception run smoothly. I'll talk about the meal, the cake, the music, the photography, the transportation, and more, as well as assisting in finding efficient people to help you.

Part Four

As you'll learn in Part Four, the weeks before a wedding boast a flurry of activity. There are numerous pre-nuptial details to tend to, including the marriage license, financial paperwork, pre-marital counseling, gift registry, various pre-wedding parties and rehearsal dinners, as well as the dreaded family feuds and prospect of "cold feet."

Part Five

By the time you reach Part Five all your planning will have paid off – your wedding day awaits! I'll take you through some example ceremony scenarios so you'll know just what to expect from your own wedding. Plus, we'll put the final touches on your honeymoon plans and learn how it will feel to begin your new lives as a married couple.

The Extras

THROUGHOUT THE BOOK you'll notice a number of boxes and symbols. They emphasize the information provided, giving you valuable insights into the world of wedding planning, while guiding you through the sometimes difficult process of putting it all together. You'll find:

Very Important Point

Some information you simply must know. If a topic deserves special attention, I'll alert you.

Complete No-No

This warning alerts you to practices or ideas that can cause you harm, discomfort, embarrassment, expense, or needless work.

Getting Technical

Wedding planning can get technical. When it does, I'll let you know so that you can read and understand more carefully.

Inside Scoop

Throughout the years I've picked up a whole host of insider wedding tips. I share them with you here.

You'll also find some little boxes that include information I think is important, useful, or just plain fun:

Trivia...

These are entertaining, thought-provoking facts that will provide you with in-depth knowledge of weddings and wedding culture.

DEFINITION

Here, I'll **define** *words and terms for you in easy-to-understand language. You'll also find a glossary at the back of the book with wedding-related lingo.*

INTERNET

www.dk.com

The internet is a fantastic place to research anything you can think of related to engagement, weddings, and marriage. I've included some of my favorite websites.

PART ONE

Creating Your Wedding

YOU'RE PLANNING A WEDDING! As you'll discover, getting married is one of the most exciting things you'll ever do. It's also one of the most detail-oriented: There are people to contact, papers to sign, help to hire, dates to choose, parties to attend, family members to mollify, rings and gowns to buy, food and flowers to decide on, and so very much more. How do you get it all done?

Chapter 1
First Things First: Engagement

Chapter 2
Envisaging Your Dream Wedding

Chapter 3
Creating a Budget

Chapter 1

First Things First: Engagement

In early Rome, engagement began the moment a woman accepted a ring, which acted as an unbreakable legal agreement. In China, betrothal was so binding that if an engaged man died before his wedding, his fiancée was treated as his widow. These days engagement provides time both to get emotionally ready for marriage and for planning the nuptial festivities. It's a heady time, when you and your new fiancé publicly acknowledge your intentions toward each other. You'll have to choose engagement and wedding rings, start to plan the wedding day itself, and deal with all the typical engagement stresses – from putting together a wedding guest list to dealing with difficult relatives. For more on the modern engagement, turn the page.

In this chapter...

- ✓ You're engaged
- ✓ Choosing a wedding ring
- ✓ Engagement stresses

You're engaged

PERHAPS YOU'VE BEEN ENGAGED for a while, or maybe the proposal occurred just an hour ago – either way, I bet you're feeling excited. I know I was. Although I've been married for more than 10 years, I remember that giddy mixture of joy, anticipation, and wonder that I felt during my engagement.

INTERNET

www.bestwedding sites.com

Think of this as one-stop-surfing: This site features contests and special deals, as well as advice on everything from inviting children to your wedding to staying organized. It also includes links to dozens of other wedding sites.

Yes, there was also a dose of nervousness and some terror, too – normal feelings when you consider what an enormous commitment marriage is. What I hope you're not feeling – at least not too heavily – is stress. True, you have a lot to do during your engagement, but planning a wedding can be enjoyable. Really! Let me prove it to you.

How long an engagement?

The fabulous thing about engagements is they can be as long or as short as you want. Their purpose in modern weddings is twofold: To give you time to prepare the wedding, honeymoon, and other marriage details, and to encourage you and your fiancé to enjoy your growing closeness.

Don't let outside parties dictate the length of your engagement. Regardless of whether you want a month-long engagement or you feel happier with something closer to two years, the decision is up to you and your future spouse.

■ **After the initial** *excitement of getting engaged, everyone will be asking you when the wedding date is set for.*

Weighing up the pros and cons

Certain cultural groups and families prefer engagements of certain lengths. For instance, in my mother's family, engagements are always short – anywhere from five days to three months. The family saying is, "The longer the ***betrothal***, the shorter the marriage."

DEFINITION

Betrothal *is an old-fashioned word for engagement. Taken from a Middle English word, it first came into use in the 14th century. It means, literally, to be true or loyal.*

My husband, on the other hand, comes from a family that prefers two- to four-year engagements; shorter betrothals are for those who "have to get married." The weddings in his family are enormous, elaborate, and very expensive – obviously it makes sense to spend a few years both planning and saving money for these galas. Other proponents of long engagements believe that rushing into marriage is reckless. Time gives you a chance to be sure of your decision and work through any relationship problems before adding the stress of marriage.

Trivia...

Though most people know what fiancé and fiancée mean, few know the words are taken from the French fiancer, *which means to trust.*

As far as I am aware, there hasn't been a study comparing engagement lengths with marriage lengths; but it doesn't matter how long you've known your partner, the first year of marriage is notoriously challenging. There is a theory that a "newer" couple is still enjoying the initial "honeymoon" phase of their relationship, which propels the duo through that difficult first year.

Making a decision

So how do you decide on the length of your engagement? Examine your needs. Are you an older couple who is anxious to start a family? Do you want to get married before one of you gets sent overseas for a job? Do either or both of you believe in waiting until marriage to have sex? A shorter engagement may be for you. On the other hand, would you like your wedding to coincide with a special future event? Are you eager to finish school before settling down? Would you like a little more "me time" before making a final commitment to someone? A longer engagement could be your best choice. And if you've got visions of an elaborate wedding, you'll need plenty of engagement time to pull the event together.

You'll need more engagement time if you're rigid in your desires, such as insisting that the ceremony be held in a particular place or performed by a specific officiant.

As for my husband and I, we came close to getting married a month after becoming engaged. But because we'd gotten engaged within only a couple of weeks of meeting, we decided that a four-and-a-half month engagement would suit us and give us time to be sure of our decision.

Engagement rings

At one time, men commonly presented an engagement ring to their beloved when they proposed. Today, it's more common for a man to propose, then take his betrothed to a jewelry store so that she can pick out her own ring. As romantic as it is to be surprised with a ring, allowing the bride to choose her own ring is more practical – she's got to live with it, after all.

Don't compare the price of your ring or the size of its stone to the depth of your fiancé's love. Not only is it crass and unattractive, it's unfair to your partner – who may be unable to afford that flashy 1.5 carat diamond you want, or may rather spend the money on something necessary, such as a home.

So let's address you ladies who will be choosing your own ring – or who will be steering your beloveds as they shop for a ring with which to surprise you. In the last few decades, diamond engagement rings have become so popular that many people don't realize there are other lovely choices available.

Different stones

Your engagement ring can be anything you want it to be. At one point in history, birth stones were the most popular choice for rings. Semi-precious stones, polished rock and glass, and various metals have also been widely used. Wood, shells, and other "found materials" are also used.

Use your imagination and find something that expresses your personality to its fullest. If you have your heart set on a diamond, be sure to learn everything you can about these gems and find a reputable dealer. There are several books and websites out there with terrific information to help you make a sound purchase. I've listed some of these in the appendices.

INTERNET

www.diamond review.com

This information-only site features in-depth research to help you find a reputable jeweler, choose a flattering and practical ring, and more.

You may hear people talk about the four "Cs" when referring to a diamond's quality. These stand for carat, clarity, color, and cut.

Remember that *you'll be wearing the ring every day. Some rings with protruding stones can catch on clothing – you may find these types are not for you.*

Why do I need an engagement ring?

Engagement rings are a hot topic among the soon-to-be engaged – and even among those who hope to eventually become engaged. Usually, the talk leans less toward whether or not to wear one than toward what size diamond the groom-to-be purchased for his beloved.

It may be hard to believe as you ogle a colleague's new ring, but there are a number of women who opt against wearing an engagement ring. If you don't want to wear a ring, the earnest advice in wedding magazines and on websites won't make you feel very secure about your decision – but don't feel pushed into having a ring if you don't want one. Many women simply aren't fond of jewelry. Others don't like the fact that some early cultures used engagement rings as a sign of subservience.

Trivia...

The first recorded diamond engagement ring was given by King Maximilian I of Germany to Mary of Burgundy in 1477.

Don't feel freakish if you're faced with other women's reactions at your ringless finger. Engagement rings are optional and going ringless is a very valid personal choice.

Then there are brides who are bothered that engagement rings are typically something a woman wears but not a man. "Why should I be visibly marked as unavailable while my fiancé is not?" said a friend of her refusal to wear an engagement ring.

It's your choice

If you love the idea of a pretty ring to mark your betrothal, that's terrific. If you are someone who isn't excited by engagement rings, that's terrific also. While many ladies choose to go ringless, a number decide to purchase engagement rings for their fiancés, allowing both partners to celebrate the engagement with special jewelry. This can be the perfect solution to a ring dilemma.

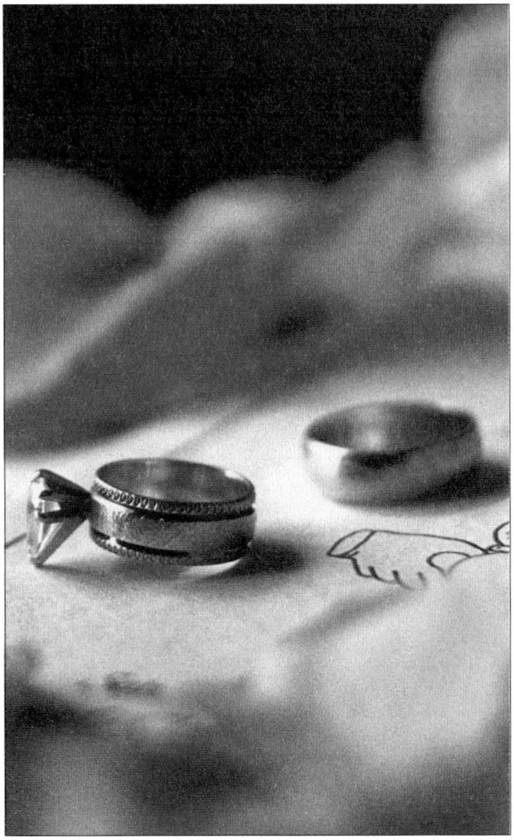

■ **The choice of** *engagement rings is huge – when you're choosing one, make sure you pick one that will complement your wedding ring, too.*

Engagement rings for men

There is a growing trend for men to wear an engagement ring. In my own circle of friends, two couples wore his-and-her engagement rings. Furthermore, when my husband proposed, he slipped a simple ring on to a chain and placed it around my neck, and then he donned a ring-accented chain himself. I was charmed by this simple gesture. "It signifies that you're engaged and I'm engaged – to each other," he said later, admitting that he'd "whipped up the ritual as a way to bring a more spiritual touch to the engagement." Spirituality aside, each time I saw the ring hanging around his neck it sent a shiver of happiness through me.

Trivia...

Approximately 60 percent of North American women are involved in choosing their engagement ring, while three percent actually pick it themselves. Furthermore, 74 percent of all brides receive (whether chosen by them or their fiancé) a diamond engagement ring.

Let's say you'd like to surprise your partner with an engagement ring but don't know the circumference of his or her finger. Ask your jeweler about buying a ring on the large size. Once your partner has the ring, he or she can have it sized down to fit.

If you and your fiancé both want to wear an engagement ring, you might like to opt for his-and-her rings. Perhaps you'll surprise your groom-to-be with a surprise engagement ring, just as he presented you with one when he asked you to marry him. If you want your fiancé to wear a ring but you're not sure of his thoughts on the matter, talk to him about the practice. If you sow the seed of a thought, there's a good chance he may decide to purchase one himself.

■ **When you go** *browsing for a ring, check out all the different jewelry stores to see the range on offer. Don't rush into any purchases. The ring you choose will be with you for the rest of your life.*

Choosing a wedding ring

FOR SOME COUPLES wedding rings are the most important element of a wedding. My husband and I spent weeks wandering through Manhattan, lingering at jewelry store windows. Too tacky we'd say, inspecting a shop's wares. Too formal. Too boring. Too this. Too that. Finally, we hit upon a small workshop that created handcrafted bands. We found exactly what we were looking for: A single design that not only complemented our respective personalities and hands, but one that could be customized. My husband ordered a band made of white gold and I took the same band in gold. We had each other's initials and our wedding date engraved inside the bands. My point is, choose a ring you love, because it will become a part of you.

What to look for

You may have an exact idea of the ring you want. If so, all you need is someone who can give it to you. Or, you may have no clue as to what you'd like. If so, shop around until you find a ring you love so much that you can't imagine anyone but you wearing it. In other words, a design you love should be the first thing you look for in a wedding ring.

Synthetic Moissanite diamonds look so much like diamonds that, using standard thermal conduction tests, jewelers cannot detect that they are fake. Fortunately, an experienced jeweler can detect one of these phonies by looking at it through a 10x loupe.

INTERNET

www.bridaltips.com

In addition to all sorts of general wedding information, you'll find a terrifically detailed primer on buying engagement and wedding rings. Included are common jewelers' scams and a diamond dealer's database featuring a list of rings (along with their prices) and jewelers.

A FAMILY HEIRLOOM

In some families it is common for a ring to be passed on from generation to generation. If you have – or are given by your fiancé – such a ring and you love the way it looks, lucky you.

Even if you own an heirloom ring but are unsure about a few of its design elements, consider yourself fortunate: A jeweler may be able to rework the ring into something you adore.

Good quality and a fair price are also important factors to consider. Unless you're a jeweler, these can be hard qualities to ascertain. Before you begin shopping, educate yourself by reading books on jewelry, searching websites for information, and asking friends for their tips and advice.

His-and-her wedding rings

I love the idea of his-and-her wedding rings. Clearly I'm not alone – this is among the fastest-growing wedding trend today. Matching rings – or rings that, if not identical, clearly resemble each other – are best for partners who have similar tastes. Yes, each person's ring can be tweaked to make it more to his or her liking – for example, one partner may want his band thicker, the other partner may want the band thinner so it will sit prettily with her engagement ring.

Trivia...

The tradition of wearing the wedding ring on the fourth finger of the left hand began with the ancient Egyptians, who believed a vein ran from there directly to the heart.

Consider having the inside of your rings engraved with your wedding date, your partner's name, a favorite saying, or anything else that celebrates your relationship and makes your rings unique to you.

Nearly all jewelry stores *carry versions of his-and-her rings – in similar styles but with subtle differences, such as one in yellow gold, and one in white or rose gold.*

A design of your own

You've searched for weeks or months and still can't find the perfect wedding ring. Don't lose hope: You can always have a ring made for you. Most urban centers and some moderately sized towns have jewelry makers.

Wear your engagement ring on your right hand during your vows. After the wedding band has been placed on your left hand, move your engagement ring to sit above it.

If you're looking for a reputable jewelry designer, do some research online or visit a bridal boutique and question the store manager to find out if he or she has any recommendations to offer you.

Placing a ring *on your partner's finger is a symbolic part of your wedding ceremony.*

FINGER FLATTERY

It's important to choose a ring that suits the shape of your finger. Here is some general advice to help you choose a ring style:

- Long, bony fingers: A large, thick band with a fairly prominent stone or stones will flatter your hand.
- Large hands with long fingers: Lucky you. You can wear larger, flashier rings, and rings with prominent settings.
- An active lifestyle: Pronged settings that sit above the ring are bad choices for anyone who works with his or her hands. The stone can snag on clothing and hair, as well as scratch hard surfaces.
- Short fingers: Avoid pronged settings in favor of a medium-sized ring with a stone that remains flat against the hand.
- Delicate fingers that are either thin or small: A thin band with a small, delicate setting will complement your hand best.

Engagement stresses

I HAVE A CONFESSION TO MAKE: My engagement was as near to stress-free as you can get. My fiancé and I agreed upon almost everything, including the notion that he should tend to an equal share of the wedding details. If I have one desire for your engagement, dear reader, it's that your betrothal is as calm as mine was. Read on and I'll share my methods.

Ladies – don't plan the wedding by yourself

Why do so many women feel wedding planning is their responsibility? There are two people getting married: Shouldn't both partners play an equal role in creating the wedding of their dreams? The argument I've heard from several brides-to-be is that men don't care about weddings, that the ceremony is really for the woman and her family, that men would rather be sitting in the nearest pub watching the World Cup.

Humans are more apt to attend to chores – wedding planning included – when the tasks are enjoyable. When I was engaged, my fiancé and I visited our favorite Chinese restaurant or rode on the Staten Island Ferry to talk about our wedding plans and come up with ideas.

■ **Planning your wedding** *should be enjoyable, rather than stressful. Instead of talking about wedding plans at every spare moment, set relaxing time aside to share your ideas for a dream wedding – and make sure you listen to your partner's views, as well as expressing your own wishes.*

The reason men seem indifferent to weddings is that events are often planned entirely without them. Wouldn't you be bored at an affair that you'd had minimal say in putting together? Your fiancé loves you. You are more fun when you are happy and calm, so he wants to help you stay stress-free. He also wants to have a say in the manner in which he marries you.

If you're in the early stages of your betrothal, you probably haven't yet decided on the type of wedding or honeymoon you want. Start with a list of what you must do at this point of your engagement.

THINGS TO DO:
Write out a guest list and discuss with family
Visit some possible wedding locations
Buy wedding magazines, to get some ideas for reception decorations
Find out about marriage license
Think about possible wedding attendants
Go shopping with girlfriends to get some ideas about possible wedding dress styles

Help yourself, your relationship, and your groom by making a list of every single thing that needs to get done, then splitting the list down the middle. He gets half and you get half – fair is fair.

■ **Carry your list** *of things to do around with you, so you can add ideas as they occur to you.*

Gentlemen – make sure you have your say

Your married friends warned you, your engaged friends warned you, even your dad warned you, and now you're seeing it first-hand: Propose to a woman, and she turns into a bossy, stressed-out, control freak. Don't be too hard on your fiancée. Planning a wedding is tough. There is an endless parade of details, unwanted suggestions from both sets of parents, and the difficulty in juggling her engagement duties while maintaining a career and enjoying time with her favorite person – you.

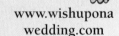

INTERNET

www.wishupona wedding.com

Like many wedding sites, this one offers planning advice, but what makes it special are the articles on staying sane and getting grooms involved.

Keeping your fiancée calm, happy, and healthy is the first reason to take over half the planning duties. Giving yourself a say in the festivities – no pink tuxedos or karaoke, definitely an open bar, and a Caribbean honeymoon – is the second, and perhaps more important, reason to get involved. You must know guys who let their partners do all the wedding work, then afterward whined about how the wedding turned out. Don't be one of those guys. Give yourself a strong voice in your own nuptials and then you'll enjoy them all the more.

After making your "to do" list, let each partner choose the tasks they're most excited about attending to – there's nothing like personal enthusiasm to spur someone into action. Divide the remaining "unclaimed" chores evenly between you.

Dealing with pushy relatives

When my new fiancé and I called my parents about our engagement, they said congratulations, asked for the date, offered to send us a check, and then told us they'd see us at the wedding. After the horror stories I'd heard from married women about their own parents, this happy exchange wasn't what I expected. Frankly, I was waiting for a bit of drama and a whole lot of unwanted advice. And I got it from my husband's family. Thank goodness I did, because it made me an uncertified expert on these matters.

Each person you talk to, and this includes professional counselors, will give you a different recommendation for dealing with aggressive familial meddling. Here's mine: Stand up for what you want. Most of the people advising you have had their big days – this wedding is yours. You want it to be everything you dreamed of. Furthermore, if you don't stay firm on your wedding plans, you send a message that you will tolerate interference. After the wedding, the advice will turn to your housekeeping, your relationship, your career, your children if you choose to have any, and so on.

Don't fret over small details. No one will care if your napkins and tablecloths don't exactly match. What is important is the wedding itself and the people who've come to share it with you.

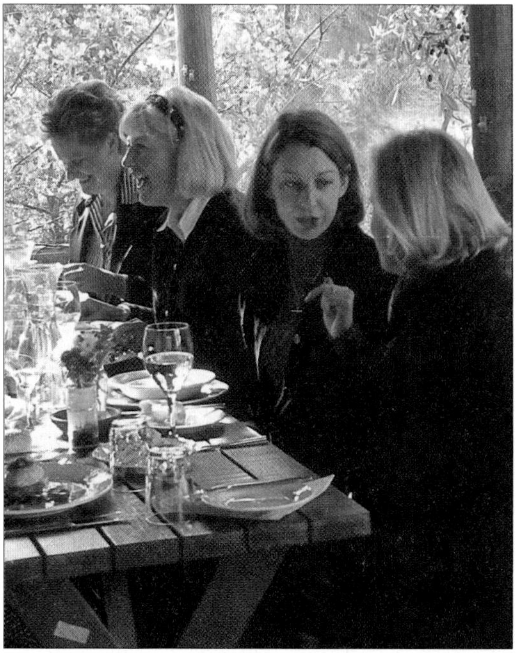

■ **Discussing wedding plans** *with your family can be helpful. Talk through your plans over a family lunch – but don't let wedding chat dominate the day.*

Sound harsh? Well, it's the only foolproof remedy for pushy relatives. Don't think you can tell your mother-in-law that you will not marry at the local church? Say it to her nicely. There is always a pleasant way to refuse someone's unwanted "help." An easy solution some couples adopt is for each partner to deal with his or her own family.

Let your family feel involved

Standing your ground is admittedly easier for couples who are paying for their own weddings. What if your parents or grandparents are contributing – or paying for the entire event? One solution is to assign them areas where their help would be appreciated.

Trivia...

In the UK in 2000 the average bride was 24 years old, the average groom 28.

For instance, perhaps you and your partner care nothing about decorations or seating arrangements or what type of cake you have. Tell your helpful relative how flummoxed you are by the decorating (or seating or cake) issue, and let it become the person's area of expertise. I have a wise friend who had parents, grandparents, and in-laws working on different areas: each "expert" proudly did his or her absolute best, easing the bride's workload and helping to ensure a gorgeous, smooth-running wedding.

Should we get expert help?

Could a ***wedding planner*** be the secret to making your big day run smoothly? It's true that people have been getting married for centuries without professional assistance, but planning a wedding was perhaps easier a few centuries ago. The couple's family did most of the work, and most brides-to-be weren't juggling wedding plans and careers in the way many women are today.

DEFINITION

A **wedding planner** *specializes in engagement, wedding, and honeymoon help. He or she may also be referred to as a wedding consultant, coordinator, advisor, or bridal consultant.*

INTERNET

www.weddingdove.com

This fun-filled site is both entertaining and informative. It contains almost everything imaginable about weddings, from engagement trivia to honeymoon help.

If your wedding is small or easily planned, you won't need a consultant. I didn't use one. Yet, turning over a portion or the entire wedding to a wedding planner makes sense if you want a large or elaborate wedding, your engagement is too short to provide adequate planning time, you and your partner have high-pressure careers that don't leave time for attending to nuptial details, or you simply want professional assistance.

■ **Relatives who are** *keen to help you prepare for your wedding can be "assigned" various tasks, thus making them feel part of the occasion while relieving you of any unwanted pressure.*

CAN I AFFORD A WEDDING CONSULTANT?

Love the idea of retaining a professional helper, but worried about the cost? Paying a consultant may be easier than you think:

- Find a wedding consultant who offers free initial consultations. Most do.
- Some wedding consultants charge 10 to 20 percent of the entire wedding cost, depending on how much coordinating they do. Others charge an hourly rate, still others prefer a flat fee. And there are some who use a combination of these methods. All are acceptable.
- If your wedding planner charges a percentage of the wedding cost, make an effort to lower wedding costs where you can. This will save you wedding day dollars as well as consultant fee dollars.
- If your consultant charges by the hour, firm up your list of wants and don't-wants before sitting down with him or her.
- Do some math before meeting with your consultant so you know what you can afford. Often he or she will find a way to give you what you want for a price you can afford. If you can't afford their services for the entire wedding, you can always hire them to coordinate specific parts of the wedding – such as entertainment, food and beverage, location, decoration, or clean-up.
- In addition to suggesting money-saving alternatives, many consultants get discounts from various wedding suppliers.

■ **Looking through** *magazines and books will give you ideas for your wedding ceremony and reception. Your consultant will then be able to advise you on costs and suggest ways to keep your expenditure down.*

Employing a wedding planner

Unlike helpful friends or family members, wedding planners coordinate weddings for a living. The advantage of this is that they know exactly which vendors are the least expensive, the most honest, the most professional, and the most likely to be available on the dates you need them.

Anyone can call themselves a bridal consultant. Look for someone associated with a professional association, such as the International Institute of Weddings or the Association of Bridal Consultants. And always ask for references!

And unlike a mother or mother-in-law, a conscientious wedding planner does not impose her taste or opinions onto your wedding. Instead, she listens to what you want and goes about making your wants reality. And if you are not really clear about what you want? Just talking through ideas will help you start to form some concrete plans of your own.

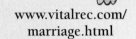

INTERNET

www.vitalrec.com/marriage.html

www.weddingdetails.com

www.usmarriagelaws.com

Wondering about marriage licenses? These three sites tell you what you need to know about marriage licenses throughout the United States.

A simple summary

- ✓ Use your engagement period constructively – make sure the planning stage is fun.
- ✓ Don't want to wear an engagement ring? Then don't.
- ✓ The best wedding ring is a ring you love.
- ✓ Brides, you must invite your groom to share planning details.
- ✓ Grooms, it's your wedding, too! Get involved in creating your day.
- ✓ Be firm yet kind with bossy, meddling relatives.
- ✓ Involve your family by giving them specific areas of your wedding to take care of.
- ✓ Reduce your stress by using a wedding planner.

Chapter 2

Envisaging Your Dream Wedding

SOME PEOPLE KNOW exactly what they want their wedding to be like – they've been envisaging it since childhood. Others have a hazy view of what their big day will be like. Still others are completely clueless. Wherever you fall in the spectrum, you'll have plenty of work to do to create the wedding you desire. But, as you'll see, the work is fun. Trying different ways to blend each partner's religious beliefs, cultural traditions, and general preferences, can be a lively lesson in teamwork and diplomacy – skills that will serve you throughout your marriage.

In this chapter...

- ✓ **A personal event**
- ✓ **Selecting a date and time**
- ✓ **The guest list**
- ✓ **Choosing attendants**

A personal event

THE VERY BEST, and the most fun, weddings are not the prim, expensive, tradition-obsessed affairs that indulge some bridal expert's fantasy. The best weddings are the ones loaded with personality – specifically, the personalities of the people getting married.

■ **Your wedding** *should express both partners' personalities and their love for each other.*

Think back to all the weddings you've attended and remember which of them were enjoyable and which were tedious: The beach-front ceremony where guests took off their shoes and stood in the gently lapping waves; the New Year's Eve cocktail party where five of the couple's favorite bands performed; the summer meadow where guests ate picnic lunches and drank champagne while the children played tag. These are the weddings that are happily remembered – by the guests as well as by the bride and groom.

INTERNET

www.wedding gazette.com

www.wedding kingdom.com

Two sites with a wide range of information designed to help you personalize your wedding day.

Finding your wedding officiant

You've decided how you want to personalize your wedding – whether it is by getting hitched in a botanical garden, being serenaded by a choir, or having ballerinas dance at the reception – now you have to find an officiant. Finding someone to marry you is easy if you belong to a congregation of some sort: Simply have the minister, priest, rabbi or other religious official oversee your wedding. People who are not religious – at least not in the sense of an organized religion – may have more trouble finding someone to do the job. You should ask your friends and local wedding vendors, visit several wedding websites (most have lists of local vendors), check out the available civil officials in your town, or see if there are any available Unitarian ministers. Going through the phone book is another way to look for an officiant, but only if you've no other options.

Civil ceremonies

A civil ceremony is one without religious overtones, performed by some type of civil officiant, such as a city hall official, a mayor, justice of the peace, notary public, ship captain, or other qualified person. Marrying can be as simple as going to city hall and having someone there marry you and your partner after you've received your marriage license. But it could also mean inviting your town's mayor to your aunt's mansion to perform the ceremony in front of 200 of your favorite people.

THEME WEDDINGS

Organizing your wedding according to a special theme – whether it happens to be romantic or downright crazy – is a great way to add some fun to your wedding. Here are a few ideas from people who have married in thematic style:

- "I got married at the beach under a canopy decorated with sea grass and shells. My dress was silvery and form-fitting and made me look like a mermaid; instead of a regular headpiece, I had a jewelry designer friend make me a headband of small shells."
- "We're both first generation Americans from Scottish-born parents. To celebrate our heritage, we had a traditional Scottish wedding, bagpipes, and a buffet of traditional highland foods."
- "We had a *Star Trek* theme wedding in Las Vegas. It wasn't traditional at all – and some might say it was kind of tacky – but it sure was fun!"
- "My wife and I both teach medieval studies at local universities, so we have a lot of interest in this time period. It seemed perfect to try to recreate a medieval European wedding, which we did. We chose a refurbished stone cellar for a location, hung large tapestries about, lit lots of candles, and hired a harpist and some lute players."

A theme wedding *can help to make your day especially memorable and good fun.*

Ethnic elements, cultural details

We all belong, somehow or another, to an ethnic group. But unless you and your partner have a shared ethnic background, you'll have to pick and choose which of the different cultural elements to weave into your wedding celebration. How you do this is completely up to you.

Don't get frazzled by the differences in your family's wedding traditions and those of your partner's family. Melding cultures should be a fun way to celebrate each, rather than a source of tension. Use the traditions that work; ignore the rest.

Let's say you are of Eastern European extraction and your partner is the son of Greek immigrants. Since rosemary has special wedding significance in the Czech Republic, Hungary, and surrounding countries, you might wish to feature the herb as part of your wedding ceremony decoration. At the reception, you could incorporate the traditional Greek wedding dance. An African-American bride may want to incorporate broom jumping (a marriage ritual created by the first Africans in America) in her wedding, while her Bermudan husband may insist upon having a very small sapling as a wedding-cake topper – to be planted after the reception in his parents' yard.

Religious overtones

Once upon a time, the religion you were born into was the religion you married within. Among certain pious groups, such as Hasidic Jews, Muslims, the Amish, devout Mormons, to name a few, this still applies. However, most modern couples are not willing to give up their true love just because their partner is of a different religion. Nor are these folk willing to convert to their partner's faith.

INTERNET

www.beliefnet.com

This great site has loads of information on the wedding ceremonies of different faiths, as well as practical ways to incorporate elements of two faiths into one wedding. It also has helpful links to sites that can assist you further.

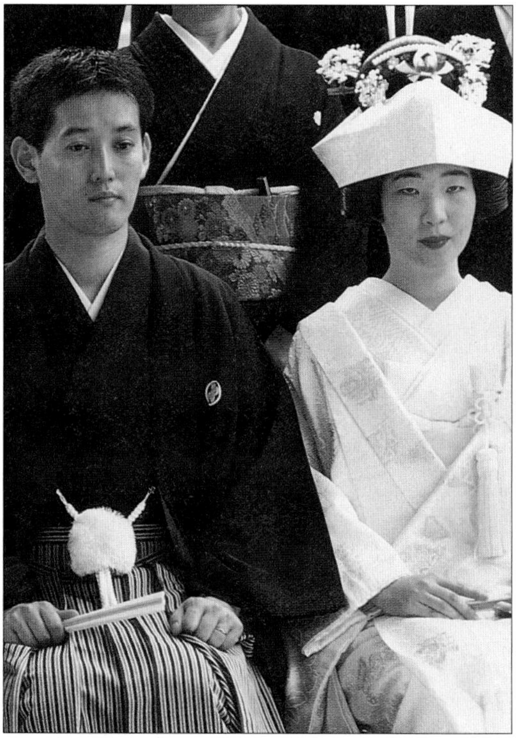

■ **Every culture** *has its own wedding traditions – relating to dress, ceremony, and celebrations. These can all add to the significance of your day.*

Enter the interfaith wedding. Blending traditional religious elements from both partners' religions, these ceremonies are often held in a location that is religiously neutral, such as a country club, a park, or a private house.

If you choose to go the interfaith route, each partner should approach his or her religious leader about possible marriage requirements. For example, many catholic priests won't co-officiate at a ceremony unless both partners attend the church's traditional marriage counseling sessions.

This is to allow these weddings to be co-officiated by a member of each partner's clergy when neither cleric is willing to perform the ceremony in a house of worship that is not their own.

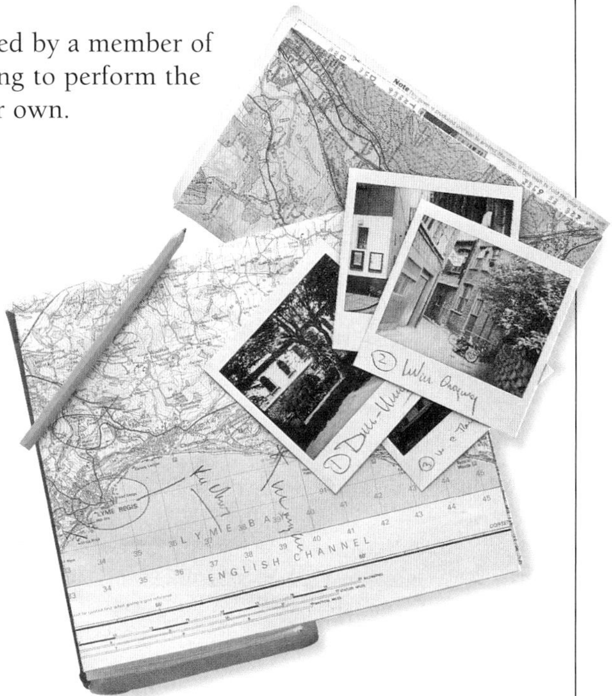

About eloping

If you're like I was, you may be seriously considering eloping. It certainly seems simpler than dealing with budgets, guest lists, timelines, and all the other issues you must slog through to create your fabulous day. Yes, eloping is easy. Just grab your honey and find yourself someone to marry the two of you. Bringing along a friend or two for support is strictly optional. So are a nice outfit, reception decorations, a caterer, and all those other extras you might be questioning at this stage in your nuptial planning.

Eloping does require a smidgen of advance planning. Check with the area where you'd like to marry to find out about obtaining a license and to confirm any other legal requirements.

■ **If you're planning** *an elopement, you could think about tying the knot overseas. Make sure you do your research.*

There's no denying the sense of romance associated with eloping, but it can also be a practical choice if the bride and groom don't have many close friends or family, or if it is important – for whatever reason – to marry immediately, or if your family strongly objects to your partner (though you might want to investigate the disapproval), or if you just cannot take another day of wedding preparations. Elopement is a valid choice. But be aware that even the word "elopement" elicits strong reactions in people. Rationally, people know that your wedding is your own, but emotionally no one wants to feel left out – and many people do when a couple elopes.

Destination weddings

Many people mistakenly call destination weddings "elopement." True, there are similarities: Both are alternatives to a traditional wedding; both require the couple to accept whatever officiant is available; and both can be performed without the presence of anyone other than the couple and the person marrying them. However, there are differences, and it is these that make destination weddings so attractive.

Destination weddings offer a kind of package deal – wedding, reception, and honeymoon all rolled into one. They are so popular that specialty travel agents organize weddings in romantic locations such as Italy, the West Indies, California's wine country, Hawaii, and even on cruise ships. With so many specialists willing to help you, it's obvious that destination weddings are fancier than a simple elopement. They require more money and more advance planning, though not as much of either as a traditional wedding does. (It is possible to book a destination wedding for the following month and pay up to half as much as you would for a traditional wedding.) As a bonus, if you want to share your wedding with a few close friends and family members, they can travel with you, attend the ceremony, and then vacation alongside you afterward.

INTERNET

www-personal.umich.edu/~kzaruba/wedding.html

A great site for those who want something different. It provides information on elopement, destination, theme, alternative, small, and interfaith weddings, plus commitment ceremonies, same-sex ceremonies, and more.

A destination wedding *can lend an exotic or romantic atmosphere to your day. And there is the advantage that you do not need to spend time traveling to your honeymoon location, too.*

Selecting a date and time

THERE IS NO MAGIC TO CHOOSING a wedding date. At its simplest, you just select a date and aim to have all your planning done and money saved by that date. If there is a time of year or a specific day that is special to you, even better; your choice has just gotten easier.

I question couples who can't marry when they want simply because they can't have their first choice of venue for their chosen day or the groom's sister has a trip to Maui planned that week and couldn't the couple please move the wedding to another time? The bottom line is, if you have a date that means something to you, do what you have to do in order to make that date work.

But what if you do not have a time in mind? If there is a venue you like (even if it is so popular that it's booked two Januarys from now), you could schedule your wedding for the site's first availability. Or you could arrange your ceremony around family members' and friends' plans. If you will be having a number of out-of-town attendants, you could even date your ceremony to coincide with their vacations, allowing them to incorporate a short holiday into their wedding duties.

If you have your heart set on a specific venue, select two substitute dates in case your first choice is unavailable. Likewise, if you have a special date you want to marry on, have two alternative wedding venues in mind.

Decide on your *priorities and stick to them. Remember that you cannot always please everyone, so concentrate on pleasing yourself and your partner.*

SITE SPECIFICS

Deciding on where to have your wedding and reception can be a big dilemma. You have so many choices! Here's the lowdown on a number of popular options:

City hall

If you want to marry in a ceremony-free way, your town's city hall is a fast, inexpensive, easy choice. After filling out the paperwork for your marriage license, most city halls will, for a small fee, allow you to be married by one of the officials on hand.

Restaurant

Restaurants are natural choices for receptions, but they are also convenient places to wed, too. Choose one with a large, private room that you can reserve.

If you have an emotional attachment to the restaurant you've chosen as your venue, your wedding will feel even more special – and the staff will go out of their way to spoil you.

Country club or other private club

Private clubs can be great places to wed and have a reception. Furthermore, if you or a family member belongs to the club, you may be able to get a discount. Check to see if the club has kitchen facilities and whether or not you can bring in your own caterer.

A rented wedding hall

In some regions, there are large halls that serve one purpose – to provide a venue for weddings and receptions. The pros are that they offer all-inclusive service, from processional organ music to food, and they are often good value for money. The downside may be the "mass-market" feel of a wedding-hall celebration.

A private home or private property

Perhaps the easiest of the lower-cost alternatives, getting married in a private home or outdoor property is a terrific option for both the ceremony and the reception. You don't have to set your wedding date with the venue's availability in mind.

Houses of worship

Another easy wedding and reception option, especially if you choose a church, synagogue, mosque, or temple that you, your partner, or either set of parents belongs to. Some houses of worship have large common rooms, with kitchens, folding chairs, and tables. Some even have plates, glasses, and silverware you can rent.

Out of the ordinary locations, such as a hot-air balloon, a yacht, etc.

An unusual wedding site can be a fun and very memorable way to get married.

If you're going to get married in an unusual way, make sure you can find an officiant who is comfortable marrying you while in a hot-air balloon or running alongside you in a marathon, or jumping out of a plane with you, or whatever else it is you'd like to do.

Your easiest bet is to get married in the way you have chosen and then follow up with a reception in a restaurant, home, park, private club, or some other venue.

Public spaces, including parks and other open areas

If you're getting married in what you are positively sure is a dry season, a public outdoor area – such as a state park – can be a fun, easy, economical option. Check with park officials about a few things, such as getting a permit, the number of people the space can accommodate, and what kind of parking will be available.

Unusual weddings *are increasingly popular, and the locations ever more daring!*

Civil wedding venues *can still include gatherings of your family and friends.*

Creating a timeline

A wedding timeline is part calendar, part "to do" list, and it helps you plan the various aspects of your wedding. These popular lists – found in bridal magazines, most wedding books, and on almost every bridal site on the internet – are somewhat subjective, but helpful nonetheless. Here's my (also subjective) addition to the wedding list genre:

Nine months prior

- Announce your engagement. This can be done with formal mailed announcements, in a newspaper or website, verbally, or through an engagement party.
- Choose a wedding date.
- Create a budget.
- Decide what type of wedding and reception you'd like. And once you've decided that, secure the necessary site.
- Start looking around for friends who will be willing to help you, or engage a wedding consultant.
- Talk about what kind of honeymoon you'd like.

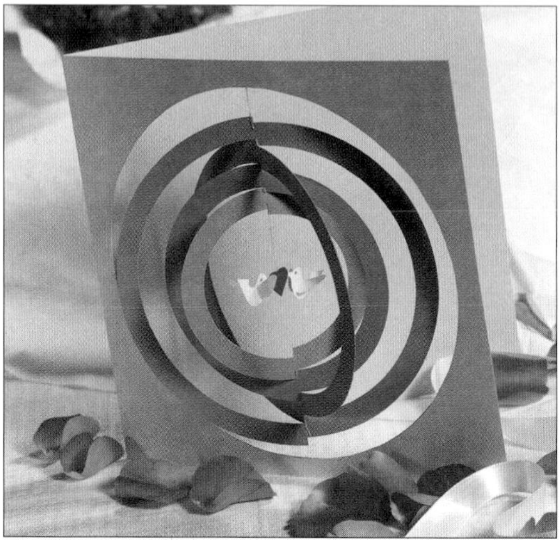

■ **The wedding invitation** *can help set the tone for the day – traditional, romantic, fun, or exotic.*

Eight months prior

- Begin searching for an officiant who complements both partners' personalities.
- Discuss attendants with your partner. Decide together who you'd like to do the honors and then contact these people.
- Get to work on your guest list.
- Start searching for wedding attire.
- If your reception site does not provide food, secure a caterer (preferably one recommended to you by family or friends).
- If you'd like a band or DJ, find one now.
- Think about how you'll be decorating your wedding and reception. Make a list of the elements you need, and go about securing what you can.
- If you'll be needing a florist, find one whose work you like. Think about the types of flowers you'd like and what will be in season. Note that if you're using wildflowers, herbs, spring blossoms, fall foliage, or winter greenery, you can get away with having an artsy friend or two to do the floral work.

Trivia...

The word trousseau literally means "bundle." It came to mean specifically the items of clothing (and sometimes also linen) that the bride, or her mother, traditionally collected or made in preparation for her marriage.

Six to eight months prior

- Decide on the design you would like for your wedding invitations and order them now.
- Purchase your wedding attire.
- Find someone to make your wedding cake – or wedding dessert, if you don't want a cake. This can be a professional wedding cake designer or a talented friend.
- Hire someone to photograph your wedding, and if you wish, another person to film your wedding.
- If you are using a **wedding registry**, sign up now.
- Remind attendants of their wedding duties.
- Decide on bridal attendants' dresses. Get attendants' measurements, or give necessary information to your attendants so they can order their own dresses.
- Decide on groomsmen's suits.
- Call out-of-town guests to remind them of your wedding date and to ask if they'll be needing lodging.
- Reserve a block of hotel rooms for out-of-town guests.
- Finalize your reception's food with the caterer or on-site food service team (or with whoever else is responsible for feeding your guests).

DEFINITION

A **wedding registry** *is a kind of wish list. It is lodged with a particular store and lists the items the bride and groom would like as presents from their guests.*

Five months prior

- Finalize honeymoon details and book the trip.
- If your caterer or an on-site staff member is not taking care of tables, chairs, and other necessary equipment, find a rental house to rent items from.
- If you don't want to spend your first married night at your home, choose a romantic venue and reserve the accommodations now.
- Book a rehearsal dinner site and decide on the menu.
- If you'd like to use a calligrapher to address your wedding invitations, find someone now.
- Pick up invitations and give them to a calligrapher if you are using one.

■ **Think about** *the kind of food you want at your wedding – it could be traditional or you may opt for a culinary theme, such as Mexican cuisine.*

Four months prior

- Mail out invitations.
- Brides: If it is important to you, decide on your bridal attendants' accessories. Make sure you give your attendants the necessary information so they can order the desired shoes, gloves, and so on.
- Grooms: Make final decisions on groomsmen's accessories, including shoes, vests, neckwear, cummerbunds, and so on. Give groomsmen the necessary information so they can order these items.
- Are there any specific ceremony decorations or elements that you need but haven't arranged for? Now is the time to do so.
- Buy your wedding rings.
- Find a graceful way to let attendants know your desired guests and preferences regarding a bridal shower, bachelorette party, and bachelor party. Make sure these last two are held well in advance of your ceremony to avoid having a bride or groom sick at the altar, or a relationship damaged by one of the night's potentially lascivious events.

Three months prior

- Finalize plans with all service providers, such as your caterer, florist, DJ or band, photographer, videographer, and so forth.
- Check to see your bridesmaids have received their dresses and accessories. Do the same with groomsmen and their attire.
- If there is someone you'd like to read a special poem, perform a musical number, or read a meaningful bit of verse, ask now.
- If you'd like your wedding bands engraved, send them out now so they'll be ready in good time.

Two months prior

- Brides: Begin your dress fittings. Purchase any special lingerie needed to wear under your gown.
- Arrange wedding-day transportation for you, the wedding party, and any out-of-town guests. If you'll be holding your wedding and reception in separate sites, make sure you take this into account.

Make sure you *have several dress fittings in the months before the wedding, so that adjustments can be made in good time before the big day.*

- Arrange parking for the wedding and reception.
- If you'll be writing your own vows – or altering existing vows – start now. This gives you time to look at your ideas with fresh eyes in a few weeks' time.
- If you want to see your wedding announcement in the newspaper, submit it now. Enclose a picture of you and your partner, if you'd like.
- If you'll be giving out wedding favors, order them now.
- Purchase a guest book and pen.

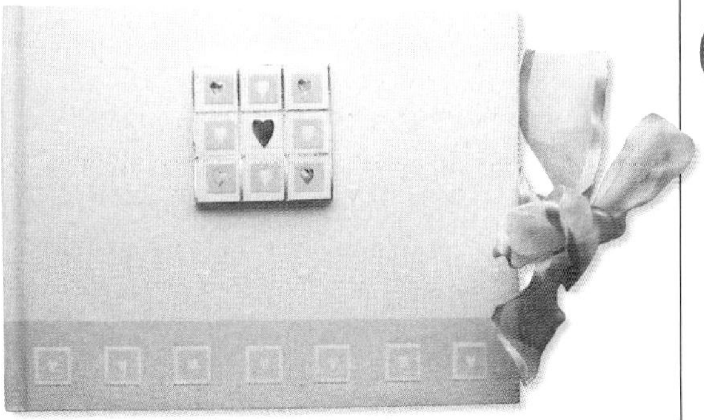

It is a nice touch *to have a guest book on display at your reception so guests can write their good wishes to you both.*

Six weeks prior

- Write thank-you notes for any gifts you received at the bridal shower.
- Bride and groom: If you'll be giving your attendants gifts, shop for them now.
- If you'll be using ceremony programs, have them printed now.
- Get the marriage license and blood test, if necessary.
- Send out your rehearsal dinner invitations.

It will help you maintain your sanity if you keep notes, reminding yourself of what you still have left to do. It's very satisfying when you start to tick things off your list, too.

Three weeks prior

- Touch base with all service providers.
- Give your band or DJ a list of songs you'd like played. If there are songs you feel are inappropriate – or that you find downright annoying – make a "Do Not Play" list.
- Confirm all hotel room reservations, including your own.
- Confirm your honeymoon plans and reservations.
- Check in with your officiant to go over any last-minute matters, or just to calm your nerves.
- If there are any traditional or cultural items you will be including in your ceremony, such as a blue garter or a unity candle, put them in a safe place.
- Contact anyone who hasn't replied to your invitation, so you have a final head count.
- If you'll be serving food at your reception, put together a seating plan. Make place cards yourself, ask a friend to make them for you, or have them made professionally.

Trivia...

The tradition of lighting a candle after exchanging vows began within Protestant churches, but it is now popular among brides and grooms of all faiths. Each partner is handed a lit taper by a member of their family, often their mother. The partners use the tapers to light one large candle, which symbolizes their two lives joining as one.

Two weeks prior

- Give your photographer a list of "must take" photographs.
- Prepare any thank-you toasts you'll be delivering to family and friends.
- Distribute wedding day directions, a schedule, and contact list to guests, attendants, and service providers.
- Contact the reception site's location manager to ensure all your service providers will have access.
- Call your officiant and remind him or her of your rehearsal and wedding day schedule.

Make sure you collect together *all the accessories that you want for your wedding in good time – and keep them in a safe place.*

One week prior

- Pack for your honeymoon.
- Put together an overnight case for your wedding night.
- Print out your honeymoon itinerary and give it to your parents, maid of honor, or someone else, in case there's an emergency.
- Put cash tips and final payments in specifically marked envelopes and give them to the best man – or whoever will be doing the honors – to distribute on your wedding day.
- Ask your maid of honor – or another responsible person – to collect the wedding gifts and wedding cash brought to the wedding.
- Brides: Check to see your gown fits and you have all the necessary accessories. Call attendants to make sure their gowns fit and they have all the necessary accessories.
- Grooms: Check to see your suit fits and you have all the necessary accessories. Call groomsmen to make sure their suits fit and they have all the necessary accessories.

The day before

- Bride and groom: Pull together all the necessary elements of your wedding day get-up.
- Rehearse the ceremony with your wedding party and officiant. (This can also be done up to a week beforehand.)
- Drop off guest book, pen, and favors at the reception site.
- Get some sleep!

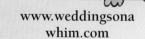

INTERNET

www.weddingsonawhim.com

Worth looking at if you've got just a short period in which to plan your wedding.

The wedding day

- Relax and enjoy your wedding!
- Make sure you spend a few moments with family members, as well as your partner. It's easy to overlook your loved ones during this busy time.

■ **Your wedding day** *will fly by in a blur – but make sure you spend a little time with close family members, so that they feel included in your day.*

When time to plan is limited

I have a soft spot for short engagements, so I am particularly sensitive to the fact that wedding magazines and other bridal-planning helpers are unequivocally biased toward yearlong – or years-long – engagements. I once complained to a cousin about this. "The wedding industry would go under if everyone had short engagements. The shorter the engagement, the less expensive the wedding," she said. It sounds cynical, I know, but I think there is some truth in her idea. Yet, I also think that wedding experts extol long engagements simply because they assume one of two things: Most people want as extravagant a wedding as they can possibly afford, thus needing extra planning and moneymaking time. Or, even those who don't want a lavish affair would at least like to plan their weddings at a less frenzied pace.

While I can't change all those wedding timelines that presume you'll be engaged for an extended time, I can offer some special suggestions to those of you who will be marrying shortly after getting engaged:

- Decide on a firm wedding date as soon as possible after the proposal.
- Start planning the day after you get engaged – this is especially important if you want a large, traditional-style wedding and reception. If possible, both partners should take a few vacation days off work to make phone calls, visit vendors, and do internet research. You may have to do in weeks what another couple would have months – or years – to do.
- Call everyone you know the day after your engagement to tell them your happy news – and to tell them your wedding date. You may not have time to send out traditional announcements.

- If you have your heart set on a traditional wedding, then why not consider using a friend's or family member's home for the ceremony and reception? This will save time in booking a space and it will also save on extra expense.
- Save time by asking for as many favors from friends as possible. Ask your photographer friend to snap wedding day pictures, your pastry school student neighbor to make your cake, your music-obsessed friend to organize the music to be played on a stereo, and so forth.
- Have someone else do the planning. Either hire a wedding consultant – preferably someone with experience in short engagements – or use an all-inclusive site that will do everything for you.
- Consider avoiding the big traditional wedding, and go for something more streamlined and more easily organized. The fewer elements you have to attend to, the less time you'll need to pull off a wedding.
- If you don't mind limiting your guests and attendants – or not having any guests present at all – consider a destination wedding at a site that will organize your ceremony, reception, and honeymoon.
- Consider eloping or getting married at your city hall, then celebrate by throwing a large reception barbecue, potluck, or cocktail party in a private home or private outdoor space.
- Many restaurants can quickly organize an on-location wedding followed by a fabulous reception – this might be the option for you.

INTERNET

www.world-wedding-traditions.net

A great site for those looking for inspiration. You'll find stories on themed weddings, as well as wedding traditions of various countries around the world.

Getting married – day or night

Most brides and grooms generally favor daytime ceremonies. In the United States the afternoon seems to be the most popular time of day for a wedding, while in the United Kingdom late morning is a favorite choice. Remember though that the time of day or night you choose to get married is a personal decision that says a lot about you and your partner.

If you get married in the afternoon, you can have a wedding reception that extends long into the evening.

As a general rule, whatever time is most popular in your area will be the hardest to book a venue for and the most expensive. For example, in the United States, wedding halls typically charge less for morning weddings than for afternoon weddings. If you're concerned with convenience, however, late morning to mid-afternoon is generally the easiest option for most guests. Early morning ceremonies can be hard to reach for people living outside the area, while evening affairs may end too late for other guests to travel home easily.

The guest list

FEW ELEMENTS CAUSE more nuptial stress than the guest list. Usually, the scenario goes something like this: You and your partner want a smallish wedding. Your parents, aware of the cost involved in putting on a wedding, agree…as long as most of the guest list is comprised of their friends and family members. Further, by the time they've given you every last name they want on that list, there is no room for any of your own friends.

Obviously, it is your wedding, so "your people" should hold priority over "your parents' people," but when it comes to guest lists it's easy to get irrational. Here we talk about guest lists in a rational way. You may want to read this section before speaking with your parents.

If you're trying to save money, having a small ceremony with a large reception probably won't help you much because the reception is the most costly part of getting married. In fact, the reception is often considerably more expensive than the honeymoon.

A small reception *for close friends and family can be intimate and charming in a way that is not so easy to achieve with larger affairs.*

Whittling the list

The easiest way to whittle your guest list is to remove everyone you haven't spoken to in a year. If it's still too large, take away anyone you haven't spoken to in three months. It doesn't matter if your college sorority sister invited you to her wedding 10 years ago. If you haven't spoken to her in two years, then she'll probably be just as relieved at not having to get herself to your wedding as you are at being able to eliminate one more name from your list. The same goes for your relatives, too. If you can't recall ever speaking to your mom's baby sister, or haven't heard from your cousin (even though you send him a Chanukah card every year) in a decade, then remove their names from your guest roster. Yes, it's ruthless, but you have to start somewhere.

After eliminating people with whom you are no longer in close contact, your list may still be large. This is when things get difficult. It may be easier if you can eliminate those who live abroad, or on the other side of the country, for whom traveling to your wedding will be difficult.

If you're feeling guilty about not inviting various cousins, second cousins, aunts, uncles, and other relatives, why not contact them and organize a family reunion? That way, you can keep your wedding small, while finding a time-honored way to bring relatives closer.

If you still need to whittle your roster further, scan the names for any "problem" people. In my own wedding, there were two: A friend of my husband's who couldn't have a glass of wine without getting out of control, and a bigoted family member. Because our wedding was so small, any type of anti-social behavior would have been disastrous, so we didn't invite these two.

Remaining firm

Traditionally, the bride's parents have paid the majority of the wedding expenses. Today, however, with more and more couples paying their own way, the rules have changed. You may need to gently remind your parents of this. Be firm if they insist you invite people they know whom you do not have personal relationships with – you'll only be resentful, especially if you haven't been able to invite someone who's special to you.

After determining what size you'd like your wedding to be, and the people in your life you'd like to include, draw up a preliminary guest list with those individuals in your parents' lives with whom you yourself have a relationship. You might want to present this to your parents as "the folks from their lives whom you'd like to invite." Remember: Your wedding should not be used by your parents as an opportunity to see a bunch of second cousins they were close to during their youth but whom you don't know. Nor should it be used to reciprocate for a parent's childhood pal's invitation to his daughter's wedding or to compliment a friend who always gives your mother extravagant Christmas gifts.

Trivia...

In many South American countries, such as Argentina and Chile, wedding rings are exchanged during the engagement. The wedding ceremony, which takes place without attendants, is strictly for exchanging vows.

The less help, financial or otherwise, you get from your family, the less entitled they'll feel to comment on your guest list.

An even easier solution is to draw up the guest list yourselves without anyone else's input and be done with it. Include, of course, a smattering of your favorite people from both your family and your groom's, as well as your important friends.

Choosing attendants

SURROUNDING YOURSELF with people you love on your wedding day is a wonderful tradition. In the not-so-distant past, the number of helpers you chose was dictated by fairly inflexible wedding etiquette: one female attendant and one male attendant for every 50 guests. Today, however, professional nuptial experts say a couple is free to have as many or as few attendants as they desire. A bride and groom can even go completely attendant-less, choosing to walk down the aisle alone and stand at the altar with only each other.

INTERNET

www.ourmarriage.com

A fun wedding site that offers helpful advice for couples planning their own weddings, as well as a few tasty wedding punch recipes.

Who does what

There are several types of attendant to choose from, each of whom has their special responsibilities, perks, and wedding uniform:

Your attendants

- **Maid of honor:** Also known as a matron of honor if she is married, this is the bride's right-hand-gal. She helps the bride plan the wedding, and supports her during the ceremony. She organizes the bridal shower and fulfills numerous wedding day responsibilities, including walking down the aisle behind the bride, holding the groom's ring on her thumb, toasting the couple, as well as collecting gift envelopes at the reception.
- **Best man**: The male equivalent to a maid of honor. He helps plan the bachelor party, making sure things don't go in a direction disrespectful of the bride.

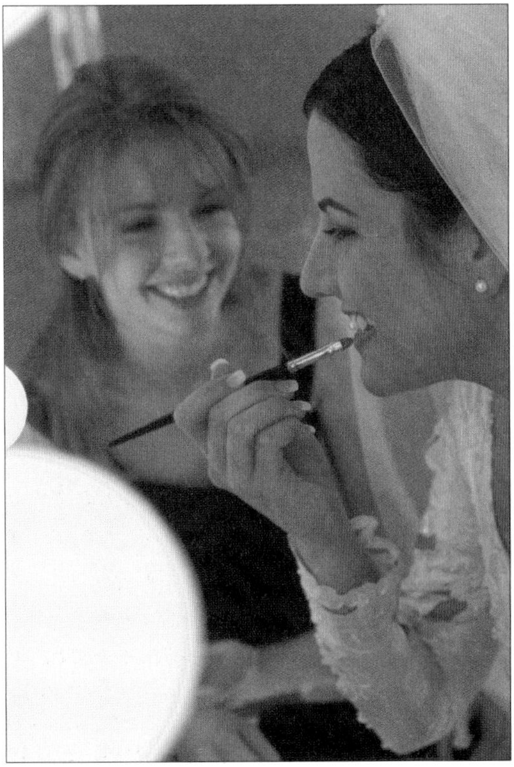

■ **Your maid of honor** *will play a particularly important role on your big day, from helping you get ready to calming your nerves before your vows.*

If there is a co-ed wedding shower, the best man helps the maid of honor with the planning. He traditionally drives the groom to the wedding, keeps the bride's ring, gives the officiant his or her fee after the ceremony, and offers a reception toast.

- **Bridesmaids**: A support group for the maid of honor, they help her organize pre-wedding parties and perform nuptial tasks. It is the bridesmaids who throw the bride a sexy bachelorette party. In keeping with their party hostess image, bridesmaids may be asked to lure guests onto the dance floor during the reception.
- **Groomsmen**: Any number of men who help the best man and the groom with wedding plans. At the ceremony, the groomsmen accompany the bridesmaids down the aisle; they may also act as ushers before joining the wedding party at the altar.
- **Flower girl**: A young girl, aged between three and eight, who walks in front of the bride with a basket of flower petals, which she scatters about. After walking down the aisle, the flower girl sits down for the duration of the ceremony. Most flower children sit with their parents after completing their ceremonial duties.

Most children *love dressing up for a wedding and then having a special part to play in the day's events and celebrations.*

When choosing attendants – especially a maid of honor and a best man – consider how competent and responsible the candidate is. Remember, these people will be entrusted with wedding plans, wedding rings, cash, and gifts. You need someone you can trust in these roles!

- **Ring bearer**: A young boy, aged between three and eight, who walks down the aisle just before the flower girl – or in front of the bride if there is no flower girl. The ring bearer carries a small, decorative pillow, on which two rings have been attached. These rings are usually fake as a precautionary measure against loss or misplacement of the real things.

- **Ushers**: For many people, the term usher is synonymous with groomsman. Some weddings, however, feature separate people whose sole job is to seat guests. In the past, ushers were exclusively male. Today, however, female ushers are becoming increasingly common.

The proud parents

- **Mother of the bride**: While not so much a position as a point of fact, the mother of the bride does incur a few responsibilities, including walking her daughter down the aisle if her daughter desires, and being reception hostess, reception toaster, and emotional support for the bride. If a bride's parents will be helping fund the wedding, the bride's mother may also act as a financial advisor of sorts.

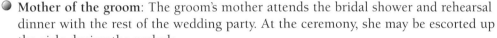

In the past, the rules dictating the roles of family members and attendants were strictly defined and adhered to. Today, the etiquette is far more flexible. Make sure that everyone knows precisely what he or she is supposed to be doing.

- **Mother of the groom**: The groom's mother attends the bridal shower and rehearsal dinner with the rest of the wedding party. At the ceremony, she may be escorted up the aisle during the prelude. And, of course, for weddings that have dancing at the reception, she gets to dance the mother-son dance with the groom.
- **Father of the bride**: He may or may not help with the funding of his daughter's wedding. Other duties might include walking his daughter down the aisle, helping the couple find a wedding site, ferrying guests to and from the wedding site and reception venue, as well as initiating "man-to-man" talks with his future son-in-law about everything from the bachelor party to the groom's place in the bride's family. Heart-felt reception toasts are commonly given by the father of the bride, as well.

■ **The mother of the bride** *traditionally has an important role to play at her daughter's wedding and is often a source of emotional support.*

- **Father of the groom**: He and the groom's mother might help the bride and groom fund various parts of the wedding – traditionally, the groom's side paid for the rehearsal dinner. The father of the groom might also help the father of the bride find a wedding location, offer wedding toasts, and address any service problems that arise during the wedding and reception.

Other important people

Of course, there are some people that you will have to have present, including your wedding officiant – the person who will conduct your wedding vows. You may also like to invite a close friend to do a reading at your ceremony. If you are having a large wedding, or are particularly sociable souls and have a large circle of loved ones, there are a few other people you can add to your nuptial lineup:

- **Very Important People**: Kind of a made-up, feel-good title given to important people who perform a variety of tasks. Depending upon your individual wedding, a VIP can be a singer, solo musician, party aide, general event coordinator, or guest-book monitor.
- **Junior bridesmaids**: Young women, typically aged between nine and 15, who dress and function as bridesmaids.
- **Junior groomsmen**: Young men, generally aged between nine and 15, who dress and act as groomsmen.
- **Junior ushers**: Usually young men, though they can be young women, aged between nine and 15, who dress the same, and perform the same duties as adult ushers.
- **Candle lighter**: In some Christian ceremonies, boys or girls aged between nine and 12 light candles at the altar just before the mother of the bride is seated. Candle lighters usually dress like the wedding party.
- **Train bearers**, also called pages: Young boys or girls, aged between six and nine, who carry the bride's extra-long train as she walks down the aisle. Do not use train bearers, however, if your dress doesn't have a train!

It can add an *intimate air to your wedding if you and your family know the officiant who will be conducting your ceremony.*

Going without wedding attendants

You can get married in a perfectly lovely way without wedding attendants. I realize I am repeating myself here; but bridesmaids, parents, ushers, ring bearers, flower girls – none is mandatory. The reasons a couple might decide to go ahead and marry without bridesmaids, groomsmen, and the rest, include economy, lack of any one or more persons "special" enough to perform the duties, a small or alternative-style ceremony, elopement, and, of course, personal preference. Many second-time and older couples forgo having folk flank them at the altar. It is perhaps more dramatic to stand alone – just you and your partner – which is why younger couples with an independent streak often also eschew attendants. It's your wedding, your choice.

Trivia...

In ancient times, it was believed brides were particularly vulnerable to evil spirits. To confuse these spirits, several young women (bride's maidens) dressed like the bride and accompanied her to the wedding.

A simple summary

✓ Make your wedding fun and memorable by adding your own personal touch to the ceremony and reception.

✓ Celebrate your heritage by weaving traditional ethnic elements into your wedding.

✓ Tempted to elope but frightened of the familial consequences? Consider having a destination wedding instead.

✓ You can reduce your nuptial stress if you get organized well in advance.

✓ You have six months or even less to plan a wedding? Reduce the amount of details you have to attend to and you'll be able to organize your big day quickly.

✓ Need or want to keep your guest list small? Pare your list down to the people you've spoken to in the last six months.

✓ Wedding day attendants are strictly optional. If you do choose to have bridesmaids, flower girls, ushers, and groomsmen, the number is completely up to you.

Chapter 3

Creating a Budget

MONEY, BUDGETS, SCRIMPING – it all sounds so unromantic. And maybe it is, but watching your money before you're married is a lot more romantic than starting your marriage in debt, or putting your family into financial difficulties. Fortunately, creating a fabulous wedding doesn't have to leave you poor. There is a wealth of easy ways to trim spending and help you organize your money. And, as you'll find, you won't have to sacrifice style just because you're saving money.

In this chapter...

- ✓ **Who pays for what**
- ✓ **How much can you afford?**
- ✓ **Prioritizing your spending**
- ✓ **How to slash spending**
- ✓ **Financing a wedding**

Who pays for what

IN THE OLD DAYS, the bride's family could be expected to pay for most of a wedding's expenses. This wasn't such a bad deal considering that, in the past, weddings didn't require a lot of spending. The wedding food was often prepared by the couple's relatives, and so were the wedding gown and bridesmaids' dresses, the cake, and the decorations. Flowers came from gardens, fields, and orchards. Musical friends and family entertained guests. There was no need to pay for hotel rooms because out-of-town relatives stayed with family members.

How things have changed since those days! Today, most modern couples have to pay for nearly every aspect of their wedding, from the dress, to the meal, to the cake, to the reception entertainment, to the honeymoon. All this hiring and purchasing can add up to enormous sums.

Getting help from parents

If your parents are truly well off, helping to fund your wedding will be less of a hardship than if they are retired or are in the middle- or lower-income brackets. It's important to consider your parents' other financial obligations. Are they putting your sibling through medical school? Do you have a younger sister who may get engaged next year? Do they foot the bill for your grandmother's nursing home? I've had the sad experience of chatting with several older couples who have used their retirement funds, maxed out their credit cards, or taken second mortgages on their homes, just to pay for a daughter's wedding. A wedding is a wonderful day – but it is not something worth upsetting your parents' financial health over. Okay, I am stepping off my soapbox now.

■ **You'll be surprised** *by how all the small details, such as accessories to go with your outfit, add up. Never underestimate wedding costs.*

Expenses the Traditional Way

If you're new to the world of weddings and don't know who should pay for what, take a look at the traditional breakdown of expenses:

Expenses of the bride and bride's family:

- The engagement party.
- Invitations, engagement and wedding announcements, enclosures, personal stationery, newsletters, postage, wedding programs, and thank-you notes.
- Bride's wedding gown, shoes, accessories, and honeymoon wardrobe.
- Formalwear for the bride's parents.
- Bridesmaids' and flower girls' dresses, shoes, and accessories.
- Bridesmaids' tea, luncheon, or dinner.
- Groom's engagement ring (if he's wearing one) and wedding ring.
- Bridal consultant's fees.
- Ceremony and reception decorations and flowers.
- Bouquets and corsages for bridesmaids and flower girls.
- Fee for ceremony space, sexton, organist or other musician, rental of aisle carpet, canopy, huppah, and any other necessary ceremonial items.
- Reception: All professional service providers, including the caterer, bartender, and musician(s) or DJ.
- Engagement and wedding photos, and wedding video.
- Transportation for the bridal attendants and bride's family to and from the ceremony and reception.
- Bride's gifts to bridesmaids and flower girl, and bride's gift to her groom.

■ **The groom** *pays for the bride's rings.*

Expenses of the groom and groom's family:

- Pre-wedding parties after the initial engagement party. This includes the bachelor dinner and the rehearsal dinner.
- Groom's wedding attire, shoes, accessories, and honeymoon wardrobe.
- Formalwear for groom's mother and father.
- Groomsmen's wedding attire, shoes, and accessories.
- Bride's engagement and wedding rings.
- Bride's bouquet; boutonnieres; and corsages for mothers and grandmothers.
- Marriage license and officiant's fee.
- Transportation and accommodations for groom's attendants and family.
- Groom's gifts to his bride, groomsmen, and ushers.
- Transportation from the reception to the honeymoon.

Avoiding falling into debt

Just as it is essential not to put your parents in debt for your wedding, it's important to avoid debt yourself. It really does make things difficult if you have to start your post-wedding life together weighed down by monthly payments.

Do you feel you must have the same elegance-obsessed wedding that all your friends have had? Examine your motives. You may find you're more concerned with impressing people than creating a unique celebration for you and your groom.

Consider your joint future goals. Do you want to buy a house? As someone who has recently purchased her first home, I'll let you in on a nasty secret: The more debt you have, the less likely you'll be to get a mortgage, which means the less likely you'll be to own a home. Do you foresee graduate school, a new car, children? All require money – especially that last option. And the more debt you have, the harder it will be for you to attain these and other goals.

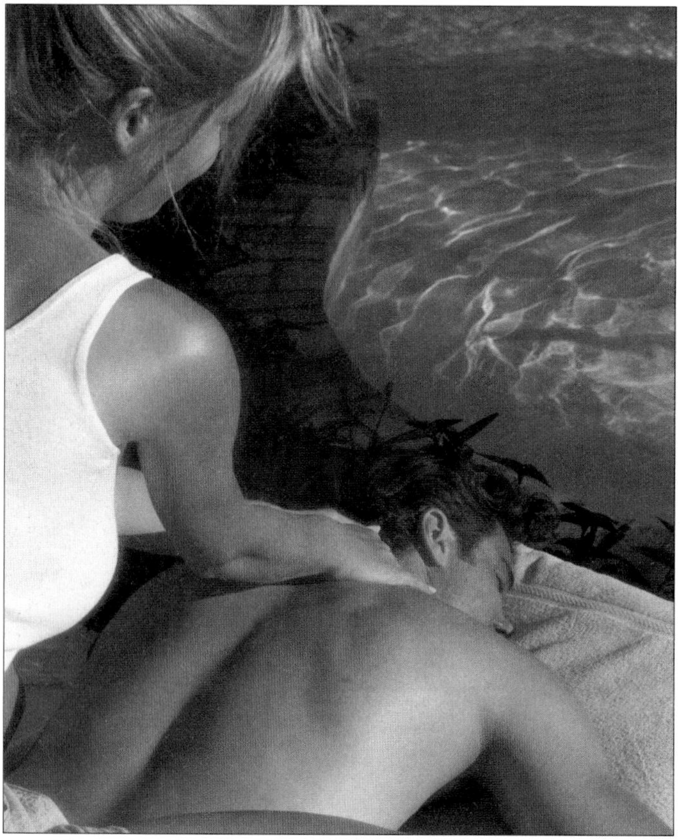

Talk about your goals

If you and your partner have never discussed your future, or you simply haven't been able to decide on some goals, take some time out to do so. Make the chat fun by pairing it with something enjoyable, such as a day-trip to a nearby state park, or a lazy afternoon at the spa. Examining your life beyond your wedding day, and sharing your ideas and expectations, can help to put the issue of nuptial debt (as well as some other more general topic) in perspective.

■ **Don't let** *money worries and wedding plans get in the way of the important things in life. Make sure you spend relaxing time together in the buildup to your wedding.*

How much can you afford?

ON TO THE FUN PART – deciding what you can afford. No, I'm not insane. Looking at your shared financial assets can be a great bonding experience. It was for my fiancé and me. We were engaged shortly after we met, so I had no idea his job paid so well. Nor did I know he had such staggering student loans to pay off. Meanwhile, he didn't know I had such an extensive savings account, or that I had never before asked my parents for money.

The talk meandered to our childhoods and our parents' attitudes toward money, to what we could afford to spend on our wedding, and ended with some shared financial goals. It was our first big money talk, and it not only gave me terrific insight into my partner's feelings about money but also created a foundation of trust and comfort that continues to this day.

Trivia...

While it's common in English-speaking countries for the bride's family to pay for most wedding expenses, in many countries, such as France, it is the groom's family who fund the festivities.

Disagreements over money remain a leading cause of divorce. By getting comfortable with financial talk before your marriage, you can lessen money conflicts after you're married.

To decide how much you can afford to spend, you need to know how much disposable cash you have. If either of your parents have pledged money, add in that amount. If your wedding is a little way off, estimate how much you can realistically save during that time, and add in that amount. Factor in any pressing debts as well. The total figure will be the amount you have to work with. Next, plan on opening a joint checking account – a wedding account – where you can safely keep this money. Separating wedding cash from personal cash will make budgeting easier.

■ **When you talk** *to your partner about money, be honest. Once you have identified your goals, start to set realistic budgets.*

Prioritizing your spending

EVERY ENGAGED PERSON has their own idea of what elements go together to make a fabulous wedding. The areas that you and your partner feel are the most important are the ones you should concentrate your cash on. For instance, if you consider a gourmet meal, dazzling wine, and a show-stopping cake essential to celebrating your big day, focus your money on these instead of wasting cash on something you're less concerned about (or even indifferent to).

If you don't have particularly strong feelings about flowers, then buy whatever pretty bloom is cheap. If you know you hate dancing at weddings, don't bother with a band or a DJ. What's my point? Don't be influenced by what you think others will expect. Decide what is important to you and spend your money on that.

I know it can be hard to pinpoint the main priorities for your wedding. To help you prioritize your desires, take a look at the following checklist. Number each of the 21 items according to its importance as you see it. Have your partner look at it and do the same. Then, compare and contrast your marked-up lists:

- Invitations
- Pre-wedding parties
- Wedding venue
- Decorations
- Engagement and wedding rings
- Large guest list
- Transportation
- Outfits
- Accessories
- The number of attendants
- Beauty/grooming
- Flowers
- Cake
- Food
- Wine
- Photography
- Videography
- Music
- Wedding reception
- Honeymoon
- Miscellaneous

If you don't have *your heart set on arriving at your wedding by limousine or horse and cart, save money by arriving in your parents', or a friend's, car.*

If you're lucky, there may be one or two items that both you and your partner have marked as high priority. But don't worry if your lists show differences. Ask your partner where he would be willing to compromise, and then ask yourself the same.

When planning your big day, think about what is necessary, and what is superfluous. Party favors, over-the-top decorations, different outfits for the ceremony and the reception, and elaborate transportation – all these items can easily be done without.

Perhaps you could each move a high priority item to a more moderate level, so that you spend some money on these items, but not as much as you'd each originally hoped. Or, maybe a relative could fund (either partially or in full) one of the high-priority items as a wedding gift. Look for ways to find compromises and solutions.

Considering your options

My husband and I were married in 1993 for less than $2,000. We came up with this (admittedly low) figure after looking at our disposable income – and our debts. This last point is important. We could have spent more on our wedding, but that would have left us unable to pay off my husband's student loans. We also needed to put some money aside for a move into a larger apartment.

Don't be shy about asking for gifts that will reduce your final wedding costs. Maybe your grandmother could give you your wedding dress, your fiancé's mother could purchase the wedding cake, and your godfather could supply some of the wine.

We agreed that our priority was fun. What we wanted was less of a ceremony and more of a party. When a friend suggested the back room of the honky-tonk restaurant she worked at, we accepted. The staff not only decorated the room, but came up with a terrific menu of appetizers, entrées, and drinks, and they even made our wedding cake – all at a very large discount.

Around 20 of our closest friends and family members attended a short ceremony, followed by a sit-down dinner. After dinner, we opened the party to include everyone we knew, and soon dozens of acquaintances, neighbors, and co-workers arrived to celebrate with us. Ten years later, guests still tell us it was the most fun wedding they've ever attended – it's nice to know that our special day was one that others remembered fondly, too.

INTERNET

www.ivillage.com/relationships/brides

Visit this site and find a wide array of advice on relationships, bridal beauty, planning, and more. Be sure to click on the budgeting subhead to see why this is one of the best money-saving resources around. Excerpts from books, professional advice, and real-life budget weddings help you save on everything from cakes to gowns to honeymoons.

How to slash spending

I HAVE ALREADY MENTIONED the evolution from homemade weddings to largely purchased weddings. What caused the shift? Theories abound: Some experts say that few modern folk have the sewing, cooking, decorating, musical, and other skills needed to create a wedding celebration. And even if we did have this expertise, who has the time in our work-packed world to use it?

There is another theory that we, as a society, are obsessed with doing things the same way everyone else does. So, if another couple goes into debt paying for an elaborate wedding, then we are quite prepared to do the exact same thing. And because of our ready access to credit cards, we have the means to create weddings that we don't have the cash to pay for. To be honest, there is some truth in all these theories.

It's hard to avoid using credit cards completely when paying for a wedding. But if you feel you must use plastic, limit its use to 15 percent of your wedding expenses.

Knowing why modern weddings are the way they are can help you see alternatives. For example, you could get married while you run the New York Marathon or from the dizzy heights of a hot-air balloon. Or you could go the old-fashioned route and get hitched in your parents' backyard, at the beach, in an uncle's apricot orchard (just imagine the spring blossoms), at city hall, or at a church or synagogue. And follow your wedding with a potluck reception, just like they did in our grandparents' day.

Saving money

Of course, there are all kinds of ways you can save on your wedding costs – regardless of how traditional or alternative it is. I'll be sprinkling cost-cutting ideas throughout this book, but I've also put together a checklist:

Put all your *calculations into a spreadsheet, so that you can juggle figures and begin to see where you can make savings.*

- Create your own wedding invitations and newsletter on your computer.
- Save money on your wedding gown and bridesmaids' dresses by shopping at a bridal outlet, renting outfits, or having them made by a seamstress.
- Do you really need six bridesmaids, a maid of honor, six ushers, and a best man? By limiting your attendants to a maid of honor and a best man, you can save considerably on clothing costs, as well as gifts.
- Venues, photographers, caterers, musicians, and other professionals often charge less for weekday weddings than for weekend weddings.
- In America Saturday is the most popular and, because of demand, the most expensive day of the week for a wedding. Choose another day.
- Get married in the morning: Afternoon and evening weddings are more expensive.

A local seamstress *can create a unique, beautifully handcrafted dress for you.*

It's easy to get discouraged by the extra sleuthing needed to save money. Well, you shouldn't. Think of saving money as a game – a good way to learn about finances ahead of your married life together.

- Instead of hosting your reception in an expensive country club or wedding hall, consider free or low-fee options, such as city gardens and arboretums.
- Consider hosting your reception at a restaurant. Most charge less than a hotel or country club. Plus, restaurants don't have the room fees that many facilities do.
- Check facilities in other areas. If you live in an expensive urban center, a nearby village or small town may be able to offer less expensive reception sites.
- The reception is the largest expense of your wedding. Concentrate your money-saving powers here.
- Providing food and drink at weddings is a costly business. Most caterers, venue kitchens, and restaurants charge per person, so invite only the people you really want to be there.
- Another way to lower your food bill is to junk the multi-course dinner in favor of high tea, brunch, luncheon, a dessert reception, or even a cocktail party.
- Many venues require you to use their catering staff, but if you're allowed to bring your own food then having family or friends – or an inexpensive caterer – prepare your meal can save you money.

Trivia...

Brunches or wedding breakfasts are the latest craze in wedding fare. They give you lots of leeway, allowing you to serve less traditional foods or even simpler wedding cuisine – from quiches to sausages to seafood platters.

- If you like the idea of a venue that does it all – from beverages and meals, to entertainment and cleanup – check out the local business hotels. Most are quiet on the weekend and are very willing to give you a good price.
- Do you need a traditional full bar? Could you feature a full bar for the first hour or two, and then switch to a cash bar?
- For those who'd like to keep drinks free, you can save money by limiting options to beer, wine, and non-alcoholic beverages.
- Wedding cakes can cost anywhere from several hundred to several thousand dollars. Save money by making enquiries at a nearby pastry school. Near- or recent-graduates could make you a gorgeous cake at a fraction of what a wedding-cake baker would charge – and they might come up with some unusual ideas, too.
- Consider using a ***display cake***. Then, your caterer or kitchen staff can serve guests slices of sheet cakes, which cost a fraction of the cost of a beautifully iced wedding cake. If you want a cake you and your groom can actually cut, have a talented friend or family member make you a small wedding cake to cut, but then serve guests slices of pre-cut sheet cake.
- DJs are generally cheaper than live bands – unless you happen to be friends with a bunch of musicians.
- If you want a band, consider contacting your local music school for references. You may get a lovely string quartet for very little money.
- Consider placing a disposable camera at each table. The guests can enjoy taking pictures of each other and you'll get dozens of fun, candid photographs as mementos at little extra cost.

DEFINITION

A **display cake** *is one that looks the part, but is actually inedible. The advantage of one of these imposters is that they can look sumptuous and ornate – but at a fraction of the cost of a real wedding cake.*

Hiring a professional photographer, *or videographer, can cost a substantial amount. Consider asking a photographer friend to do the honors for you – perhaps as a wedding present.*

Financing a wedding

YOU'VE CHARTED YOUR PRIORITIES, you're thinking about different wedding and reception options, and you've begun investigating costs. You're now ready to make a commitment to financing your wedding. If you haven't yet opened a separate checking account for wedding expenses, now's the time to do it.

Is your wedding date more than nine months away? It might also be worth opening a high-yield savings account where your money can earn interest. Make sure the savings account is linked to your wedding checking account; you'll need to transfer funds when you write checks.

A high-yield savings account is an account that boasts a higher-than-average interest rate. Most have certain requisites, such as a fairly high minimum balance and a limited number of monthly withdrawals before you're charged a fee.

Remember that priority list you and your partner made? It's time to look at it again. As you investigate your options for each item on the list, it's important to note each option's cost. If you've done extensive homework – which you should have done – you'll notice wide discrepancies in the costs of items, sites, and services. Remembering your priorities, record what you're comfortable paying for each item. Add up these last numbers. Does the total figure match the budget you drew up earlier in the chapter? If you're like most of us, it will probably exceed your budget. Not to worry! You'll either have to find ways to find additional funds, or you'll need to whittle the costs associated with each item of your wedding.

INTERNET

www.wedfrugal.com

The name says it all: If you want to streamline wedding costs, this site is a must.

Helping to fund your wedding

Taking on freelance work, moving to a cheaper apartment, renegotiating your mortgage or lease, giving up a few restaurant meals here and there, and renting videos rather than going to the movies are all ways to help increase your income. Negotiating down the price of wedding services, asking your friends and family to help create some of the items for your wedding, bartering for bridal services, doing away with superfluous extras, and limiting your guest list are easy ways to shave wedding costs.

There is no magic formula to determine how much to spend on specific bridal services. It depends solely on your preferences and pocketbook.

REAL-WORLD ADVICE

Don't know how you can possibly have the wedding of your dreams while staying within your budget? Here's what these real-life couples did:

- "We had always dreamed of getting married outdoors, surrounded by the people we love. We ended up marrying on a hill in California's wine country. Each guest carried a picnic basket and, after reciting our vows, we all sat and ate the picnic and drank wine. We had a fantastic time."
- "My godparents have a gorgeous old plantation house they were trying to sell. I convinced them to wait until after my wedding, which I had at the house, before they put the mansion on the market. Not only did I get a stunning space for my wedding and reception, I didn't have to pay for a thing. Well, actually, I paid a clean-up crew to clean the house after we were finished."
- "For me, buying the dress was a huge issue. Everything I liked was so expensive! I ended up going onto eBay and purchasing one of the very gowns that I had tried on in a boutique, where it had cost $1,100 – I paid only $190!"
- "We wanted a late spring wedding. My grandparents have an enormous backyard, so a few months before the ceremony, we planted 220 tulip bulbs. They were in full bloom by the time we got married. There were so many growing that I cut enough to use for my bouquet and for all the table decorations."

Choosing seasonal *blooms that can be picked locally will help you cut costs.*

- "I fell in love with the idea of getting married in the Caribbean. After some research, I found a resort in the U.S. Virgin Islands that put together a wedding-honeymoon package, with an on-the-beach sunset wedding and great food – all at a $4,000 saving over a New York wedding and separate island honeymoon. Plus, our parents, siblings, and eight of our close friends all used the occasion as an excuse for a vacation."
- "We planned to get married in my in-law's church and then stay put for the reception, too. The church has a large recreation room, which our friends and family decorated the night before. For a small fee, the church let us use their tables, chairs, plates, and silver. We simply hired a caterer to bring in the food."

Trivia...

It's a frightening thought, but the average wedding in the United States costs $20,000. And with that type of peer pressure to live up to, it's no wonder that many couples find that debt is a very real consequence of their wedding ceremonies.

A sponsored wedding

Yet another option is a sponsored wedding. This involves approaching various local businesses – such as florists, stationers, photographers, caterers, bakeries, bridal boutiques, and so on – and asking for reduced or free services in exchange for public acknowledgment. This acknowledgment can be anything from the florist's logo printed on all bouquet ribbons, to a mention in the couple's wedding brochure, or a public announcement to the guests by the bride and groom. If you're interested, approach newer, smaller, or less popular businesses – they may be hungry for publicity. But before you begin approaching local vendors, ask yourself: Does it feel strange having company logos plastered over your reception?

If your total budget is $10,000 and your reception site, reception meal, and your honeymoon are your top priorities, you might plan to spend $7,000 on these three items together (or around 70 percent) and find a way to economize, barter, or receive as gifts the remaining elements of your wedding.

A simple summary

- ✓ Don't let your parents go into debt over your wedding.
- ✓ You'll need money to start a married life together, so don't blow it all on your wedding.
- ✓ Talk about what you can and can't afford before you start making definite wedding plans.
- ✓ Prioritize your wedding wants and you'll have an idea of where to focus your spending.
- ✓ There are dozens of easy ways to save money on your wedding and reception.
- ✓ Make sure you do your research – costs of wedding sites and services can vary widely.
- ✓ Creativity is the easiest way to shave wedding costs. With ingenuity, you can save money on everything from dresses and photography, to flowers and food.

Part Two

Looking Good on the Day

A lot of work goes into your wedding-day look. There's your outfit, hairdo, makeup, and manicure to think of. You'll also need to get your skin in order and firm up whatever body part may need attention. But don't worry, you will pull your look together in the most gorgeous of ways. After all, have you ever seen a bride who wasn't beautiful? A groom who wasn't dashing?

Chapter 4
Deciding What to Wear: The Bride

Chapter 5
Deciding What to Wear: The Groom

Chapter 6
Outfitting the Wedding Party

Chapter 4

Deciding What to Wear: The Bride

WHAT BRIDE DOESN'T HAVE an image of how she'd like to look on her wedding day? Resplendent in white satin, glowing in ecru silk, pretty in pastel chiffon, sophisticated in red or black couture; hair softly waved, in a gentle upsweep, or styled more dramatically; with flawless skin, picture-perfect makeup, an immaculate manicure. It really doesn't matter whether your bridal tastes lean toward traditional conservatism or personal self-expression, achieving your dream look is easy to do – with a bit of advance preparation.

In this chapter...

- ✓ Finding a wedding gown
- ✓ Some help in getting ready
- ✓ Beauty care
- ✓ Getting into shape

Finding a wedding gown

IF YOU'RE LIKE MANY WOMEN, one of your first concerns when you get engaged is finding the perfect wedding gown. I don't need to tell you that for every woman this gown is different. In fact, for some it isn't a gown at all, but a suit. A large number of today's brides choose white or off-white, which, for those with warm skin coloring, happens to be much more flattering than white.

Your wedding attire can be any color you like, such as subtle pastels, bright red, a deep jewel-tone (think burgundy, emerald, or sapphire), or dramatic black. I've seen gowns in silver velvet, chocolate organza, pale gold taffeta, and even flattering prints – all of which were even more gorgeous than the popular white gown because they were correctly chosen with the bride's personality in mind. Here follows the low-down on your wedding-dress options.

Wearing a family heirloom

My mother got married in the wedding dress that her two aunts and sister had worn. With each bride, the dress – a tea-length, ecru number with boat neck and dolman sleeves – was slightly resized and reworked by my seamstress grandmother. I haven't seen photographs of my aunt and great aunts wearing the dress, but my mother's wedding pictures show a stunning shift that is as flattering as it was fashion-forward. I tell this story to erase any prejudices you may have against "hand-me-down" dresses. Not only did my mother save a lot of money on her gown, she says it made her feel lucky to wear something that had brought so much happiness to three women before her. Plus the cut and workmanship were of much better quality than in any of the new gowns she had considered.

Trivia...

Wedding dresses as we know them today are a purely 20th-century creation. Before the 1900s most women either wore their prettiest gown, or had someone make a dress for them.

If you wear *a dress from a particular era, choose accessories, such as shoes and headwear, that are in keeping with that look.*

Wearing a family wedding gown is also a lovely gesture. Many people feel that it brings good luck, especially if the first person who owned the gown went on to have a successful marriage (my mom is still happily married, as are all the aunts who wore the dress). It's also an inexpensive option. The only outlay is your tailor's fee to have the gown resized and possibly refashioned a bit. Furthermore, dressmaking was once taken more seriously than it is now, meaning most older gowns boast extremely high-quality workmanship, tailoring, and materials.

No, you don't have to get married in a long dress – nor do you have to wear a dress at all. Wedding suits were once wildly popular; there have even been brides who marry in pantsuits. Your wedding is your big day. Wear whatever makes you feel fabulous.

WEDDING-DRESS TRADITIONS

Why does the old rhyme urge brides to wear something blue? And is there a reason why white is associated with weddings? Here is an insight into what lies behind those wedding-dress traditions:

- You've probably heard the saying "something old, something new, something borrowed, something blue," which originated in Victorian England. Many historians believe the blue refers to royal blood – blue blood. It's explained that both bride and groom were once looked upon as "royalty" on their wedding day. However, blue has been associated with weddings since at least biblical days. For brides in ancient Israel, blue signaled purity and fidelity, which explains the blue ribbons brides-to-be would sew onto their clothing and weave into their hair.
- The "something old" that many Anglo brides wore was often an heirloom or family piece of jewelry.
- In many Asian countries brides wear red, which is associated with good luck.
- Early Roman brides usually wore yellow.
- Though white dresses were occasionally worn by early brides, colored fabric was more common. In 1840, however, when Queen Victoria of England married Prince Albert, she wore a white gown to signify purity and virginity. (Until then, royalty typically wore gowns heavily embroidered with silver thread.) From that point on, white and off-white grew in popularity.
- From the first days of the church into the early 19th century, many church leaders condemned white dresses, saying they were indecent and vulgar because they advertised sexual status.

■ **If you are tall** *and slender, a floor-length gown in a draping, elegant material, such as silk or satin, can be very flattering.*

Figure flattery

You may be familiar with a concept called "dressing for one's figure." A popular topic among women's magazines, the idea espouses specific silhouettes for specific body shapes.

If you are short, consider avoiding overly long dresses, or gowns with large details – these styles can overwhelm a slight figure.

For instance, big women shouldn't wear anything ruffled or puffy or too billowy, for fear of looking even bigger. Women with short waists shouldn't obliterate what waist they have with wide waistbands. If you have generous hips, avoid anything that cuts across the pelvis's width, and if you have broad shoulders, don't wear shoulder pads. And, of course, you should avoid emphasizing an ample backside with ruffles or butt bows, and so on.

Wear what you like

There is some truth to these bossy bits of advice – though not enough for you to avoid that lovely tea-length gown you're so infatuated with, even though it does display your solid ankles.

If you love a dress, if the dress seems to be created with your personality in mind, by all means go ahead and try the thing on – even if it is low-cut and you have no bosom to speak of. You may be pleasantly surprised by what you see in the mirror. The worst that can happen is that it'll flatter you so wildly that whatever could seem like a fault becomes just another gorgeous part of you.

Wearing something different

I am going to let you in on a bridal secret: There are women who hate wedding gowns. Despite this, some of these ladies will go against their personal preferences and wear a long white dress, even though they hate the way it looks. However, some will choose to veer from the path slightly and wear a light-colored suit. Still others will find dresses that look more like something you'd see in *Vogue* than in a bridal magazine. Then there are women who will marry in the pretty sundress they wore upon meeting their fiancé or in the taffeta skirt and silk blouse their partner loves so much.

WEDDING ACCESSORIES

■ **Headwear can** *come in many guises, including jewelry, lace, or flowers.*

Veils, trains, headpieces, garter belts, and other wedding wardrobe extras are strictly optional. Wear them or ignore them – but perhaps you'd like to read the following before making your choice:

- While face-covering veils aren't often worn today, they were standard bridal equipment in the past. Historians disagree over their origin, but some believe that they were used to hide the bride's identity from evil spirits. Others believe that, in the days of arranged marriages, veils hid a bride's face until after the marriage, thus protecting her and her family from a groom who may have preferred a different-looking bride.
- Headdresses of various forms have been popular throughout history. Some historians say this tradition goes back to the time when many Northern European tribes chose wives by force. The headdress represents the blanket, rug, or sack that was used to throw over and subdue a captured bride.
- The garter is thought to be one of the oldest surviving symbols from early European marriage ceremonies. It is descended from one of two old traditions. The first is from the ancient practice of having witnesses present at the marriage bed. These voyeurs were deemed necessary to ensure that a couple consummated their marriage – the witnesses carried away the bride's garter as proof. Another possibility is the belief that it was lucky to have a piece of the bride's clothing: Ill-behaved town folk took it upon themselves to grab something of her clothing – sometimes even her dress. After watching her gown being shredded to bits by aggressive males, the bride or her groom would remove her garter and throw it to the masses to appease them.
- In the days when fabric was expensive and hard to come by, a train was one way to give a nice dress an opulent, wedding-ready look.

Dressing for your big day as you'd like to is how it should be. Really. There is no single good reason you should wear a standard wedding dress if you'd rather wear a cocktail gown, or a pantsuit, or a designer shift. Or some other non-conventional choice. But what will people say, you might wonder?

I'll be honest: You may get some not-so-nice feedback from your judgmental aunt Agatha, but then again, when she sees how stupendous you look in your signature wedding get-up, she may have nothing but accolades for you. After all, few people can resist a gloriously happy, glowing bride – no matter what she's wearing. Three of my married friends – like me – chose wedding-day attire that was nothing like what you'd see in a bridal magazine.

Some brides *prefer to wear something less conventional – and choose dramatic jewelry and makeup to match their stunning look.*

Trivia...

It's not just the bride who may opt for non-conventional dress. Bridesmaids traditionally wear matching outfits, but nowadays you might see them in differing gowns (perhaps in matching material) specifically chosen to flatter their individual looks. Alternatively, some brides choose to be demure in white, contrasting with bridesmaids in black.

One friend wore a form-fitting, pale silver Betsey Johnson number. Another chose a vintage Pucci caftan from her aunt's "young days." The third friend climbed up a wine-country hill in an ethereal, custom-made sundress fashioned in gauzy layers of cornflower blue (to match her eyes). I chose to wear a long, sleeveless, close-fitting evening gown – it was black – from Nicole Miller. Do I need to add how amazing each of us looked?

Where to look

If you're going the traditional route and wearing a modern white or near-white gown designed especially to get married in, you'll probably visit some sort of wedding dress store. Not before, I'm sure, a peek at several bridal magazines to study what's available. This is a smart idea. Having a general picture of what you want, such as slim or billowy sleeves (and if so, what length?), calf-grazing or floor-sweeping, and so on, can make your search easier.

Online auction sites, such as eBay, can be great places to buy your wedding dresses. Most garments have been very gently used – after all, wedding dresses are usually worn only once.

Bridal boutiques, department stores, upscale dress shops, and designer showrooms are terrific places to visit. You can try on dresses, cross off those models that you don't care for, and make note of those you love. Before buying at one of these stores, however, you may want to save yourself some money – up to 60 percent is not unheard of – and search for your favorite dress at a bridal outlet, online bridal discount store, consignment shop, upscale thrift store, or auction website.

Bring your dress with you when you go shoe shopping just to ensure you get a good match. Also, buy your shoes toward the end of the day, when your feet are at their largest. You don't want a pair of toe-pinching shoes on your wedding day.

INTERNET

www.egowns.com

www.wedding discountstore.com

www.isaidyes.com

www.onefineday.com

Try these sites if you're interested in finding your wedding dress at a discount.

Your dress-buying options widen considerably when you take a more individual path, dropping the modern wedding dress in favor of something more personal. Designer boutiques, trendy dress shops, and department stores are easy places to search for your ideal dress, but don't limit yourself. Vintage stores, your mother's collection of 60s frocks, designer sample sales, your fashion-stylist friend's closet, and websites specializing in luxury clothing are also worth exploring.

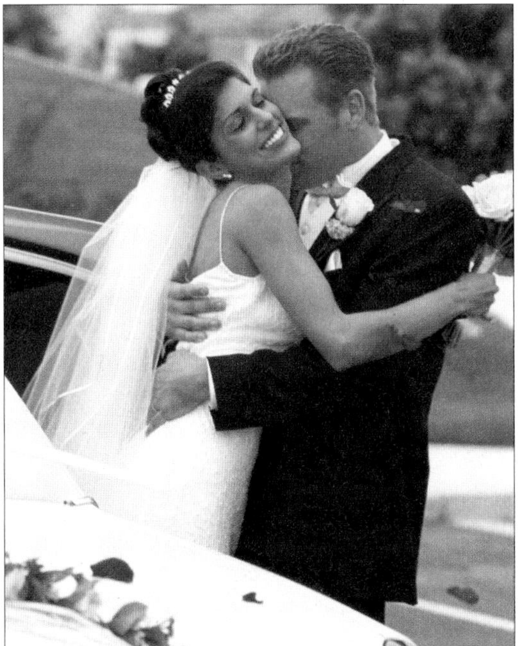

Reception gowns

In some cultures, it is common for the bride to go through several changes of clothing on her wedding day: A ceremony gown, a reception dress, a suit when leaving the reception for the honeymoon. For women who like dressing up, this can be a fun way to show off several gorgeous outfits. However, most women wear their wedding attire for the whole day.

What's nice about sticking to one outfit is not only economy and certainly ease, but the chance to show off your gorgeous self in what's probably a wildly flattering get-up. Furthermore, people like to see brides in their bridal clothes.

■ **A wedding outfit** *is fun to wear. It's also fun for your guests to see you in something special.*

Some help in getting ready

GOOD BEAUTY THERAPY can make the difference between feeling gorgeous and confident about yourself and feeling self-conscious, reserved, and less than fabulous. I know this firsthand. Not blessed with perfect skin, well-behaved hair, or good nails, I must rely on other people to help me look my best. It was my marriage that taught me just what a difference skilled beauty treatment could make to my looks.

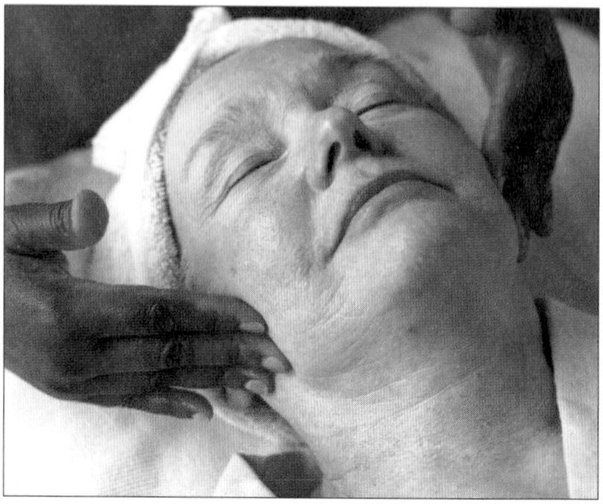

Treat yourself *to some beauty therapies in the months running up to your wedding.*

DEFINITION

A **beauty timeline** *is a kind of "to do" list to help you prepare for an important future event. Think of a beauty timeline as a personal goal sheet that reminds you, haircut by haircut, facial by facial, how far in advance and how often to schedule specific beauty treatments in order to reach your goal.*

I happened to be working for a beauty magazine when I got engaged – an incredibly lucky bridal break. Lucky, because my editor asked me to write a story on my bridal ***beauty timeline***. Before she had approached me, I had given no thought to preparing my looks for my wedding; I'd certainly never heard of a beauty timeline.

Pre-wedding beauty treatments

I had figured I'd paint my nails the night before, do a quick facial mask on the morning of the wedding, do something with my hair, and hope that it would all turn out well. Like any dedicated journalist, I immersed myself in research – hair appointments, spa treatments, manicures, pedicures, facials, and more. Thank goodness I did, because when my wedding day arrived, I looked and felt more exquisite than I ever knew I could. I did not have a single pimple, my skin was dewy, my nails were perfectly groomed, my décolleté and backside were smooth and spotless, my hair shone, and my makeup was long lasting and perfectly designed for my face and personality. I have all those wonderful hair, skin, makeup, and nail professionals to thank for my healthy good looks that day.

Don't assume you must pay extravagant amounts for good beauty treatment. If you have a stylist or makeup artist in your family, perhaps you could ask for their help as a gift? Or perhaps you have a cousin who is talented with makeup or updos?

Wedding-day help

I didn't have my hairstylist or makeup artist at my wedding, but it's something worth considering if you feel clumsy with hair or makeup, you are wearing an intricate coif, you will be outside where an unexpected breeze could mess up your hair before the photographer arrives, or you just want beauty assistance at hand.

Many stylists and makeup artists will happily come to your wedding – for a price. I'd love to quote you this price, but there isn't a set fee: These vary wildly according to locale, the professional's experience, and how busy he or she is. Some charge a flat fee, others ask anywhere from $50 to $200 an hour. Some charge for their commuting time and transportation costs, some would like to be fed, some will fix mom-in-law's lipliner gratis, while others back away from anyone who isn't a paid customer. Make sure you know exactly what you're getting for your money – and what amount of money that will be.

If you're weren't a contract expert before your engagement, you will be by the time you get married. You may not think to get a contract from your hairdresser, but protect yourself, as well as him or her, by insisting on a service agreement. True professionals will happily oblige.

FINDING PROFESSIONALS

Where do you find a good wedding stylist? Or makeup artist? Start with recommendations from other local brides, bridal boutique owners, wedding florists, and others in the bridal business. The internet is also a terrific place to suss out talented – and not-so-talented – individuals in your locale. Lastly, you could contact a beauty association, such as Intercoiffure, and ask for references in your area.

Book your stylist and makeup artist (if you are using one) for the morning of your wedding. Many professionals invite you (and your attendants) to their salon, where you can be beautified in relative comfort. Most ask you to bring your bridal clothing, so you can get dressed at the salon and go straight to the wedding with fresh hair and makeup. Other artists prefer to visit you at your home or hotel suite.

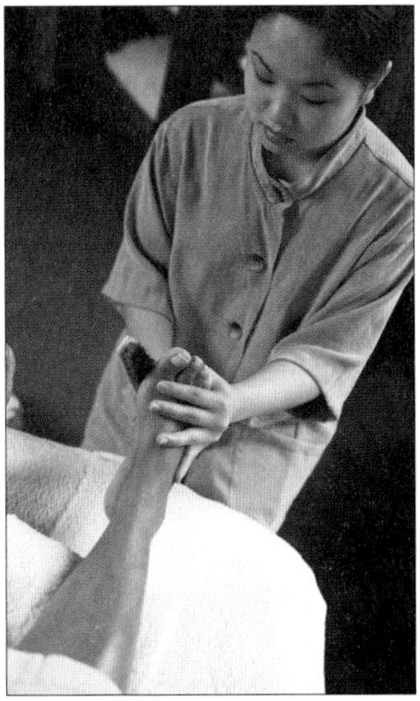

Your feet *may not be on view on the day, but you want to feel perfect from head to toe.*

Beauty care

IT'S NEVER TOO EARLY to start honing your beauty. In fact, the earlier you get a haircare, skincare, and nail care routine in place, the easier it will be to get ready on your big day, the fewer unexpected glitches will get in your way, and the more beautiful you'll be. Here's a sample timeline to consider. Of course, if your engagement is shorter or longer, then you'll have to adjust the schedule accordingly:

Six months prior

Get your nails *into good shape as soon as possible, and then work on keeping them that way.*

- Find a hair stylist, esthetician, dermatologist (if needed), nail technician, and makeup artist you can trust.
- Begin taking better care of your hair with weekly deep conditioning treatments, gentler handling, cooler water, and shampooing no more than every other day.
- Get your hair trimmed every six weeks.
- If you want to experiment with a particular hair color, do it now. This will give you time to fix it if you don't like the shade.
- Make a skincare treatment schedule with your esthetician. Depending on your complexion, this might be twice monthly or monthly facials designed for your skin type. If you are concerned with the quality of your décolleté or any other area where skin will be bared, talk to your esthetician about treatment options.
- Research and invest in a skincare regimen for your skin type. If necessary, ask your esthetician to recommend a daily skincare routine.
- Do a full body exfoliation (either with a loofah, a washcloth, or scrubbing grains) with each shower.
- If necessary, consult a dermatologist about any skin problems.
- Visit a makeup artist and "play" with possible wedding looks. If you'll be doing your own bridal makeup, be sure to schedule a makeup lesson so you can learn how to recreate the look on your big day.
- If your nails are in poor shape, indulge in weekly or twice-monthly manicures – and pedicures, if you need or want them.

Two to three months prior

- Visit the dentist for a full teeth-cleaning session. If you'd like to have your teeth whitened, now is the time to start.
- Visit your stylist to finalize your bridal coif. If you'll be wearing some kind of wedding headgear, bring it with you to your appointment, so your stylist gets a chance to work with it.
- Visit your esthetician for a day of body treatments – salt scrub, body wrap, full massage.
- If you'll be doing your own wedding makeup, make sure you have the know-how and all necessary cosmetics. If you're not confident in this area of expertise, revisit your makeup artist.

Trivia...

The most popular wedding day headpiece and hairstyle combination in the United States is a tiara-upsweep duo.

One month prior

- Book a trial-run session with your makeup artist.
- Book a trial-run session with your hair stylist. Bring any headgear you'll be wearing with you.
- Settle on a "nail look," including whether or not to wear acrylics and what nail color you'll be wearing.
- Schedule a full day of body treatments.
- Watch your diet for excess caffeine and alcohol, as well as processed or overly salty food, sweets, and other foods that can leave you looking bloated.

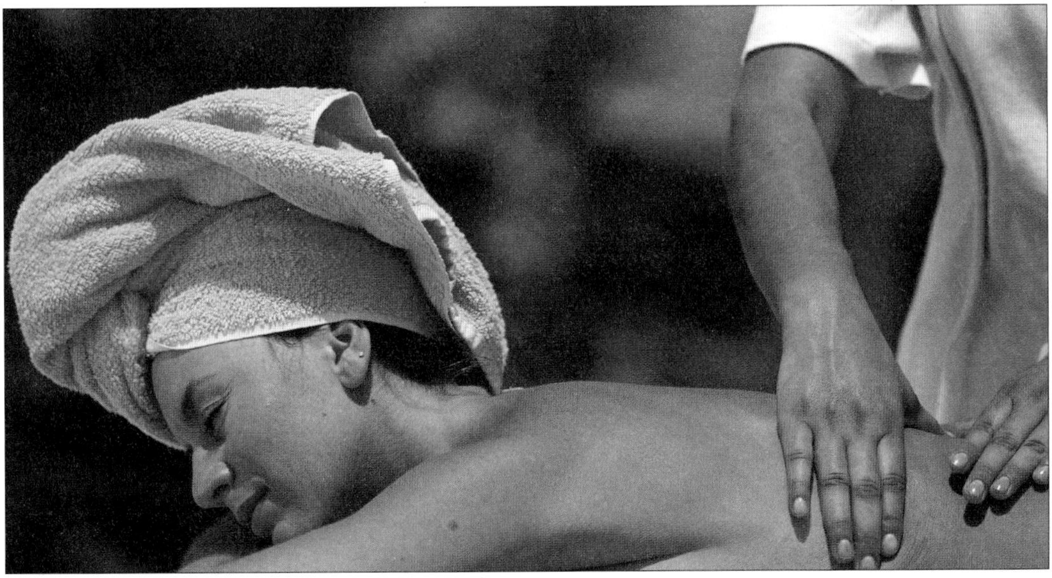

The months leading up *to a wedding can be very stressful – and stress will have an effect on your looks. Money spent on relaxing massages and beauty treatments will pay off on your big day.*

Two weeks prior

- Be diligent about moisturizing all areas of your skin, from your face to your cuticles to your calves.
- Get at least eight hours of sleep a night – this will help keep your skin and undereye area healthy and looking its best.
- Be sure to drink enough water.
- If you feel like a little hair boost, treat yourself to a colorless glossing treatment to make your tresses shiny.

Don't be afraid to switch beauty plans if you change your mind about your wedding-day hairstyle or makeup, or if you suddenly feel uncomfortable with one of the beauty professionals who is helping you in your countdown to the big day.

DEFINITION

Threading *is an ancient form of hair removal used in Israel and the Middle East. A skilled practitioner uses a length of thread to quickly lasso and pull individual hairs.* **Sugaring**, *also from the Middle East, involves painting skin with a resinous paste, which is rubbed off, pulling hair away with it.*

Ten days prior

- Get all relevant parts of your body waxed – or you may like to try ***threading*** or ***sugaring*** instead.
- Have your eyebrows shaped – this is an inexpensive treatment, but it can alter your whole facial appearance in a striking yet subtle way.
- Book a day of body treatments for the same day as your facial.
- Call your hair stylist for any last-minute instructions. He or she may want you to deep condition your hair the night before your wedding, or suggest you forgo washing it to make it easier to style.

Threading and sugaring keep skin hair-free for as long as waxing does, but may be more comfortable for delicate skin.

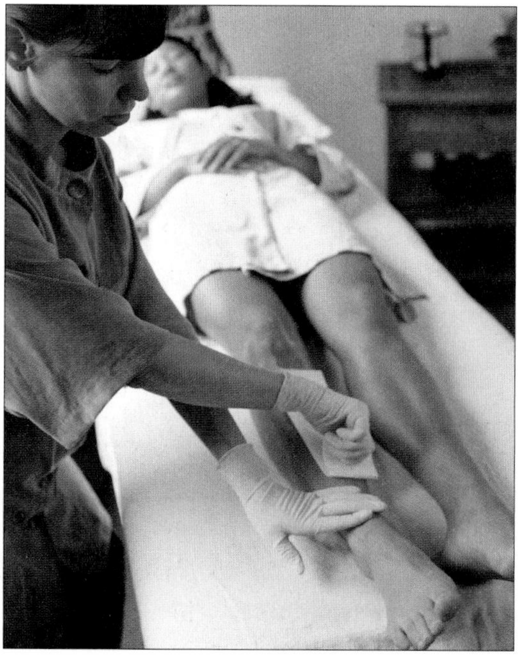

■ **Book your waxing** *session well in advance – and schedule it to be as close to your wedding day as possible, so that your skin is at its silky smoothest on your big day.*

One day prior

- Have a manicure and a pedicure.
- Have a massage.
- Take a moisturizing bubble bath.
- Eat well.
- Drink plenty of water.
- Relax.
- Get plenty of sleep!

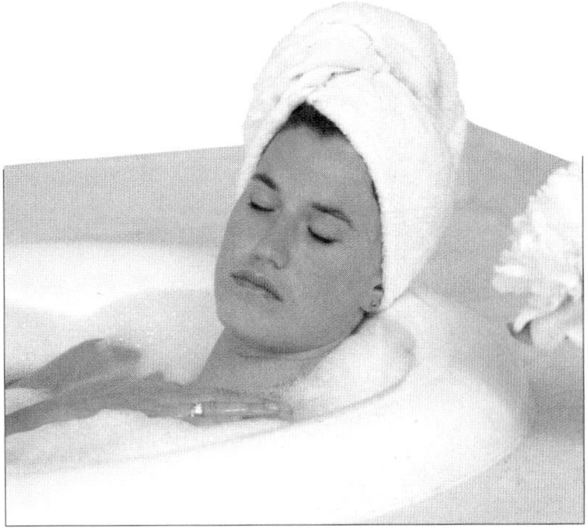

A relaxing bubble bath *will leave your skin feeling glowing and radiant, while calming any last-minute nerves.*

Experimenting with hair styles

When you think of wedding hair, what springs to mind? Updos? Waves? Something soft and face-framing? It's true that there is a sort of "wedding do" out there, although the exact elements of the coif will depend on your hair's type and length.

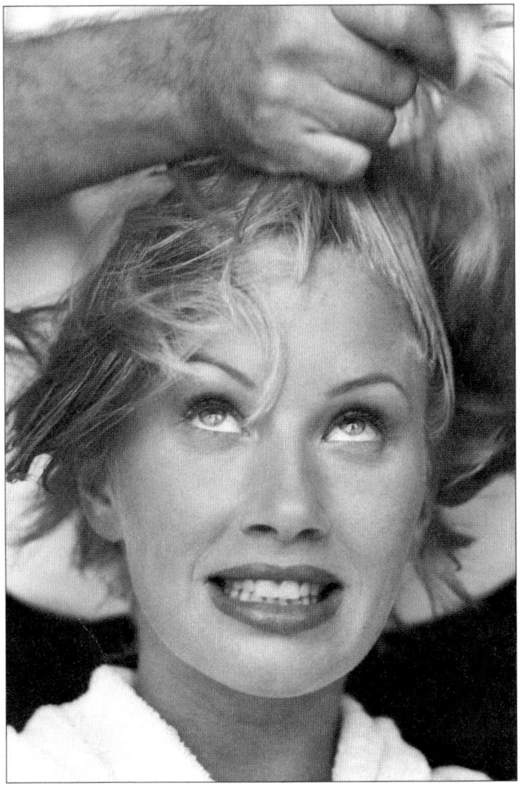

If you'd like to follow suit with a similarly romantic style, you'll find lots of inspiration in bridal magazines and at your salon, where there may be someone on the staff who specializes in "bridal upsweeps." For fun, book an appointment with one of these updo designers to see what he or she can do with your hair.

If you have your dress or a photograph of it, all the better – the stylist will have something to work with. If you don't yet have your wedding outfit, book another appointment when you do. The earlier you're able to find and start meeting with a stylist who specializes in the kind of look you want for your wedding, the better off you'll be.

If you're changing *your hair style or coloring for your wedding, experiment with the new look well in advance – just in case you don't like it.*

If you'll be wearing your hair short, or prefer something a bit less traditional and romantic, it still helps to study magazines for ideas. Furthermore, there's no reason why you, too, shouldn't be visiting your stylist regularly for "ideas" sessions. Try to find someone whose esthetic sensibilities match your own – if you don't, you may end up with soft and full on your special day, when what you really wanted was smooth and sleek.

INTERNET

www.weddingmakeup.com

This smart site lists a directory of makeup and hair artists working near you. Each artist specializes in women's wedding-day needs.

Rethinking wedding makeup

Conventional wedding wisdom recommends soft, pink-tinted makeup. For many women, this works beautifully – these may be particularly flattering colors, which you already wear in everyday life. Yet, for some women, pink seems more girly than womanly, and many brides do not want to look girly. I know I didn't, so I wore a lipstick that was both bright and deep – a dark red touched with a bit of brown. And instead of the peach or pink or lavender eye shadow so many bridal magazines were pushing, my makeup artist covered my eye with a neutral beige, smudged a smoky brown in the crease, then gave me winged black eyeliner, heavy black lashes, and just-dramatic-enough brows. I looked strong and glamorous – which is exactly the way I wanted to appear. Why am I telling you this? To show you that there is more than one way to face your wedding day.

If you're wearing mascara on your special day, make sure it's waterproof. You never know when an emotional moment may strike.

Ignore the wedding planners, those relentless wedding magazines, the makeup artist in the salon where you get your hair done, your mother, and your cousin. Instead, think about what you find beautiful. After all, marriage is a very personal step. It's nice to look like an individual when you walk down the aisle.

■ **Outline the shape** *of your lips with a lip pencil, and then apply your lipstick in layers – dab the first layer with a tissue for longer-lasting lips.*

LOOKS-BOOSTERS FOR THE BIG DAY

Whether you have on-site beauty help or you're going it alone, make sure you pack a beauty emergency kit and that it's ready the day before your wedding. You'll feel more secure if you have grooming supplies stashed under your maid of honor's chair. Here are some ideas of what to include:

- An extra pair of stockings, in case of a run.
- A sample-sized bottle of clear nail polish, to stop a snag in your stockings before it becomes a run.
- An emery board or nail file, plus a sample-sized bottle of the polish you are wearing, in case you chip or break a nail.
- A makeup remover pen or makeup remover wipes, to clean up tear-smeared eye makeup or kiss-upset lipstick.
- Cotton swabs.
- The lipstick, lipliner, and gloss you are wearing. Any of these can double as blush, should you suddenly look pale.

You'll be photographed at numerous times during your wedding day – it's always worth touching up your makeup at a few well-chosen moments, so that you look your glowing best from the start of the ceremony to the moment you leave the reception.

- Translucent powder.
- A wide-toothed comb.
- A sample-sized jar of moisturizer.
- A travel-sized can of hairspray.
- A few bobby pins.
- Eye drops.
- Mints, for stale breath.
- A granola bar or other healthy snack, in case you start to feel weak before the ceremony.

Collect your wedding *makeup in a bag and ask your maid of honor to put it in an accessible place at your wedding venue.*

Getting into shape

THE PRESSURE TO BE A CERTAIN SIZE on your wedding day is enormous, even among those women who have few pounds to spare. This is simply a by-product of today's insane preoccupation with size but it's hard to resist the pressure, even if you know how unhealthy it is. So what to do?

If you don't need to lose any weight, resist slimming down further simply for the sake of being "super skinny" in your wedding gown. If you let your weight dip too low, you can disrupt your sleep patterns, your fertility cycle (important, if you'll be trying for a child after the ceremony), and your immune system function. It will also affect your skin, give you dark circles under your eyes, and contribute to temporary hair loss.

No makeup artist or hair stylist can cover up these last conditions and you will not look your best in either your wedding photos or in front of your guests. So it is important to eat well and healthily in the months leading up to your wedding.

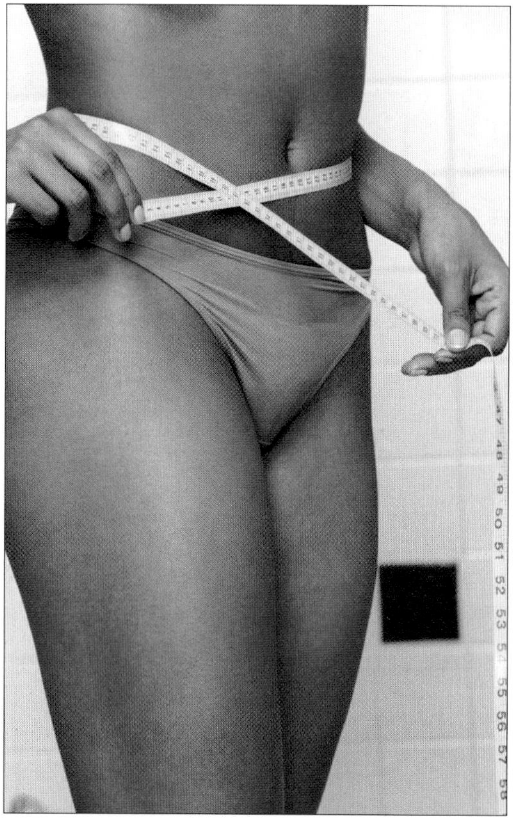

Don't be tempted to lose weight by adopting extreme eating regimes, such as protein- or grapefruit-only diets, or any plan that severely restricts your calorie intake. Weight loss is not worth compromising your health or your looks for.

But what if you are carrying extra pounds? Well, your engagement is as good a time as any to shed them, as long as you do so sensibly. I suspect that you know exactly what I mean by sensible: No more than a one- to two-pound loss each week.

■ **Keep an eye** *on your weight and your waistline before your wedding, so that you know you will be able to fit into your dress – but don't force yourself into extreme weight-loss regimes.*

Watching your weight

Before you attempt to lose any weight, pay attention to what I've told you about the effect on your looks if you force your body to lose weight faster than it should. It has been proven that the best way to lose weight while enhancing your beauty is to combine exercise and diet.

If it's been a while since you worked out, you have a health condition, or you're severely overweight, do not embark on any kind of fitness program without first contacting your doctor for guidelines.

To be effective, exercise must be performed several times a week over a sustained period of time. A good workout won't help you if you get to the gym only once or twice.

While moderate ***aerobic*** exercise performed for 20 to 60 minutes three times a week is enough to maintain fitness, you'll need to work a bit harder in order to trim down. The key is to be disciplined and to stick to an (achievable) routine.

DEFINITION

Aerobic *is a Greek term meaning "with air" or "with oxygen." Aerobic exercise is any activity that uses large muscle groups, is generally maintained for 15 minutes or more, and is rhythmic in nature – think running, walking, and aerobic dance.*

You can go to *aerobics classes, or you can learn a few useful exercises and do these at home – whichever suits your lifestyle (and your motivation levels) better.*

An exercise program

According to the experts at the American Heart Association, the Surgeon General's Office, and the Centers for Disease Control, you should aim for five to seven sessions of aerobic exercise a week, along with at least two weekly 30-minute strengthening workouts to build metabolism-boosting muscle.

In case you need extra motivation, bear in mind that strengthening work – which includes weightlifting, push-ups, and pull-ups – is terrific for toning up flabby arms, a loose tummy, or a soft backside.

Join a gym *and do some weights sessions a few times a week.*

Eating sensibly

Eating for weight loss requires nothing more than common sense, I promise. You probably already know that eating fresh fruit and vegetables, wholegrains, legumes, and lean protein is better for your body – and your beauty – than eating processed foods, fast foods, sweets, and other nutrient-low foods.

Replace the questionable foods in your diet with wholesome foods, and you'll naturally reduce your intake of calories, fat, and sodium while shedding pounds. If it helps keep you on track, let me remind you of all the looks-stealing side effects of a poor diet, such as thinning hair, scaly skin, breakouts, a pale complexion, and nail conditions. Furthermore, a high-fat, nutrient-weak diet can exacerbate existing conditions such as psoriasis and rosacea.

The key to eating well *is to eat a varied diet with plenty of fresh fruit and vegetables, so that you are getting all the recommended daily amounts of vitamins and nutrients.*

Drinking healthily

You may also know that water is a more healthful choice than sugary soft drinks or alcohol. I'm not suggesting that you should deprive yourself of the occasional sugar boost or that relaxing glass of wine once in a while, but remember that it's important to keep your intake of water high. Drink at least eight glasses of water a day to flush out any toxins from your system.

INTERNET

www.healthwell.com

This comprehensive site features articles on beauty, nutrition, fitness, and lifestyle issues – information that you'll find useful before, and after, your wedding.

How much weight you can expect to lose depends on how much time there is before your wedding and how motivated you are. Make sure your goals are realistic.

A simple summary

- ✓ Your wedding gown should reflect your taste and personality.
- ✓ Don't feel pressured to get married in a specific style of dress – choose something you love!
- ✓ The key to finding a flattering gown is trying it on. Despite preconceived rules about what looks good on whom, you'll never know how flattering a dress is until you slip it on.
- ✓ The path to a gorgeous – and effortless – wedding-day look is advanced planning. Come up with a beauty plan and start taking care of yourself shortly after you get engaged.
- ✓ Professional beauty personnel can make the difference between feeling beautiful on your wedding day and regretting the way you look.
- ✓ Safe, lasting weight loss means taking a slow, steady approach. Frantic exercise can lead to injury while fast-acting fad diets can cause hair loss, skin disruptions, brittle nails, bad breath, and other very unfortunate beauty glitches.

Chapter 5

Deciding What to Wear: The Groom

THERE'S SOMETHING ABOUT a well-heeled groom that makes me swoon. Maybe it's this: For many men, the day they get married is the most important – or at least the dressiest – day of their lives. At no other time does a man pay closer attention to his looks: Tresses are shiny and done with care; extraneous facial hair is carefully shaved, clipped, or plucked (depending on where this hair is); nails are cleaned up, and perhaps even manicured; the shoes are good ones – shiny, solid, and elegant; and the suit – well, I simply can't resist a man in a well-cut, perfectly fitted suit.

In this chapter...

- ✓ Choosing what to wear
- ✓ Grooming for grooms
- ✓ Getting into shape

Choosing what to wear

WITH SO MUCH HOOPLA surrounding the bride, it's easy for you, dear groom, to forget how essential you are to the wedding. You are one half of the happy couple – the handsome counterpoint to your bride's luminous beauty. In other words, it's your big day, too, and people are as interested in you as they are in the bride.

So what to wear to play up your devastating good looks? Assuming you are not getting married while snorkeling, running a marathon, or during some other activity that makes wearing formalwear difficult, you'll probably wed in some type of suit or tuxedo. There is a dizzying array of both – and of accompanying accessories, such as ascots, ties, cummerbunds, vests, shoes, cuff links, socks, handkerchiefs, and so on.

This variety means two things: You have a lot of stuff to choose from, and you have a lot of stuff to learn about before you can do any choosing. Keep reading here for a few of your options, though be sure to go online or visit a menswear store to examine the matter further.

Take the shoes *you'll be wearing at your wedding to your suit fitting, so that the tailor can take an accurate leg measurement.*

INTERNET

www.theknot.com

A great-looking, fun-reading site that has information on every aspect of being engaged, getting married, and going on a honeymoon. But what I love about this site is the in-depth stories on groom's attire, including illustrations and photographs of the many styles of suits, tuxedos, and accessories.

Your wedding shoes

A fine pair of shoes can really make or break an outfit. But apart from how they look, your shoes must feel good to wear, too. If you find the shoes you've chosen for your wedding are uncomfortable, even after you've worn them in for a while, return them for a better-fitting pair. You'll be on your feet a good portion of your wedding day. The last thing you need is ill-fitting shoes that pinch your feet.

Don't wear uncomfortable shoes! If you are renting shoes or buying new shoes for the ceremony, be sure to get them well in advance so you can spend time breaking them in.

What are your options?

It's mind-blowing how many different dress-up options grooms have these days. Be sure to explore all yours before committing to a specific style. Here are a few popular wedding outfits, but these are by no means the only choices out there:

DEFINITION

In tux-talk, **collar** *refers to three types: peaked, notched, or shawl. A peaked lapel features broad, V-shaped lapel points that go up and out just below the collar line. A notched lapel has a triangular indentation where the lapel joins the collar; it is the least formal lapel style. A shawl collar is a smooth, rounded lapel with no notch; it is almost universally flattering.*

Jackets

- **Tuxedo:** Also known as a tux, the tuxedo jacket comes in a few variations, including single-breasted with anywhere from one to four buttons at the front, or double-breasted with two to six buttons. You can further customize a jacket with a different ***collar***. The jacket is traditionally worn at formal or semi-formal weddings with black, satin-striped trousers, which are commonly called tuxedo pants.
- **Tails:** An ultra formal tuxedo jacket that is short in the front and extends to two tails in the back.

You might want to choose an outfit that reflects your ancestral roots. For example, if you have familial links with Scotland then a full Highland costume – complete with kilt and sporran – will convey this.

- **Stroller coat:** A semi-formal suit jacket that is cut in a similar way to a tuxedo. It is typically worn for daytime weddings and it is most popular in gray or black.
- **Dinner jacket:** Cut in a similar way to the tuxedo jacket, this flattering jacket has a shawl collar.

■ **When you're choosing** *what to wear, bear in mind what the rest of the wedding party will be wearing so that you complement each other in the wedding photographs. You may not know what your bride-to-be will be stepping out in, but you may be in the know about the attendants' outfits.*

- **Cutaway morning coat:** Also called a morning coat or a cutaway, this is a popular choice for formal daytime weddings. The long coat tapers from the waistline button to one broad tail in the back. Most cutaway coats are black or gray and are worn with matching striped trousers.
- **Spencer coat:** An open coat without buttons, it is cut at the waistline.
- **Mandarin, or Nehru, jacket:** Also known as a Mao jacket, this coat features a stand-up collar with no lapel. It is worn with a Mandarin-collared shirt.

Your bride can be a great help when it comes to choosing a suit. But what about letting her have the final say on your wedding-day attire? Personally, I think if you're old enough to propose to someone, you're old enough to wear the suit you want to the wedding. Choosing a nuptial get-up is ultimately your responsibility. Just make sure it doesn't clash with her dress!

Shirts

- **Wing collar:** The most formal choice and the shirt most often worn with tuxedo jackets. It features a stand-up collar that has downward points.
- **Mandarin collar:** Also called a band collar, it features a collar that stands up around the neck, above the tux's buttons.
- **Spread collar:** This resembles a standard, button-front shirt but folds over and around the neck, with a wide division between the points in the front. The wider collar makes it a good choice to pair with a Euro tie or a standard necktie tied Windsor-style.
- **White-pique shirt:** A standard style dress shirt fashioned from white-pique fabric. Typically worn with a white tie and vest.
- **Crosswyck:** The collar crosses in front and is fastened with a shiny button.

The mandarin collared *shirt is the most contemporary of the styles that can be combined with a tuxedo. It is worn without a tie.*

- **Classic collar:** This traditional, formal shirt is white with buttons or stud closures. It may or may not have French cuffs and it usually has pleats on either side of the buttons or studs.
- **Wing collar:** Similar to a band collar, but with two turned-down points in front.

Shirt-sleeve cuffs

- **Standard dress-shirt cuffs:** Worn with cuff links.
- **French cuffs:** Folded over and secured with cuff links.
- **Buttoned-closed cuffs.** Worn as their name suggests.

Trivia...

Tradition dictates that tuxedos cannot be worn before 6 p.m. So what do you do if you're marrying earlier in the day and you want to wear a tux? It's your call, but I say break any wedding tradition that doesn't work for you. After all, who's the more important player in your wedding? Tradition, or you, the groom?

There is a lot of paraphernalia that goes with your wedding suit. Well before the ceremony, practice putting on and doing up all these accessories. You don't want to leave your bride waiting at the altar because you can't tie your bow tie or fasten your cummerbund.

Neckwear

- **Bow tie:** A short tie shaped like a bow that can be worn with a wing or spread collar. Bow ties come in a range of colors and usually match the vest or cummerbund.
- **Ascot tie:** This wide, formal tie – almost a scarf, really – is usually patterned, folded over, and fastened with a stickpin or tie tack. Usually reserved for ultra-formal daytime weddings and worn with a cutaway coat and striped, gray trousers.

A bow tie *is the most accepted piece of neckwear to wear with a tuxedo.*

- **Bolo tie:** Popular in cowboy and rockabilly circles, this stringy tie is typically tipped in silver and gathered below the neck with a fastener that can be made of semi-precious stone (such as turquoise), a silverwork design, feathers, or some other original design. Best worn with a Western-cut wedding suit.
- **Euro tie:** This is a hybrid between an ascot tie and a regular, workaday necktie. It has a long square-bottom, is knotted at the neck, and worn with a wing collar or spread collar shirt. Although it is not as dressy as an Ascot, a Euro offers a more formal look, which you might prefer.
- **Four-in-hand tie:** A standard tie worn in a more elegant way. For wedding wear, it looks best fastened with a tie tack of your choice.

Accessories

- **Vests:** Also known as waistcoats, these are much favored in Britain and are becoming more popular in North America. White vests are perfect for ultra-formal white-tie weddings, while colored vests can lend personality to more informal affairs.

Though it's important to have your own suit and those of your groomsmen fitted well in advance, the rule is different for any children in your wedding party. A child's tuxedo should be fitted two to three weeks before the wedding because children grow so fast.

Choose cuff links *you love: Even if you're wearing a traditional outfit, accessories make the outfit unique to you.*

- **Cummerbunds:** Very popular in the United States, these pleated swathes of fabric are worn around the waist like a wide belt. They can be black, white, in a color to match your groomsmen's ties, or in a print. (Wear it with the pleats facing up.)
- **Cuff links:** Worn with a French cuff or standard dress-shirt cuffs. The traditional choice is gold, or black outlined in gold, but you can wear whatever kind of cuff links you want.
- **Studs:** Similar to cuff links, studs are a type of formal fastener used to close the front of a formal tuxedo shirt, which traditionally has no buttons down the front. Studs usually come in sets of three or four, and can be jeweled, gold, silver, or enameled.
- **Suspenders:** Two supporting bands worn over the shoulders, these come in various colors or prints.

Should I rent?

There are definite advantages to renting your suit. It's relatively cheap – up to 25 to 30 percent of the price of a new tuxedo. Depending on where you're renting from, you can change your mind about what suit you'd like, and if your weight goes drastically up or down, you can swap for an entirely new suit. Furthermore, many suit rentals include a variety of accessories, which means fewer things to purchase. Lastly, renting ensures that you and your groomsmen look well coordinated.

When renting attire for yourself, your groomsmen, and your father, try to hire all suits from the same store. This will ensure a measure of consistency and make fittings, payments, and other details convenient.

Trivia...

In the United States, the black tuxedo with white wing-collar shirt remains the most popular choice for grooms. However, in a growing number of cases, groomsmen are outfitted with bow ties and cummerbunds made to match the bridesmaids' dresses.

WHAT LOOKS GOOD ON WHOM

In Chapter 4 I talked a little bit about the concept of dressing for one's body type. I personally believe that it's more important to wear something based on how much you love it, rather than limiting yourself to a style that some expert says looks best on your body type. That said, I realize that some of you guys wouldn't mind having some guidance on the subject, so here it is. Feel free to use this information or ignore it as you wish.

- **Tall and slim:** You're the lucky guy who can wear pretty much anything and make it look good. Experiment with different looks, but always make sure your sleeves and trousers are long enough.
- **Slim and tall-to-average height:** Double-breasted styles will help you look beefier.
- **Short and slim:** Steer clear of loose-fitting styles that can overwhelm you, making you look smaller than you are. Elongating styles include a jacket with two or three low-set buttons, pleated trousers, or classic tuxedo pants. Avoid styles that look too large on your frame, and cummerbunds, which visually cut your body in two.
- **Short and wide:** The right suit will give you a sleeker, streamlined look. Experiment with button jackets with a shawl collar. Avoid cummerbunds, which can draw attention to a wide midsection.
- **Tall and wide:** Avoid anything that might add bulk, such as shirts with frills, double-breasted jackets, and suits with winged collars. Try sleek suits, such as a single-breasted coat with a shawl collar.

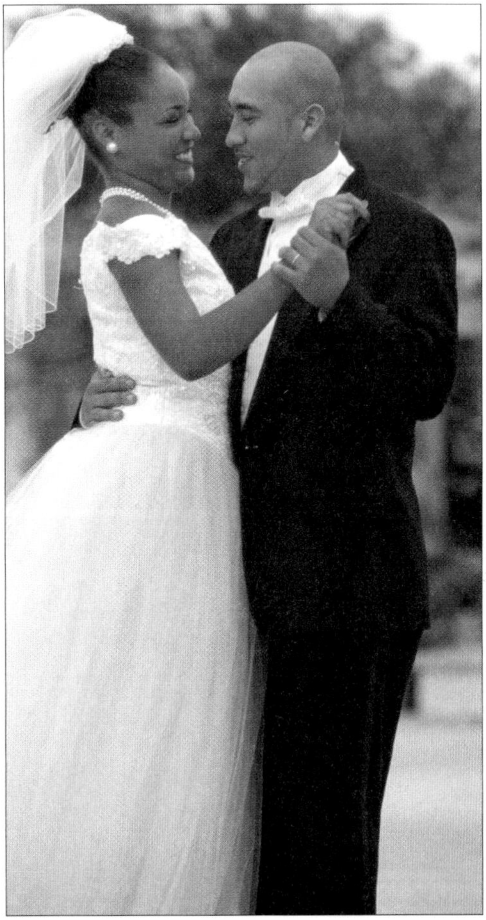

If you're tall, *single-breasted styles will flatter your figure, but double-breasted designs may also look good on you.*

Should I buy?

Buying a suit or tux makes sense cost-wise if you think you'll have two or three occasions a year to wear it. Another benefit of buying: You can have your suit fitted much more precisely than when you rent. Few tux rentals include anything more than lengthening or shortening trousers, sleeves, and jackets; some also include minor work on the jacket's width. But for anything more fitted – perhaps you have especially narrow shoulders, or are a bodybuilder with an exaggerated shape – you'd be better off buying a suit (even if you rent your attendants' attire) and having it fitted by a professional tailor.

FINDING A FIT THAT WORKS

- **Pants:** Avoid snugness at all costs! Better to err on the side of looseness than wear pants that ride up at the crotch, are too snug in the seat, and that cut into the waist. Not only does a snug fit make for an uncomfortable wedding, it also makes for an unappealing groom. Few things look as bad on a man as a pair of too-tight pants.
- **Shirt:** Make sure there is a comfortable amount of room in the neck and that you can easily lift your arms – and rotate them.
- **Coat:** The back and shoulders should not feel or look tight. You should be able to move easily in the jacket. The coat sleeve should allow a very small amount of the shirt cuff to show.

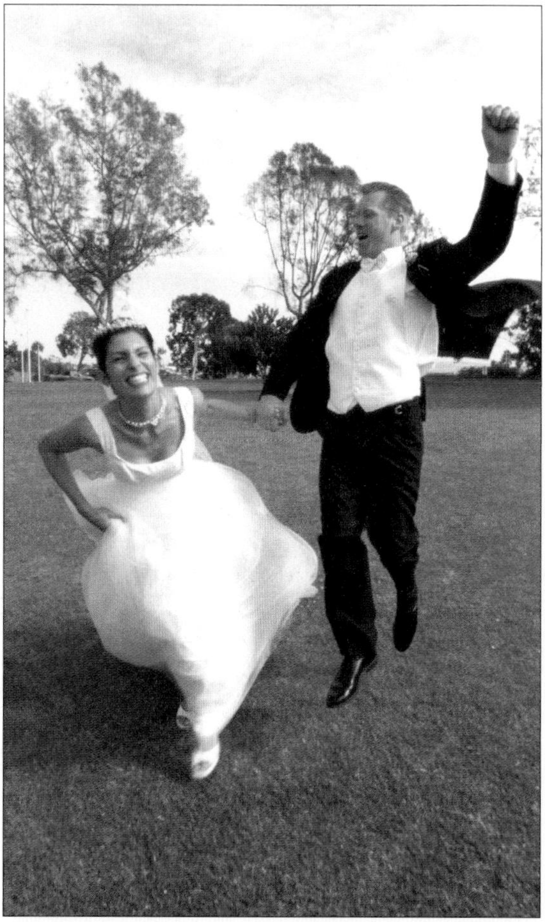

■ **Make sure you** *have room to move in your wedding attire. You need to be free to express your emotions, as well as dance!*

Grooming for grooms

SOME MEN ARE completely comfortable with grooming. They experiment with hairstyles and styling products, wear cologne, and may even get the occasional male manicure, facial, or back wax. Others consider toothbrushing, applying deodorant, and toenail clipping to be prepping enough.

A fun way to attend to your looks or a chore grudgingly done to keep yourself from being overrun by body odors and excess hair – however you feel about grooming, it's smart to step up your efforts in preparation for your big day. For an idea of just what treatments are available to you, and when to have them done, consider the following timeline; if your engagement is especially long or short, go ahead and adjust the suggestions accordingly.

If you've never been for treatments before, and you feel a little unsure, go with a male friend who has, and let him show you the ropes.

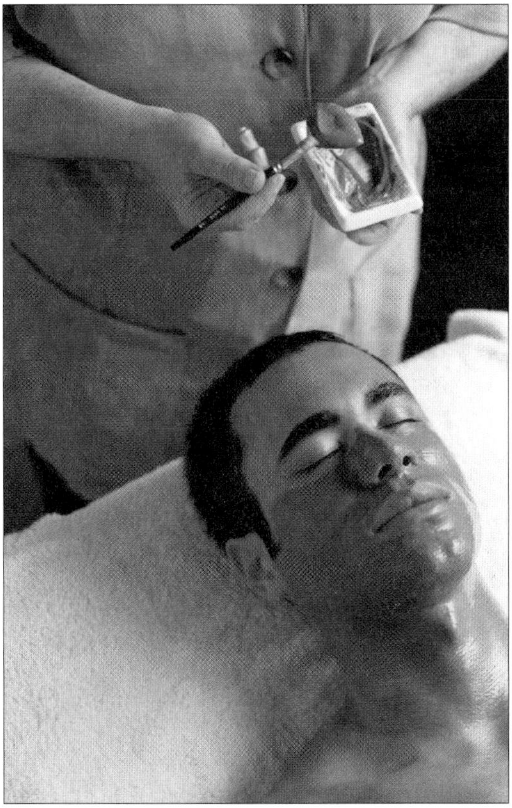

A program of facials *in the months leading up to your wedding will help sort out any blocked pores and get your skin looking its very best.*

Six months prior

- If you don't already have a barber or hairstylist you love, start looking now.
- If you're tired of your haircut and are thinking about something different, now's the time to experiment. You'll have plenty of time to try a few new looks and grow them out, should they turn out to be not what you want.
- If necessary, consult a dermatologist about any skin problems, such as acne, ingrown hairs, or eczema.
- Consider visiting an esthetician for a facial. He or she will help you draw up a skincare treatment schedule based on your complexion's needs. Depending on your skin, this might be twice-monthly or monthly facials designed for your skin type.

- Ask your esthetician to recommend a daily skincare regimen. To ensure that you will actually perform the daily steps, make sure it is simple to carry out.
- Do a full body exfoliation (either with a loofah, a washcloth, or scrubbing grains) when you take a shower – you'll soon notice the difference in how your skin feels.

INTERNET

www.1stspot.com/topic_nailcare.html

Learn about nailcare, products, and health on this helpful website, so that you are fully clued up for your wedding nailcare regimen.

Four months prior

- If your nails are in poor shape, indulge in weekly or twice-monthly male manicures, sometimes called "sports manicures." If you're uncomfortable going to a busy salon filled with women, seek out a men's spa or a nail technician who specializes in male manicures.
- Stick a bottle of body lotion in your bathroom and use it everyday on hands, feet, elbows, and other dry spots.

Two to three months prior

- If you're particularly hirsute, ask your esthetician about back waxing – and knuckle waxing, stomach waxing, and waxing for any other particularly furry locale. It helps to start these treatments in advance and have a few run-ins with the wax before your wedding and honeymoon.

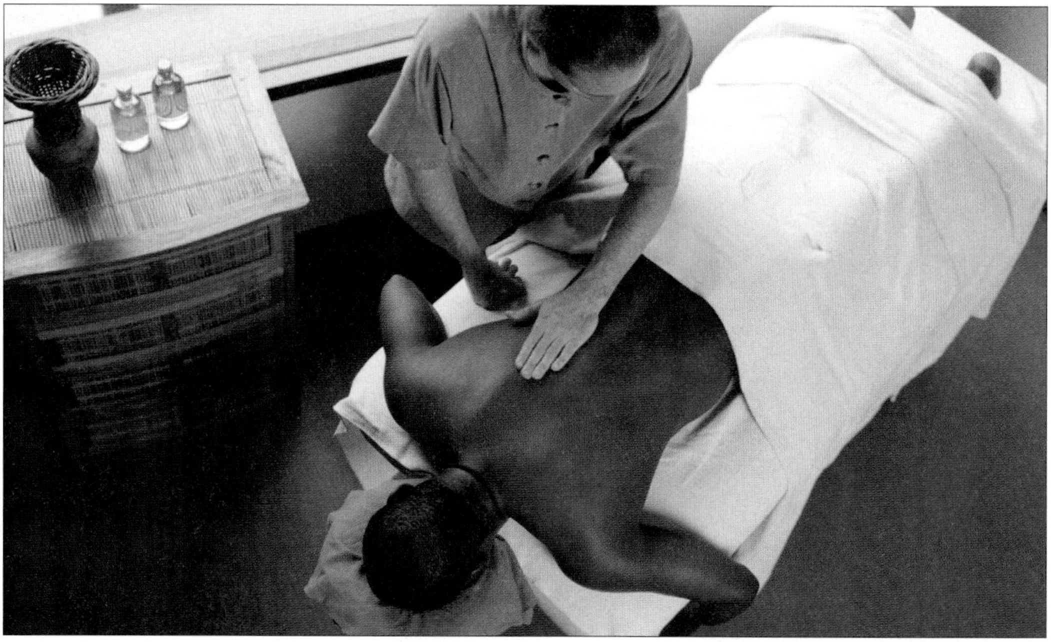

■ **Massages and body treaments** *can really help you during the stressful time leading up to your wedding – book a series of appointments, and think of these sessions as an opportunity to wind down.*

- Visit the dentist for a full teeth-cleaning session. If you're interested in whitening treatments, now's the time to book these in.
- To reduce stress (and reward yourself for being brave enough to get yourself waxed) schedule regular body massages. Depending on how tense you are, book a rubdown weekly to fortnightly.

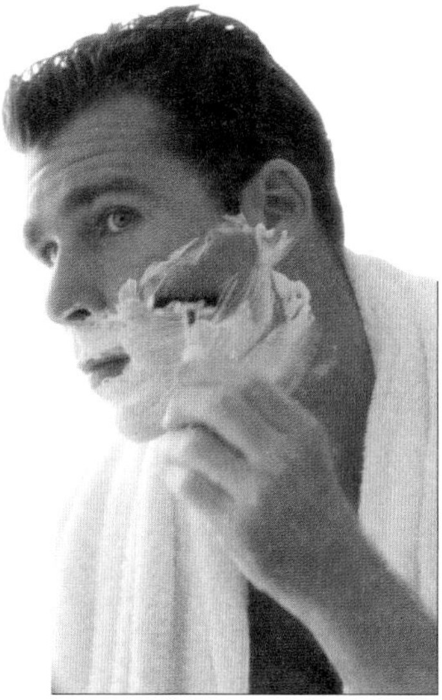

Try out new *shaving products well in advance in case you develop an allergy.*

One month prior

- Decide exactly what you'll be doing with your hair for the wedding. Pick up any necessary styling products you'll need.
- Watch your diet for excess caffeine and alcohol, as well as processed and overly salty foods, sweets, and other foods that can leave you looking bloated.
- Buy yourself a stiff shaving brush, some coconut-based shaving soap, and a good razor. Experience what a luxury shaving can be.
- Continue with your regular facial and nail appointments.
- If your town has a shaving shop with shaving services, or a skilled barber, consider booking an appointment.

If you have the time, plan on procuring your suit – whether bought or rented – and your groomsmen's attire three months before the wedding. Contact at least three formalwear companies before settling on the one with the best selection, prices, and service.

Two weeks prior

- Be diligent about moisturizing everything from your face to your cuticles to your calves every morning and night.
- Get at least eight hours of sleep a night.
- Be sure to drink plenty of water.

Drinking water *is good for your health. For zest, you can always add a little cordial or some ice and lemon.*

One week prior

- Get all relevant parts waxed.
- Book a day of body treatments to go with your facial.
- Take some regular exercise – it will help you sleep well and eat well, too.

It is worth considering booking a day at a spa with your bride-to-be, so that you can enjoy a relaxing day out together, getting pampered, in the run up to the big day.

GETTING HELP GETTING READY

It's common for brides to have at least a hairdresser on hand to help them get ready on their wedding day. After all, most bridal coifs are elaborate affairs that need a professional's hand. Furthermore, there's the bridal makeup to consider, which explains why some women also hire a makeup artist to help them get ready before the ceremony. Some even go a step further and ask their hair and makeup professionals to accompany them to the festivities for any necessary beauty repairs during the day.

Take your time *getting ready: It's all part of the build up to the ceremony – enjoy it!*

So what about you? Do you need help getting ready? My first impulse is to say "probably not." Few men wear their hair in an elaborate way for their weddings, and fewer still wear makeup. That said, my husband had help. At the time, he had a very big, busy coif. Although my groom's best man was a fashion photographer, he'd been a rock n' roll hairstylist early in his life. He flat-ironed and back-combed and sprayed and back-combed and sprayed my fiancé's hair. My groom could never have gotten that kind of volume working alone. So there you have it. If you have a friend or a cousin who wouldn't mind giving you some free help, take advantage of the extra hands. Or, if you'd really like some grooming assistance and don't mind paying whatever your stylist charges, go ahead. Otherwise, I think you'll do fine on your own. It's all up to you. I'm sure you'll look fabulous no matter what option you choose.

AN ESSENTIAL GROOMING KIT

On your way to the wedding? Consider bringing a small traincase or other small portable bag filled with a few grooming essentials in case of an emergency. In it stash travel-sized containers of deodorant and medicated powder, a small comb, a sample-sized tube of hair gel or whatever other styling product you use, mints, and a few aspirin.

One day prior

- Get a manicure and a pedicure.
- Have a massage.
- If your wedding is early the next day, consider getting a professional shave late in the day.
- Eat well.
- Drink water.
- Relax.
- Get plenty of sleep!

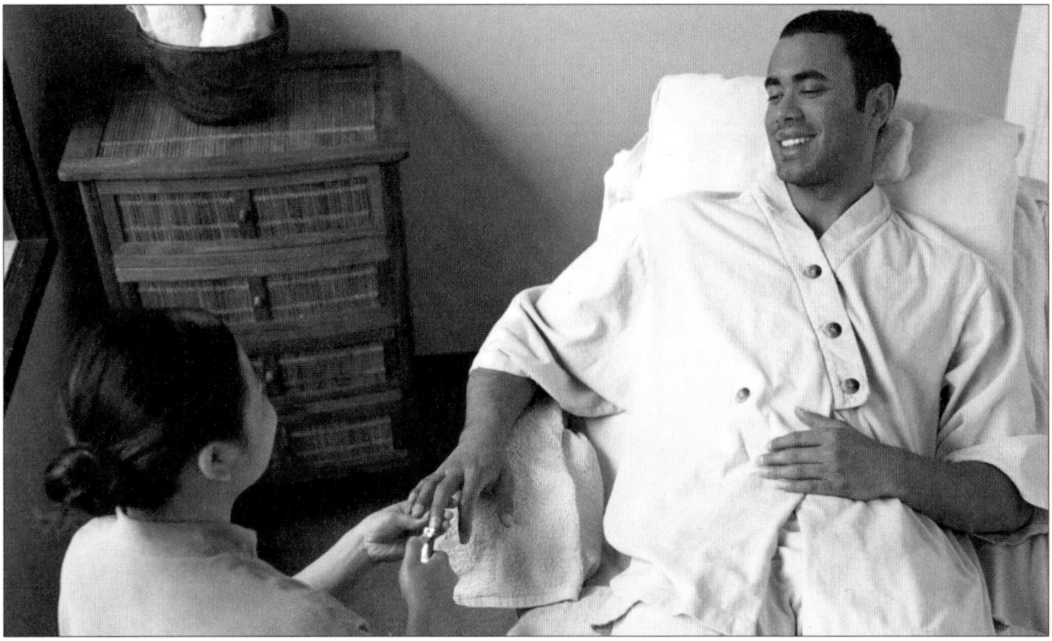

■ **Have your nails** *manicured before your wedding day so that they are looking their best when you exchange rings with your bride.*

Getting into shape

ON YOUR WEDDING DAY you are the center of attention (well, your bride shares the limelight with you). It's normal to want to look your best. For some guys, this means losing a few pounds and firming up some flab. For starters, see Chapter 4; all the specifics listed here apply to you as well as your bride.

Eat plenty of *fresh vegetables – mixed salads are a good, quick-to-prepare option.*

However, I'd also like to offer you a personal pep talk: There's no magic to losing weight. It's actually easy if you remember that it's all about common sense: Eat less, move more. That's it.

Don't try following any odd diets, or living at the gym. Simply eat fewer calories – preferably by cutting out fatty foods, processed stuff, sweets, or other nutrient-weak food, and replacing them with wholesome fruits and vegetables, wholegrains, and lean protein.

An exercise routine

Exercise boosts your metabolism, which helps keep you healthy – and it also increases your energy levels.

Create a varied exercise regime so that you benefit from aerobic exercise – such as swimming or cycling. Also include strengthening and toning exercise – such as jogging and gym work.

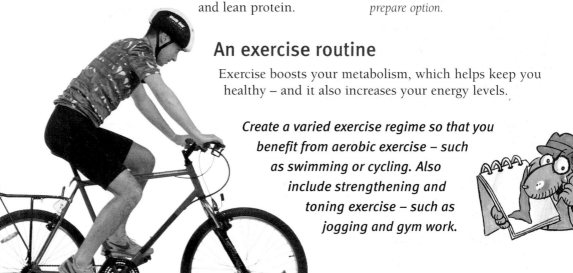

If you find it *difficult to make time to exercise, try working it into your everyday life instead – such as cycling to work, or walking those few blocks to your local store.*

To boost your metabolism into burning more calories, firm up saggy spots, and increase heart-healthy circulation, exercise five to seven days a week. Run, cycle, do a boxing workout at the gym, ski, grab a friend for a game of handball – all are simple ways to sneak exercise into your busy life.

Another get-moving idea: Spend the day walking around town with your fiancée; just the two of you, with no wedding talk allowed. You'll be reconnecting with each other, and firming up at the same time.

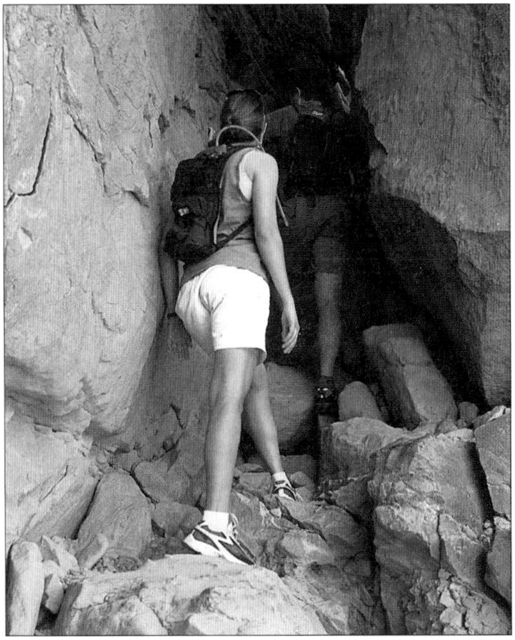

■ **Spending the day** *hiking with your partner is a great way to de-stress, enjoy some fresh air, and get some exercise – all in one.*

A simple summary

✓ As a groom, you're an important part of the ceremony. Dress yourself up and enjoy the attention you receive.

✓ Don't be satisfied with just any old wedding suit. The number of options available is staggering: Take a little time and have fun choosing the perfect look.

✓ The right suit can disguise any "figure flaws" you'd like to camouflage.

✓ Grooming is all about pampering yourself – it's a great way to help get rid of any pre-wedding anxieties, too.

✓ Advance planning is essential if you want to look your best for the wedding.

✓ Don't wait until the last minute to lose a few pounds before your walk down the aisle. It's essential that you start getting in shape well ahead of the big day.

Chapter 6

Outfitting the Wedding Party

IT'S EASY TO FEEL SORRY for wedding attendants. So much is expected of them, both in terms of nuptial duties and costs. In fact, the average bridesmaid has to spend $900 – just for the honor of appearing in someone else's wedding! The icing on the wedding cake, though, is the hideous outfits that wedding attendants often have to wear. This is the chapter where we discuss these getups, and encourage you, dear outfit-choosing bride and groom, to treat your attendants with kindness.

In this chapter...

- ✓ **Dressing the bridesmaids**
- ✓ **Outfitting the men**
- ✓ **Outfitting other members of the wedding party**
- ✓ **Picking beautiful bouquets**

Dressing the bridesmaids

LET'S BE FRANK: There are a lot of ugly bridesmaids' dresses out there, and unfortunately, a lot of bridesmaids who have no choice but to wear them. Indeed, there is a theory that choosing strange-looking attendants' gowns is a purposeful ploy by the bride – if you dress the bridesmaids in hideous garb, the bride looks that much better. It could be true. It could also be that some brides actually like fuchsia tea gowns, neon coral butt bows, or smocked dirndls.

The only thing I can say is, brides, be kind to your bridal attendants. They help make your special day happen, so it would be a nice gesture to outfit them in something they'd be happy to own themselves. If I can't appeal to your sense of kindness, consider this: Bridesmaids can seek revenge for whatever embarrassing getup you make them wear. One of the most popular ways of retaliating is to decorate the bride at the bachelorette party in various outrageous, phallic-themed accessories, then take her to a pub or other very public place. Another retribution involves posting pictures of the attendants' outfits – with wicked descriptions – on one of the many websites devoted to ugly bridesmaids' dresses.

■ **Make sure your bridesmaids feel** *as elegant and stylish as you do on your wedding day by dressing them in something they feel comfortable in and would be pleased to wear again in the future.*

Find outfits that everyone loves

Okay, you promise to dress your pals in something they'll be happy to wear. But how do you do that? All your attendants are so different – different body types, different coloring, different tastes. Can you find a dress that they will all love? Well, possibly. But you are more likely to find a dress that one absolutely loves, one likes well enough not to hold it against you, and one likes but not in a breathless kind of way. This is pretty good.

INTERNET

www.uglydress.com

This is one of the funniest sites I've ever visited. Here you'll find dozens of different bridesmaids' outfits categorized in various ways, such as "Hip Widening," "Poofy Sleeves," and "Swimcap Head."

When in doubt – or when having to please a large number of bridesmaids – stay moderate. No severe silhouettes, extreme colors, or designs that will widen hips or waists. Nothing that requires a bust of a certain size, and nothing that shows off large areas of skin – because not everyone likes to show off their bodies in this way. Furthermore, try to avoid anything that is too fashion-forward, or that will date too quickly.

The more attendants you have, the less likely you'll be to find a dress they all like. The best you can do is to find something that doesn't make too strong a statement – that won't embarrass the wearer and that won't make her look fat.

Bridesmaids' dresses are getting better and better looking. It's not impossible to find a few middle-of-the-road styles that can be worn by your entire bridal team. My personal suggestion: Go online and do some sleuthing. Investigate not only those sites professing to sell bridesmaids' gowns, but everyday and luxury fashion sites as well. Look for classic styles in mid-tones – nothing too dark, nothing too light, nothing too cool-shaded, nothing too warm-hued. This way, everyone looks as good as everyone else in the dress. Of course, if you've chosen a color scheme, you'll want to find dresses that incorporate your colors.

Letting the ladies choose

There are brides out there who do not care deeply about what their attendants wear. They care, but only moderately. If you are one of these women, why not involve your attendants in choosing their own garb? There are many ways to do this:

- If it doesn't matter whether all the dresses are the same, send each of your bridesmaids a ***color swatch*** with notes of any particular requirements or requests that you have – long sleeves, ankle length, no rhinestones. Let each attendant find her own dress.

DEFINITION

A **color swatch** *is a small piece of fabric, which is used to find exact shade matches. Many bridal stores offer these free to brides. Alternatively, you can visit a fabric store and buy a small amount of appropriately colored material.*

- Go to a few online sites, or to a few stores (make sure the stores are national chains if you've got attendants living in other areas of the country), and choose a number of dresses you wouldn't mind seeing your bridesmaids in. Tell your bridesmaids where they can go to look at – and try on – these dresses, then have the ladies vote for their favorites. The dress with the most votes is your wedding's official bridesmaids' dress.
- Many bridal stores have bridesmaids' dresses made of the same fabric but with various differences in detail. Let each attendant choose and wear her favorite version of the dress.
- Let your bridesmaids get together and find the gown they will wear. If you have any requirements, such as color, cut, sleeve length, fabric, and so on, be sure to relay this to your attendants before they begin their search.

INTERNET

www.bridesmaidaid.com

This fun site is a great place for maids of honor, bridesmaids, and brides, too. You'll find lots of advice on things like common attendants' gripes (such as bossy brides and going broke paying for showers), how to throw a shower, helping a stressed bride, and what to do with an ugly bridesmaid's dress once you're done wearing it.

If you are letting attendants choose their own gowns, remind them of your power to veto – or redirect – their choices. Study each attendant's dress before she orders it. This ensures that nothing inappropriate (the maid of honor distracting the groomsmen with her cleavage) or just plain wrong (sequins, anyone?) will mar your time at the altar.

The maid of honor's dress

What the maid of honor wears depends on the bride's decision. But if a bride has only a maid of honor and no bridesmaids, it is common for her to allow her attendant to choose her own dress. Of course the bride may have guidelines, such as nothing above calf-length, nothing strapless, no sparkles, and so on. Even brides having several bridesmaids may allow their maid of honor to choose her own gown, as long as she adheres to guidelines and finds something that harmonizes with the bridesmaids' dresses.

■ **The maid of honor** *may deliberately decide to choose a dress that makes her look strikingly different from the other bridesmaids.*

Outfitting the men

IN MY EXPERIENCE, grooms give very little thought to their groomsmen's and best man's getups for the big day. "As long as it fits, he'll wear it," many a groom has said, insinuating that, because he's a guy, the groomsman has little or no concern with fashion or figure flattery. I'm sure that's true of a large number of males, but it's not true of many others.

When you're choosing suits *for male attendants, think about whether their outfits will match yours, or whether you want a contrast.*

The groomsmen

It is best to assume the groomsmen – and ushers if you're having separate ushers – in your party have a desire to look their best, and then go about finding a single suit style that will flatter them all. Remember in Chapter 5 we talked about different styles of suits for different body types? If your attendants are the same build – perhaps you're all on the football team or in a modern dance troupe together – you're in luck: One suit style will fit all. But most groomsmen don't have similar bodies. They may not even be near in height.

If your attendants live in different parts of the country, consider using a chain store with outposts in each person's area. This way, each attendant can get fitted for the same suit with no worries or hassles.

Ask the advice of whomever you'll be renting the suits from – finding and fitting suits is their profession, so they should come up with something that will look, if not fabulous, at least good on the majority of attendants. Or you can look for something yourself: A classic, sleek, single-breasted style, without extreme details and with a shawl collar, works on most body types. Of course, you can be a little more daring – even if this means choosing a lavender tuxedo with tails. It's your wedding, after all.

What should the best man wear?

Many grooms have just a best man – no groomsmen. In this situation, the best man usually wears a suit that may or may not match the groom's. One option is to have something slightly different. For instance, three buttons instead of the groom's two, with a vest that is a different color from the groom's.

Until recently, ushers have always been male. Today, however, an usher can be a woman or a man. But how to dress female ushers? Don't try dressing them in some kind of tuxedo getup. Instead, clothe them in classic, moderate dresses that coordinate with the bridesmaids' attire.

When the groom has groomsmen, and perhaps separate ushers, the best man can dress like the rest of the male attendants, or he can sport something just different enough to set him apart and emphasize his "honor" status. Again, this could be a different number of buttons, or a distinctively colored tie and cummerbund, or even a shirt with a cut that differs slightly from those of the groomsmen.

■ **If the best man** *is wearing a similar suit to the groom, he could choose to accessorize differently – so that he's following the style of the groom, while allowing him to stand out from the crowd on his big day.*

Fathers of the bride and groom

Can the father of the bride and the father of the groom wear what they want? Sure, the dads can wear whatever they want if you and your partner are happy with that. If you'd like to ensure a bit of wardrobe order, however, find a suit that will look good on both men and then have them fitted and taken care of by the same company that is outfitting your groomsmen.

If the dads have wildly different tastes or bodies, you could allow each man to wear a slightly different suit, but in the same fabric and color, and with the same accessories, thus maintaining a coordinated look.

Men often make mistakes with shoes – in thinking about the suit they forget about the need to arrange appropriate footwear.

■ **The father of the bride** *has a special part to play, so he can wear a suit that is individual but still complements the rest of the wedding party.*

WHO PAYS FOR WHAT?

So who pays for the attendants' suit rentals and dress purchases? In the old days, the attendants simply wore their best garb, meaning no one had to pay to be in a wedding. Today, however, a bridesmaid's dress can cost upward of several hundred dollars, as can suit rental for a day or two. Is the attendant responsible for the cost? Well, it depends on whom you ask. There are experts who believe that the bride and groom should pay for their people's getups. Common practice, however, is for each attendant to pay his or her own way – at least where clothing is concerned. Just to be sure there is no confusion, find a way to make your preference known to your attendants. Perhaps you could say something like, "I'm looking at bridesmaids' dresses. It would help me narrow down the choices if I knew how much you can afford to spend on a dress."

Outfitting other members of the wedding party

OUTFITTING BRIDESMAIDS and groomsmen is one thing, but what about ring bearers, flower girls, train carriers, musicians, VIPs, and any other wedding party member? This is where things can get tricky – especially if you're someone who wants everyone's getup to match, or at least coordinate. If this kind of thing is important to you, it's best to use a dress store that has a large selection of coordinating choices.

By using one store, you can find flower-girl dresses and gowns for any other female wedding attendants that will harmonize with your maid of honor's and bridesmaids' looks. The same goes for any male attendants. Ring bearers, train carriers, and any other children can get fitted for suits at the same shop that the adults are using, thus ensuring everyone will at least be wearing the same color and fabric.

Because children can grow so quickly, it's worth waiting until two weeks before the ceremony to have child attendants fitted.

Of course, if you aren't picky about these things, you can simply give a color swatch and a general idea to the flower girls' and ring bearer's parents and have them find something for the children. Suggesting a color, dress style, or type of suit is also your best option for VIPs and anyone else attending the ceremony. True, their outfits may not match those of other members of the wedding party. So if you worry about this kind of thing – and you have the money to spend – then get their measurements and pay to have them outfitted in matching garb.

■ **Even if you choose** *quite a simple dress for your flower girl, you can accessorize with flowers for her hair and little satin shoes.*

Can our moms wear what they want?

If you're okay with both mothers wearing what they want to your wedding, then great. You're probably not okay with this, though – few brides and grooms are. To ensure that neither mother shows up in a color that clashes with your theme, or an outfit that is somehow inappropriate (how inappropriate depends on the particular mom), it helps to offer them a few guidelines. These guidelines will depend entirely on your wedding's theme and your personal style.

Trivia...

Just as blue is associated with good luck, superstition has it that, unless the bride is Irish, green is unlucky. It is thought this may be because of its association with fairies. In some places, green is deemed to bode so ill that not even the guests would consider wearing it to a wedding.

Shopping for mother-of-the-bride and mother-of-the-groom outfits could be a fun outing for the three of you, and a great way for your mother and your partner's mom to become better acquainted with each other.

■ **Especially if you and your mother** *have similar hair and skin coloring, you may want to ensure your outfits blend in tone, so that your mom looks part of the wedding party.*

If you want some guidance, here are some hints: Mothers of both the bride and the groom traditionally wear some type of light-colored suit, or a conservative dress, with matching stockings, shoes, handbag, and sometimes a hat. Should either – or both – of the mothers be joining you at the altar, you may want to request they each wear something similar, perhaps even dresses in one of your wedding's colors.

If you decide not to stipulate colors or designs, make sure that each mother knows what the other is intending to wear – it will be embarrassing for them if they turn up wearing outfits that clash with each other.

Both mothers should avoid wearing loud, wide-brimmed hats. These distract attention from the rest of the wedding party, while even obscuring the bride and groom during the photographs.

Picking beautiful bouquets

FLOWERS ARE AN important feature of most weddings. Not only are they used as room and table decorations, they are what the bride and bridesmaids carry when they walk down the aisle, and they are also worn on the lapel of each male wedding attendant, as well as the fathers of the bride and groom. Here are just a few things to consider before purchasing all your floral accessories.

■ **Carnations** *have always been a popular choice at weddings, but there are many other stylish options.*

Before you even talk to a florist, think about your wedding. Does it have a theme? A color scheme? Does either partner have a strong affinity for a particular blossom? It helps to have a few ideas before approaching a florist. Then you can tell them what you want, instead of the florist telling you what you want.

■ **Bridal bouquets and posies** *can be designed with a particular color or theme in mind, but avoid using blooms that will wilt quickly. Scented flowers are especially romantic.*

Some floral tips

Decide what you need: A bouquet for the bride, a single flower or a ***boutonniere*** for all male attendants, and a corsage each for both mothers. You could also give the maid of honor and bridesmaids a bouquet that is similar to but smaller and simpler than yours. If you have a flower girl, you may want to have a small garland of flowers made for her hair. Lastly, any VIPs, musicians, and other wedding performers will look spiffier with a single wedding flower on his or her collar.

DEFINITION

A **boutonniere** *is a small flower arrangement, much smaller than a corsage, designed for men's lapels. It's a much dressier alternative to simply wearing a single flower.*

Do not use flowers that you, your partner, or someone in your wedding party is allergic to. Before deciding on any blooms, contact your attendants and other wedding party members and ask what, if anything, makes them sneeze.

Generally, your floral accessories should be the same flowers (or herbs, or plants, or whatever else you're using) as those you are using to decorate the venue with. While most couples rely on the same florist to create both the room decorations and the wardrobe accessories, it isn't uncommon to employ a special florist to arrange the bouquet, boutonnieres, and any other floral wardrobe accessories. This includes creating corsages for the mothers, and floral garlands for the bride's, bridesmaids', or flower girl's hair.

Your best floral bet for accessorizing an outfit is something a bit sturdy. Tulips, for instance, tend to fall apart, while rose buds or orchids hold up just fine.

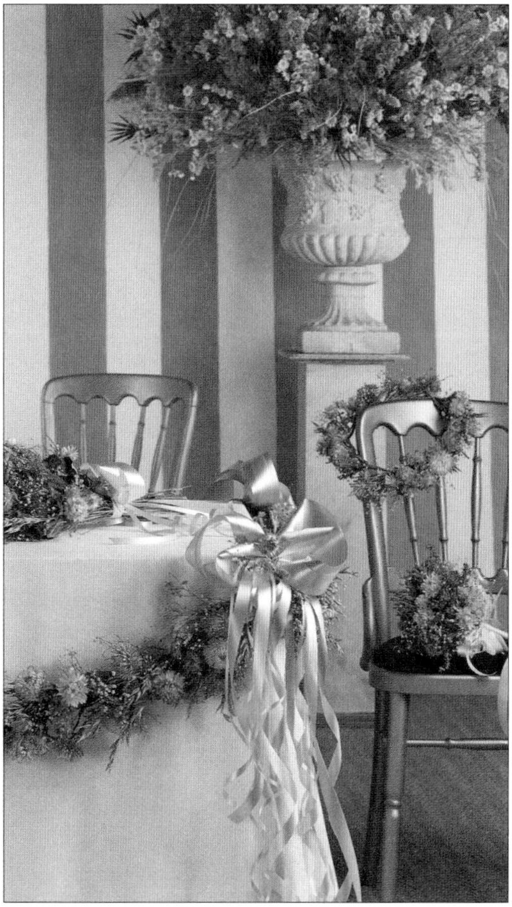

Floral decorations *can cost a fortune, especially if you want exotic blooms. In-season flowers are cheaper and just as elegant.*

FLOWERS: YOUR OPTIONS

When it comes to decorating your wedding party and your wedding space, flowers from a florist aren't your only option. Here's what else you could do:

- If you're lucky enough to have a flower farmer at your local greenmarket, ask him or her what it would cost for enough flowers for your wedding and reception site, and your wedding party. Of course, you or a friend will be responsible for turning these flowers into gorgeous decorations, but many of the posies grown by flower farmers are so outstanding that it will take little work to make the blooms look good.
- Consider growing the flowers needed. The great thing about this option is you can plant some of the more dramatic, harder-to-find blooms. Just be sure that they will be blossoming in time for your wedding!
- If you know of an area that contains a large number of wildflowers, or even spring orchard blossoms, get permission to pluck what you need. If the property is private, then you'll need to track down the landowner. Just be sure to ignore endangered or state flowers (such as the California poppy), both of which carry a fine for picking.

■ **Wildflowers** *can make a simple yet elegant statement. However, most wilt more quickly than cultivated blooms.*

Corsages for both mothers

A corsage is a small bouquet of flowers that is traditionally worn by women at the waist or bodice, but is more frequently attached to the shoulder or wrist, or pinned to a handbag.

The corsage is constructed by a florist from the heads of flowers and with added foliage – usually all tied together with a ribbon.

Make sure you discuss your choice of wedding blooms with both mothers in good time before the wedding, so that the corsages don't clash with their outfits.

■ **Before you have** *the corsages made, talk to both mothers about how they would like to wear them.*

A simple summary

- ✓ Consider your attendants' feelings when deciding what your maid of honor and bridesmaids should wear.
- ✓ Think about involving your maid of honor and bridesmaids in the choosing of their dresses. This way, they are much more likely to be pleased with their gowns (and to look good in them).
- ✓ If matching matters to you, get everyone's outfits at a place that specializes in bridal party attire. That way, the maid of honor, bridesmaids, flower girl, and any female ushers will all coordinate.
- ✓ Grooms, your groomsmen *do* care what they look like. Make an effort to find a suit that looks good on all of them.
- ✓ Mothers of the couple, as well as both fathers, should wear whatever they want. Or, you can help them carefully select an outfit that will complement those of the other attendants.
- ✓ Floral accessories are an important part of the bridal party's attire. The flowers you wear should be the same, or similar to, those used to decorate your wedding and reception.

Part Three

Getting Organized

Chapter 7
Invitation Basics

Chapter 8
Giving and Receiving Gifts

Chapter 9
Eat, Drink, and Be Married

Chapter 10
Setting the Stage

Chapter 11
A Picture's Worth a Thousand Words

Chapter 12
Sweet Melodies

Chapter 13
Coming and Going in Style

Chapter 7

Invitation Basics

THERE IS A LOT OF EMPHASIS these days on how announcements and invitations must or must not be done. More emphasis, in my opinion, than is needed – the amount of invitation etiquette, instruction, and "do's and don'ts" floating around does nothing more than frighten people. Which is too bad, because there are enough things to be anxious about when getting married without worrying about whether you've used the wrong kind of envelope or worded something incorrectly. So let's simplify the entire invitation business, starting right now!

In this chapter...

- ✓ **Share the news**
- ✓ **Wedding invitations**

Share the news

ONE OF THE MOST ENJOYABLE things about getting engaged was sharing our wonderful news. Immediately after my husband proposed to me, we called up his closest friend and asked him and his wife to meet us at a nearby pub. The next day, we spent the morning and afternoon telephoning our family, our friends – really, anyone we could think of – to tell them we were engaged.

INTERNET

www.weddingguide.co.uk

Gives advice on engagement announcement etiquette.

Many other people announce their engagement in a similar manner – using a combination of phone calls, e-mails, and face-to-face meetings. There is no convention dictating how to spread your happy news. That said, for those who prefer something more ceremonial, there are more formal methods of getting the word out.

Many couples prefer to tell their engagement news in person – if your parents don't live too far away from you, hold back on making that phone call. It's worth paying them a visit just to share the news face to face.

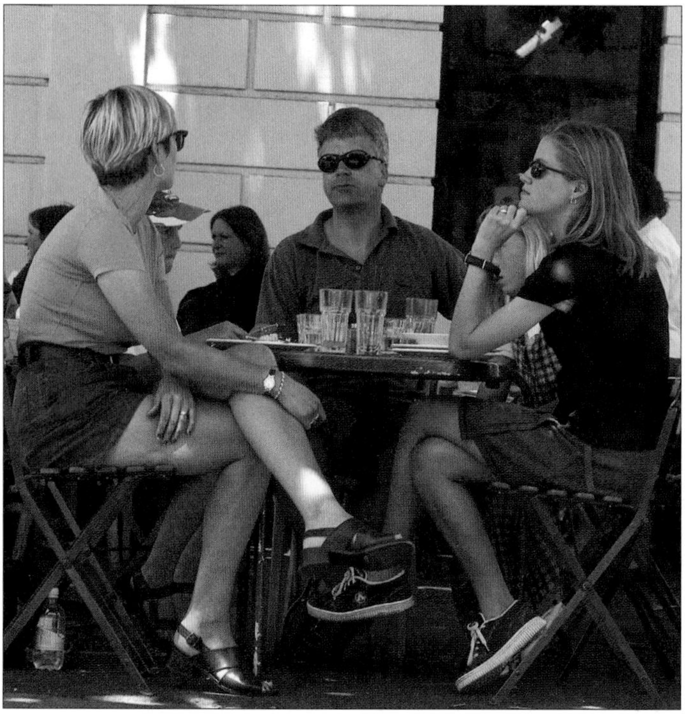

Engagement cards

Engagement announcements are smallish, important-looking cards set in fancy type. They are sent to family and friends as a way of sharing news of your betrothal.

These cards can be made by a local printer or photocopy shop. Or, if you have the time, you might like to create them yourself.

■ **After announcing your** *engagement, you'll want to talk about your wedding plans with friends.*

Engagement announcements are usually mailed somewhere between the time of the proposal to six months before the wedding. They can be sent to close family and friends, as well as to more distant relatives and acquaintances. In the past, it was the bride's family who sent out engagement announcements. Today, it may be either the bride's or the groom's family – or even the engaged couple – who does the honors.

Trivia...

During European feudal times, marriages were publicly proclaimed a week or more before the ceremony. This practice helped prevent unknowingly related persons marrying. Descended from this is the wedding command, "If anyone knows of any reason why these two should not be wed, speak now or forever hold your peace."

Newspaper announcements

If you've ever scanned your local newspaper for news on who has recently gotten betrothed, you've seen another form of engagement announcement. Usually posted somewhere between the actual engagement and two months before the wedding ceremony, these words are traditionally placed by the bride's family in their local hometown paper. However, it is growing more common for the groom's family to post an additional announcement in their town's periodical. Interestingly enough, many etiquette specialists insist that it is the bride's family's responsibility to provide the wording for any announcement that the groom's family decides to place.

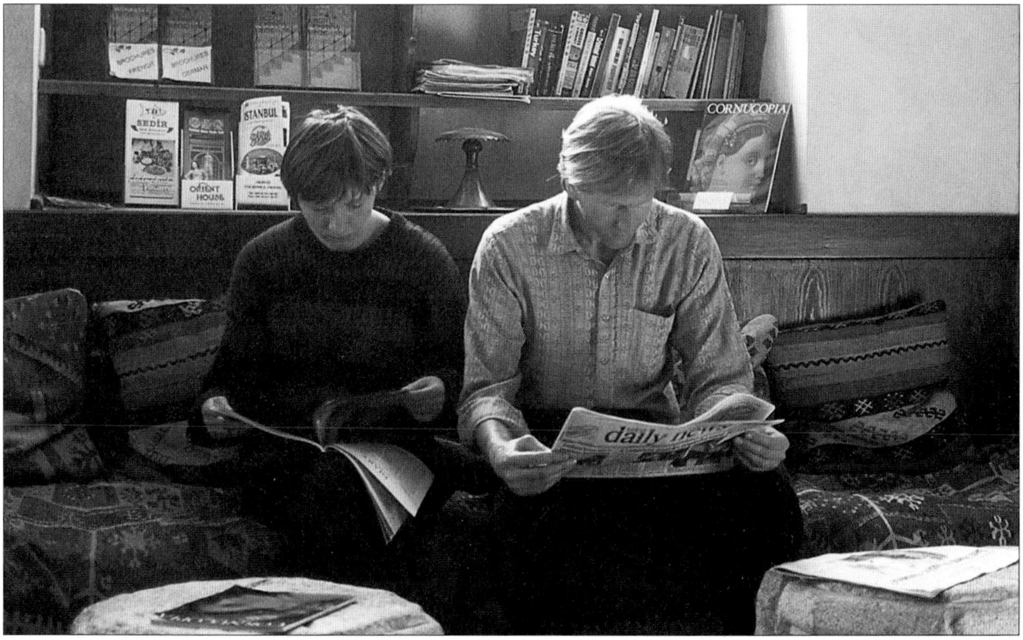

■ **Scan the social columns** *in several newspapers, just to get an idea of how other people have gone about wording their engagement announcements.*

Of course, an announcement can also be placed by the couple. To do this yourself, simply call the newspaper office. Typically, you'll be directed to bring in your engagement information typed up or on a computer disk – if you have a printed engagement announcement that you mailed out, you could give this to the newspaper to copy. Posting your engagement on one of the many wedding websites is another fun option. Many sites give couples their own web pages at no charge.

INTERNET

www.bridesandgrooms.com/engagements/addit.shtml

www.todays-weddings.com/engagements.php

Brides and Grooms allows you to create and post a free web page announcing your engagement. Today's Weddings offers examples of engagement announcements for you to study, as well as letting you submit your own announcement for posting.

Consider forgoing a public newspaper announcement if your family or your partner's family is mourning the loss of a family member. Etiquette experts say this is the one instance when a public announcement is in poor taste.

City newspapers aren't the only publications that are willing to publish engagement announcements. Why not get in touch with the writers and editors of university alumni bulletins, sorority and fraternity newsletters, industry publications, and regional religious periodicals, all of which regularly include personal news.

Writing Your Engagement Announcement

Although an engagement announcement can say anything you want it to there is a standard format to follow. However, you can personalize your announcement in any way you'd like. And you may also have to play around with the standard wording if you and your partner are sending the announcements yourselves.

An additional paragraph may be added telling where the bride and groom went to school, their work titles, how they met, and anything else worth sharing.

Mr. Robert Smith &
Ms. Alice Davis-Smith
of Anytown, Anystate,
announce the engagement
of their daughter,

MS. MARY SMITH,
to MR. JAMES DOE,

son of
Mr. John Doe & Ms. Jane Brown, of
Anothertown, Anotherstate.

A SAMPLE ANNOUNCEMENT

Wedding invitations

THE ENTIRE WEDDING invitation business can be very confusing. Do you need envelopes and reply cards and perhaps a piece of tissue, as well as the invitation itself? Should the card be a single-fold or double-fold or some other style altogether? Before you get yourself too worked up, I'd like to pass on a wise piece of advice: A wedding invitation is just that – a friendly summons inviting someone to share your wedding with you. Puts things in perspective, doesn't it?

If you're having *a small wedding, you might like to make your wedding invites yourself.*

Use a stationer or do it yourself?

The benefits of using an invitation professional are convenience and choice. If you want a special paper (maybe tinted or textured), ink other than the traditional black or dark gray, or an avant garde type, then it's easier to let a professional take care of your invites than to chase around for the special components you'll need to create the look yourself.

So where can you have wedding invitations made? Most towns, however small, have a business that can create wedding invitations. This might be your corner stationer, a bridal consultant, or a print and copy shop. Or you can try accessing an internet wedding stationer. Depending on your town's offerings, these online companies can be less expensive and offer a greater selection than a traditional business.

An invitation professional *can help you with all aspects of card design, from your choice of paper, to ink preference, to selecting your favorite font type.*

Invitation essentials

Whether you're making your own invitations or ordering them, make sure you include the following:

- Wedding date, including day of the week.
- Wedding time.
- Ceremony location.
- Reception location, if separate from the ceremony.
- All four parents' names, including both mothers' first names.
- Both partner's full names, including any middle names.
- A response date by which time acceptances should be received.

Trivia...

It's estimated that 180 guests are invited to the average wedding, so the cost of getting invitations designed and printed can be high. This is one point worth considering when you are budgeting and whittling down on the number of guests invited to your wedding.

Don't forget to proof your invitation carefully for spelling, typographical, or any other possible errors. You don't want to risk sending your guests to the wrong venue on the wrong date.

If you're a do-it-yourself type, creating your own wedding invitations should be an easy project – especially with invitation software available at most office supply stores and many internet party-planning sites. But will these self-done cards look as good as professionally made invitations? Well, yes, they can look as good or even better. But beware: they can also look worse if you don't have access to a quality printer or are unable to buy the heavy stock paper that contributes to the look of the finished result.

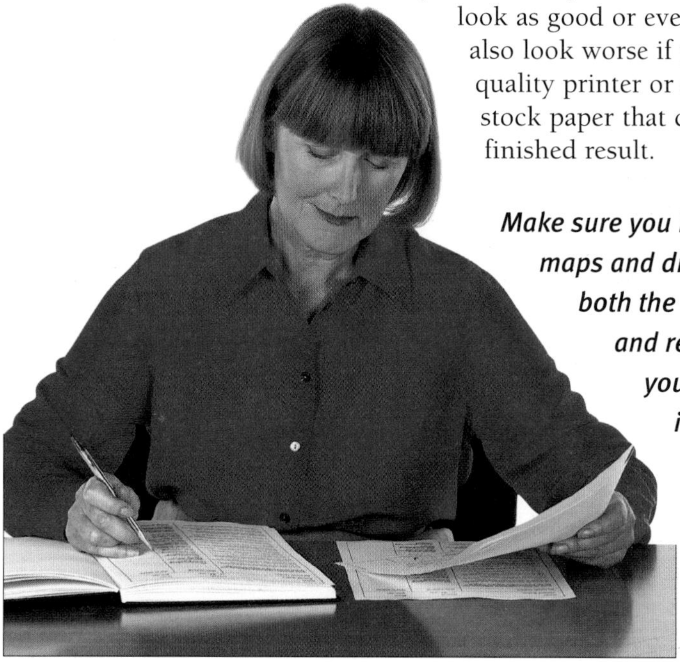

Make sure you include any maps and directions to both the ceremony and reception with your wedding invitations.

It's vital to *double check the information you use to create your invitations (such as location addresses), as well as casting an eye over the finished product.*

Word play

An invitation's primary purpose is to relay information accurately, without offending anyone. To ensure your invitations can do just that, follow (however loosely you'd like) the universal models shown below:

Although there's no hard and fast rule to invitation styling, the bride and groom's names are typically placed on separate lines. Play around with the design and decide on what works best for you.

Sarah Jane Brown
and
Laurence Olivier Smith

request the pleasure of your company at their marriage
Saturday, July 20
2005
at 3:00 p.m.

Smarttown Country Club, Inequity, Anystate
Reception immediately following ceremony

INVITATION FROM THE BRIDE AND GROOM

Mr. James Brown and Dr. Susan Quick Brown
request the honor of your presence
at the marriage of their daughter

Sarah Jane Brown
to
Laurence Olivier Smith

Saturday, the twentieth of July
Two thousand five
at three o' clock in the afternoon

Smarttown Country Club, Inequity, Anystate
Reception immediately following ceremony

INVITATION FROM THE BRIDE'S PARENTS

Addressing etiquette

Here's how to avoid offending any of your invitees:

- When addressing a female, consider using the term Ms. This fail-safe option is the feminine equivalent to Mr., and can be used regardless of the individual's age or marital status.
- Avoid using nicknames, no matter how long you've known the person. Make a phone call or two and find out Muffy's or Junior's real name.
- Either use both first names when addressing a married couple, or no first names at all. Avoid the old-fashioned "Mr. and Mrs. John Doe." Only one member of this couple is named John, and it's rarely the female half. Every woman I know – including those my mother's age – hates having her husband's first name stand in for hers. "It makes me feel like my husband owns me," says a grandmother I know.
- If one of your guests is a doctor, use the title Dr., instead of Mr. or Ms. If both members of a couple are doctors, use Drs. – so, for example, Drs. Leonard Johnston and Renee Thomas. The same rule applies to the bride and groom – if either are doctors, use the title before his or her name in the body of the invitation; use Mr. or Ms. with the non-doctor so his or her name won't look naked.
- If a married woman uses both her surname and her husband's surname, your invitation should use both as well.

ELEMENTS OF STYLE

There are various things you should know about invitation styles:

- **Paper:** The most formal paper options are ecru and white. That said, invitations can be any color you'd like. More and more couples are choosing paper in one of the wedding's theme colors.
- **Ink:** Black and dark gray are the most popular ink colors, though gold and silver are also favorites. For semi-formal or informal weddings, many couples opt for using an ink in the same shade or tone as the wedding colors.
- **Type style:** There are few social restrictions put on type style, meaning even an invitation to the most formal wedding can be festooned with flowery script, or branded with bold, all-capital type.

Don't stress too much over style. Simply remember that, like the love you share with your partner, your wedding invitations should be unique.

- **Print style:** The most popular option is straight printing, although engraved print is another wedding favorite.
- **About the folds:** Most invitations are single-fold, double-fold, or single card. The single-fold wedding invitation is probably the most common. It resembles a greeting card with a single fold on the left hand-side. The invitation itself is printed or engraved on the front and the inside is left blank. The double-fold wedding invitation consists of a single-fold invitation that is folded in half again, from top to bottom. The single card is exactly that – a single card, equal in size to the front page of the single-fold invitation. The invitation is printed on the front of the card.
- **Keep things consistent:** All your various announcements and invitations should use the same paper and ink color.

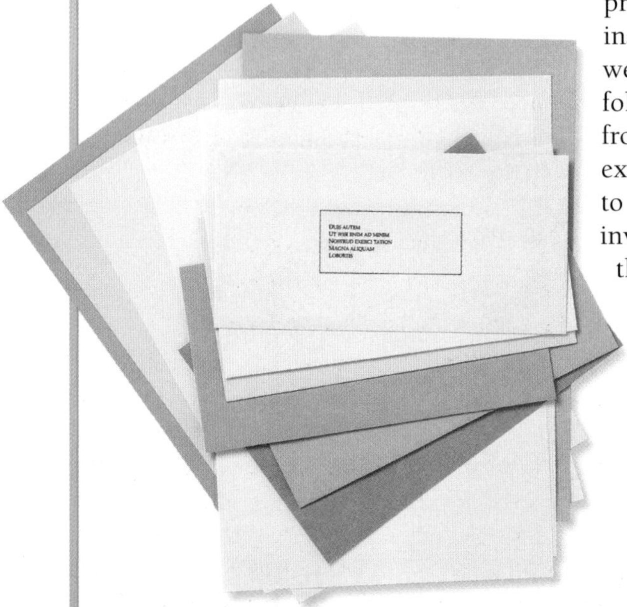

■ **Why not choose** *paper for your invitations in a different shade or texture to your envelopes? For a really plush look, opt for envelopes lined in tissue paper.*

- When inviting the adult, home-residing son or daughter of a couple, he or she should get a separate invitation from his or her parents. A general rule is every single person over 18 should receive his or her own invitation.
- If a married woman never uses her husband's surname when referring to herself, neither should you. Try "Mr. Charlie Williams and Ms. Sandra Bronwyn."
- If a guest was or is in the service, use his or her rank: Lieutenant Scott Davis or Colonel Adam Marshall. The same rule applies to the bride and groom – if either are in the military, use the title before his or her name in the body of the invitation; use Mr. or Ms. with the civilian so his or her name won't look naked.

Keep a copy *of your invitation to store in your wedding photo album.*

Ordering basics

If you've chosen to have someone else make your invitations for you, the ordering process can be a bit daunting. Basically, what you need is a certain number of invitations, the same number of invitation envelopes, and as many ***reply cards*** and separate envelopes for the reply cards. Some brides choose to mail all the above in a slightly larger, outer envelope – this saves marring the invitation envelope, in which everything else will be snuggled. The choice is yours – one option is dressier, the other is much more ecologically sound, as well as costing less in postage.

DEFINITION

Reply cards *are small cards, accompanied by pre-addressed, stamped envelopes and tucked into the wedding invitations. Your guests are expected to record their name and their answer – "yes, they will attend," or "no, they will not attend" – on the card, place it in its special envelope, then send it back to you. It makes planning easier if you request a reply no less than 30 days before the wedding. Incidentally, if you are making your own wedding invitations, don't forget to make up as many reply cards, too.*

Heard of "save the date" cards? These are cards that are sent out by couples with long engagements to remind guests to set aside time to attend the wedding. These can be sent before the wedding invitations are posted.

Most suppliers deliver these items to you in batches of 25. Better to be safe than sorry and over-order, even if it means having to exceed the number you need by 15 or 20. The little extra you pay now will give you peace of mind in the long-term. You never know how many mistakes you may make addressing envelopes, or who in your family will want a souvenir invitation for their scrapbooks.

Assembling the invitations

Now you can begin putting together the "invitation packet." Start by placing stamps on all of your response envelopes. Next, clear off a large space and place the items in the order in which they go, from the bottom of the stack to top: wedding invitation, tissue if using, reception card if using, map if using, and reply envelope with the reply card tucked under the flap. Place all this in the invitation envelope, with the printed side of all the contents facing the envelope's flap.

> **Trivia...**
>
> *Ever wonder why many invitations come with a piece of tissue enclosed? The practice began as a way to blot excess ink in the days when ink was slower drying than it is now. This ensured the invitation wouldn't be a smeary mess by the time it reached its destination. Though it holds no use in this day and age, many couples continue to enclose tissue with their cards.*

Before you sit down to assemble your invitations, make one complete "invitation packet" and take it to the post office for weighing. If you know exactly how much postage the bundle will require then you can choose stamps that are complementary to your wedding theme.

If you are not using a separate outer wrapper, then hand write the guest's name and address on the envelope – officially called "the invitation envelope" – and that's it, you're finished.

If, however, you decide to use a separate outer envelope – in this book referred to as "the outer wrapper" – then hand write the guest's name on the invitation envelope and place it unsealed in the outer wrapper. You should ensure that the guest's name faces the flap of the outer wrapper. (Incidentally, I continue to do so but I still haven't found a proper explanation of why the invitation envelope should be left unsealed.) Then simply hand write the guest's name and address on the outer wrapper and take it to the post office. If your handwriting is dreadful – no judgments here, mine is too – consider hiring a calligrapher to do the duties.

Directions to your wedding and reception can be typed up and photocopied or printed up in a formal way by your invitation maker. These can then be included with your wedding and reception invitations.

■ **Putting your invitations** *together is a little like working on an assembly line, but the process will be fun if you set aside plenty of time to do it.*

Reception invitations

Don't worry about reception invitations if your reception will be held in the same location as your ceremony. You will, however, need a reception card if the reception is separate from the wedding. A simple card, it can be tucked into your wedding invitation for those guests invited to both functions; a reception card can be sent alone to individuals invited to the reception only. Most reception cards begin with "Reception immediately following ceremony," at the top of the card, proceeded by the site's name (such as Kingdom Wedding Hall, or the home of Ms. Layla Doud), street address, and city.

Invitations to the wedding rehearsal dinner

Most weddings require a rehearsal, where all attendants, officiants, and the marrying couple come together to practice their wedding-day roles. It's become a happy tradition to follow up the rehearsal with a group meal. Extending an invitation to the rehearsal meal is commonly done by telephone, or nowadays, via e-mail. Both methods are perfectly acceptable. In fact, it's only in recent years that wedding stationers have begun marketing what they call "wedding rehearsal dinner invitations."

Ask your stationer to print up wedding rehearsal dinner invitations using the same paper stock and ink color as your wedding invitations.

A simple summary

- ✓ Sharing your news with friends is one of the most enjoyable parts of your engagement – have fun spreading the word!
- ✓ Formal engagement announcements are not necessary if you contact your friends and family directly.
- ✓ Wedding invitations can be personalized in any way you see fit. Why not match the invitation to your wedding theme?
- ✓ When addressing the envelopes, take into account the name each guest uses. Now's not the time to offend someone.
- ✓ Only send out separate reception invitations if you are holding your reception at a different place from your ceremony.
- ✓ Assembling invitations is easier if you think of the invitation as a "packet" and work in an assembly-line fashion.

Chapter 8

Giving and Receiving Gifts

As with other joyous occasions, weddings offer an opportunity for people to give thoughtful gifts. Wedding guests genuinely want to help you and your partner start your married life comfortably, which explains traditional wedding-gift choices of cash and household items. So yes, presents are an important – and fun – part of getting married. You'll get them during your shower, your bachelorette and bachelor parties, and during your wedding. But as you'll find out in this chapter, getting married is also about giving – both gifts and thanks.

In this chapter...

- ✓ **Gift registry: tacky or practical?**
- ✓ **Sending thank-you cards**
- ✓ **You mean *we* have to give presents to people?**

SET A TABLE UP AT YOUR RECEPTION SO THAT GUESTS HAVE SOMEWHERE TO LEAVE THEIR GIFTS

Gift registry: tacky or practical?

ONCE UPON A TIME, gift registries were not as commonly used as they are now. In fact, the very mention of a ***wedding registry*** *would often prompt discussion about the tackiness of these things. A gift registry implies two things: One, that you expect a gift, which is seen in many etiquette circles as the height of gauche behavior. Two, it attempts to guide a person's gift-buying choices, which many find offensive.*

DEFINITION

A **wedding registry** *is like an extensive wish list. When you register with a store, you make a list of those items that you would like to own. Your wedding guests can then peruse your list, and buy one or more of the articles from it. The store updates the list by removing items as they are purchased.*

Today, rare is the couple who does not register. Every online wedding site has links to at least one store registry; bridal magazines publish article after article on how to register to your best advantage; and it's common to receive bridal shower invitations with the bride and groom's store registry details included.

Want to register for cold, hard cash? There are cash registries available in most countries. For instance, in the United States, the Department of Housing and Urban Development has created a bridal registry savings account with participating Federal Housing Administration-approved banks nationwide. If you open one of these accounts, guests can then deposit cash gifts directly into it.

The stigma registry once carried has been all but erased. Yes, there are individuals out there who maintain that gift registries are tacky, but there are many more people who find registries practical and helpful.

■ **Many guests** *find purchasing gifts from a wedding registry very convenient, especially if the store has a catalog that they can browse from the comfort of their own home.*

Registering know-how

You've decided to register, but want help in going about it. Here are a few ideas:

- Perhaps the most obvious place to start is with a store you and your partner both like, thus ensuring you'll get gifts you actually enjoy. If you can't agree on a single store, you can open a registry at two different stores – one your favorite, one your partner's choice – as long as the stores sell different types of goods.

Keep things simple with your registry. Up to 70 percent of wedding gifts that the bride and groom receive are items that weren't on their original list. Why? Because guests had found the process too complicated.

- Register shortly after you get engaged, so the list will be available for early shoppers.
- Be sure the store is convenient for as many of your wedding guests as possible. National chains or stores with online shopping sites are easiest for a large number of far-flung people to use.
- Before you decide on a particular registry, ask about the store's policy regarding the following: Will the store ship to your address – or any other address you'd like gifts sent to? What is the store's return policy? How long will you have to return items you don't want – will you have enough time after arriving home from your honeymoon to deal with returns?
- Will the store update your list automatically every time a purchase is made? It should, so make sure yours does.
- How long after your wedding will the registry remain active? Since people have up to a year after your wedding to buy you a gift, you should look for a program that remains usable for at least as long.

Registering responsibly

When registering, it's important to follow a few guidelines:

- Make sure you have on your list a number of items that cost, say, $25 or less, for those people who cannot afford to give you costlier gifts. At the same time, you can always add a few more expensive wish list items – your friends might surprise you!
- Etiquette states that you, yourself, cannot tell your guests where you are registered. What you can do is have your parents, best man or maid of honor, attendants, and others spread the word. You can also include registry information on your personal wedding page or wedding newsletter.
- Keep your list at least twice as large as your wedding's guest list to allow a wide range of gift choices. Add new selections to your list periodically to maintain its size.

INTERNET

www.weddinggazette.com

Great advice on thank-you cards, gift giving, registry, and other facets of wedding planning.

- Make a note of who helped you set up your registry. This way, you'll have a contact person in case you have a question or problem.
- Remember that guests are not obliged to use your registry. Many will forgo even looking at it and get you cash or something else of their own choosing. This is perfectly acceptable.
- Do not register without your partner's knowledge. Before making out your list, the two of you should sit down and write a thorough list of all the things you do – and don't – need. Wedding gifts are for the couple, not just the bride.
- If you and your partner do not need housewares, then don't feel you must register at a store carrying them. Electronic stores, music stores, bookstores, sporting goods stores, clothing stores, and hardware stores are some of your other options.

■ **Visit a store** *with your partner and make notes of the items you would like.*

Deciding not to register

Traditionally, just-married couples received an array of household goods, which makes sense when you consider that long ago, most people went straight from their parents' houses to their married home. This gave them little opportunity to amass a collection of cups, serving utensils, electronics, linens, and other homemaking items. Today, however, many brides and grooms have been on their own or living together for a number of years before marrying. If that's the case for you, there's a good chance you already have all the household items you need and registering may seem somewhat superfluous.

If you're not registering but there's an item you'd love to receive, ask your mother or maid of honor to tell a guest of your desire. Make sure your helper doesn't repeat the information to several people – you don't want to get five of the same item.

If you have any qualms about the whole registry business – perhaps it feels more opportunistic than you're really comfortable with – then simply don't register. It's not a necessary part of getting married. You need to be aware that couples have been getting hitched for centuries without ever having felt the need to create a gift wish list. Decide between you.

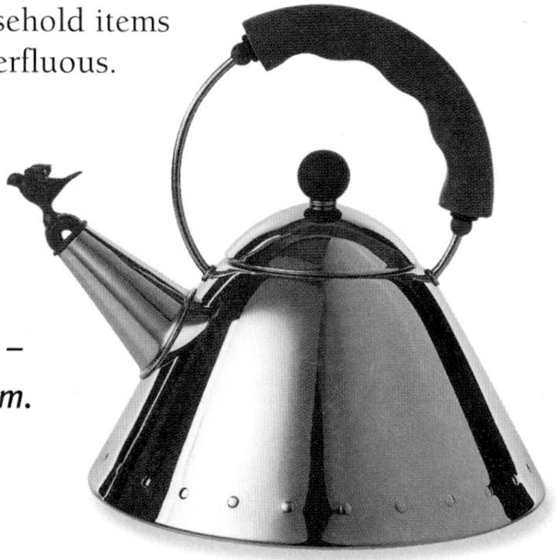

■ **Writing a list** *means being able to choose household items you really need – rather than items that aren't to your taste.*

Sending thank-you cards

SAYING THANK YOU is an under-appreciated art. Expressing gratitude for the nice things people do for you – and buy for you – is as important from an etiquette standpoint as it is from a human standpoint. But how do you go about thanking those who've presented you with gifts? There is some etiquette involved, so here's what you need to know:

- Gifts received before the wedding should be acknowledged with a thank-you card within two weeks of receipt.
- Having thank-you cards printed up that match your wedding invitations is a nice-looking way to send your thanks – but it isn't necessary. Store-bought cards will do – especially if you need to send cards out before you'll be getting your matching thank-you cards back from the printer.
- If you received a gift, it should be specifically mentioned in your thank-you card. For instance, "Thank you so much for the lovely toaster. It matches the rest of my appliances beautifully and looks great in my kitchen."
- If you receive a monetary gift, your thank-you should mention how you plan to use that money. For instance, "Thanks so much for your generous gift. We are planning to buy a new bed soon and your gift will help us do that."
- When it comes to receiving gifts, remember it is the thought that counts. This means that all presents, regardless of how small or large they might be, should be received with equal enthusiasm. After all, the person buying you a $25 gift may have had to save and scrimp more than the individual who is giving you a $200 gift.
- Presents received on your wedding day or in the days following the occasion should be acknowledged with a thank-you card within three months after you return from your honeymoon.

Trivia...

Not that this is going to happen to you, but it's good to know: If a wedding is called off after gifts have started to arrive, it's considered standard etiquette to return those presents, even if they are cash gifts.

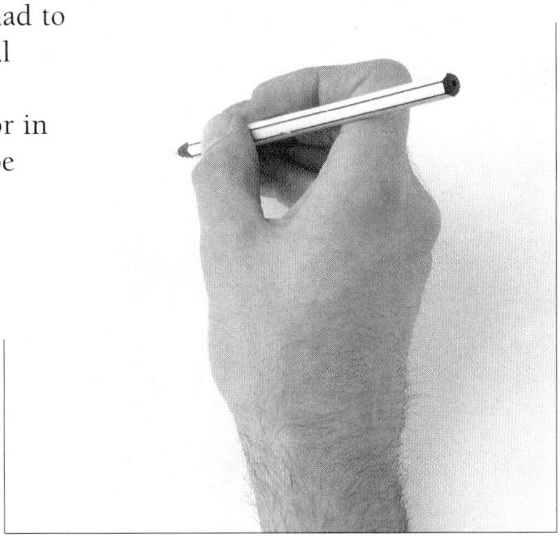

■ **Put time aside to write** *thank-you cards to those who've presented you with gifts to celebrate your wedding.*

You mean *we* have to give presents to people?

YOUR ATTENDANTS DO A LOT FOR YOU – they travel for you; they spend a lot of money on clothing they may never wear again; they make phone calls and help write out invitations and organize parties. They also do lots of other things, including dealing with you at your most stressed. For all this, they deserve something. A kind of "thank you for all you've done" present, this can be anything you'd like it to be and cost whatever you feel is appropriate.

Gifts for bridal attendants

Buying gifts for your bridal attendants should be easy: Just get them each something you think they would like. Typically, these are "one-size-fits-all" gifts, meaning that each person receives the same gift. But, if your attendants all have wildly different tastes, then you can give each attendant a different – but monetarily comparable – present. Some popular ideas include:

- A day of pampering at a local spa. Why not book all of you on the same day, at a time when everyone will be in the same place?
- Gift certificates to lingerie stores, clothing boutiques, cosmetic shops, and so on.

Treating your bridal attendants *to a day of pampering is not only a good way of thanking them, it's a chance for them to get to know each other, too.*

- Buy them something they can wear with their attendants' outfits, such as a cashmere shawl or earrings from Tiffany's.
- Take all of your attendants out to a day at the theatre, followed by a nice dinner afterward.

Train bearers, ring bearers, flower girls, junior bridesmaids and ushers, groomsmen, ushers, and VIPs also should be presented with gifts. As with any other gift-giving occasion, choose something age-appropriate that you believe the individual would enjoy.

- A case of wine each.
- Handmade quilts, or high-quality bed linens.
- Kitchenware.
- An oversized gift basket of luxury bath products.

Gifts for groomsmen

Traditionally, the best man was the guy solely responsible for helping the groom. All the groomsmen did was show up at the wedding, where they worked as ushers, bridal attendant escorts, and dance partners to your great aunts. Things have changed a bit since then – groomsmen can be asked to help with a variety of pre-wedding tasks, such as accompanying the groom to check out site locations or helping to decorate the venue – but most find they have fewer responsibilities than bridal attendants. That said, these important helpers still have to get fitted for and rent a suit, as well as give up time to help you with your big day. For these reasons, they deserve a gift. Here are a few suggestions:

- A car-cleaning kit, including a range of products for both the inside and outside of a vehicle.
- A DVD player – perhaps with a selection of DVDs.
- Gift certificates to spend at their favorite department stores.

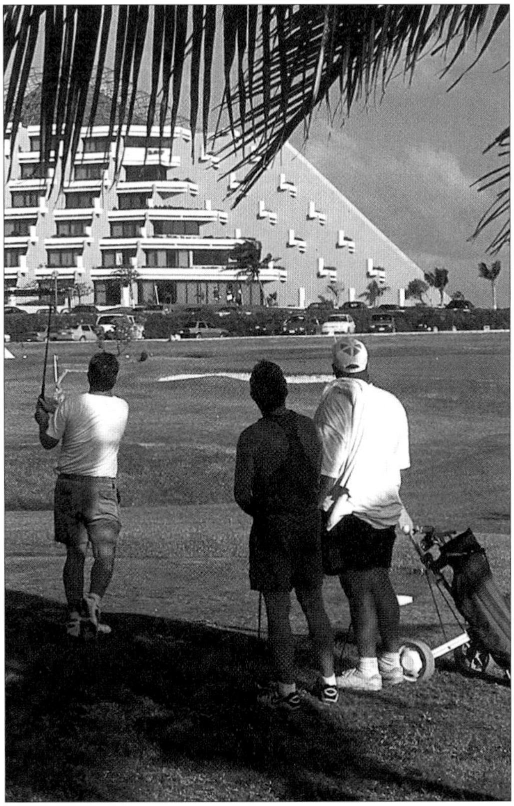

Why not arrange a day at the links *for your groomsmen? It's your chance to thank them, as well as spend some quality time together.*

- Something to wear at the wedding, such as cuff links.
- A boxed CD set, as well as tickets to see a band in concert.

Traditionally, you give attendants their gifts at the rehearsal dinner – unless, however, your gift is a spa day, a concert ticket, or some other kind of outing.

- A stainless steel flask engraved with their initials.
- A grooming kit placed in a high-quality shaving kit.

Gift for the groom, gift for the bride

It has developed into a tradition of sorts for brides and grooms to present each other with a wedding gift. This can be as simple as a box of chocolates sent by the groom to the salon where his bride is getting ready for the ceremony or as extravagant as a new set of windsurfing gear sent by the bride to the couple's honeymoon room for her groom. But please be aware that this gift giving is by no means mandatory. There isn't an etiquette maven alive who says you must do this. Furthermore, many brides and grooms believe their love and support to be the greatest gift they can give their partner.

A BIG THANK YOU

For the simple reason that they bear the heaviest responsibilities, honor attendants, such as your maid of honor and the best man, should receive slightly more extravagant gifts than the other attendants. For instance, if you buy your bridal attendants necklaces, your maid of honor should receive a necklace and earrings. If you're buying your groomsmen aged single-barrel scotch, your best man should receive a larger bottle, as well as a hand-cut decanter and high ball glasses.

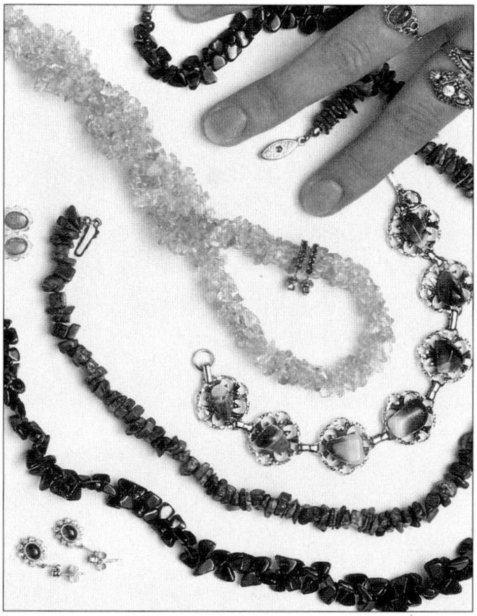

■ **A set of earrings and a necklace** *make an ideal gift for your maid of honor.*

Something for your parents

Giving gifts to your parents is not traditional, nor is it mandatory. What it is, is nice – especially if your parents have helped make your wedding happen, whether with financial contributions, emotional support, or lots of volunteered hours spent decorating or cooking. What you give these special people, and how you give it to them, is completely up to you.

Treat both sets of parents *to a champagne dinner or a meal out, as a way of saying thank you for their help.*

You could give each mother and father a separate gift at the rehearsal meal – if you're having a rehearsal meal – when you give the attendants their gifts. Perhaps you could invite them all to your place for a lovely home-cooked brunch. Or you could do something else entirely. The point is not what you do, but that you do something – that's what will show your parents how much you love them.

A simple summary

- ✓ Wedding registry is a practical way of ensuring you get both what you want and what you need on your wedding day.
- ✓ While most couples these days choose to register for gifts, not registering is an honorable option for those who aren't comfortable with the idea – or who simply don't need anything specific.
- ✓ Gratitude is an important quality for brides and grooms to cultivate. Thank-you cards are an expression of this gratitude.
- ✓ All members of your wedding party – ring bearer, flower girl, and VIP included – should each receive a token of your appreciation for their efforts.
- ✓ Gift exchanging between bride and groom is strictly optional.
- ✓ Giving your parents a gift is a lovely way to thank them for their support.

Chapter 9

Eat, Drink, and Be Married

WEDDINGS ARE THE ULTIMATE CELEBRATION. And, as you probably know, wherever and whenever people come together to celebrate good fortune, there are good things to eat and drink. What good things are offered at your wedding is up to you and your partner. Like the type of ceremony you have, and the bridal attire, decorations, and entertainment you choose, what you serve at your wedding is a personal reflection and will depend on your taste, as well as your budget. As you'll see, you have a wide array of choices!

In this chapter...

- ✓ Your wedding meal
- ✓ Finding a caterer
- ✓ Beverage service
- ✓ A piece of cake
- ✓ Finding a cake maker
- ✓ The cake table

Your wedding meal

WEDDING MEALS ARE time-dependent. What this means is that a morning wedding will be followed by a breakfast or brunch reception, an early afternoon ceremony will precede a lunch reception, a late afternoon wedding is best followed by tea, an evening ceremony can be paired with a dinner reception, while a late evening wedding could even be matched with a champagne dessert reception. The choice is yours.

Obviously, the types of food and style of service will also be affected by which kind of meal you decide on. And there are many options available to you. Keep reading this chapter and I'll fill you in on the possibilities.

IT'S CHOW TIME!

To help you decide what shape your wedding food may take, here are some typical times for certain meals:

If you're getting married in the summer, you could opt for a late ceremony, followed by a midnight feast.

- Breakfast: 9 a.m. – 11:30 a.m.
- Brunch: 11 a.m. – 1:30 p.m.
- Lunch: 12 p.m. – 3:00 p.m.
- Tea: 2 p.m. – 4 p.m.
- Dinner: 6 p.m. onward
- Cocktail reception: 8 p.m. onward
- Dessert and champagne reception: 8 p.m. onward

■ **A wedding tea** *can be the perfect way to follow an afternoon ceremony.*

Different types of meal

You can offer your guests an elegant meal in any number of ways. Your decision depends on your preferences and how formal your wedding is.

- **Hors d'oeuvres:** When the wedding and reception take place at the same site, it is customary to offer hors d'oeuvres to guests while the bride and groom finish up with wedding business, such as having photographs taken. Hors d'oeuvres also keep guests busy – and mingling – while the kitchen is finishing the main meal. These appetizers can be offered in one of two ways: Passed by tray-carrying waiters or set up on tables as "hors d'oeuvres stations." Using waiters keeps people from crowding the food tables, and it also makes the guests feel as if they're being taken care of. However, using appetizer stations is cheaper because you don't have to pay for waitstaff.
- **Seated or standard sit-down service:** This is the type of service you're probably most familiar with. It's used often in restaurants and at many weddings. The food is plated and portioned in the kitchen and guests are served while sitting down at tables. This is a versatile option that can be used at both informal and formal weddings.
- **Russian-style service:** Here, the server sets up platters of food at the table, then prepares one guest's plate at a time. This is slower than sit-down service, but more flexible because it allows guests to ask only for those items they are interested in. It's a formal option.
- **French-style service:** Platters of food are brought to each table, where they are presented to the guests, who then pass around the platters and serve themselves. The advantage of this is that guests can take what they want, and leave what they don't want. A semi formal to formal option, this type of service requires a certain amount of space, and service can be slow.
- **Family style:** This is similar to the way that food is served in most homes. Items are placed in serving platters in the middle of the table; guests help themselves. This is an informal option that cuts down on waitstaff, since only periodic platter-replenishing visits to each table are necessary.

Canapés are often *served with champagne, after the ceremony. They are a good option if you are expecting a long wait before a sit-down meal.*

Most caterers and site food service staff add gratuities to their final bill – if in doubt, simply ask. However, you may want to give something extra (anywhere from $35 on up) to individual servers or bartenders who have gone out of their way to be kind and attentive to you and your guests.

- **Buffet style:** Food is laid out on a table, and guests stand in a line for the opportunity to serve themselves or be served by one or two "food dishers." An easy way to save on waitstaff, this is a strictly informal option.
- **Food stations:** This option is similar to buffets, but more lavish. An increasingly popular option, food stations are often created around specific cuisines or food trends, such as the Thai food station, the wrap food station, the Chinese food station, the pasta station, the salad station, and so on.

Trivia...

In some countries, it is traditional to give each guest a small bundle of sugared almonds, wrapped in linen or something similar. Each of the sugared almonds – traditionally, five – is meant to represent an aspect of married life: health, wealth, happiness, long life, and fertility.

Catering for different diets

People's tastes differ. Many don't eat meat, including fish or poultry. There are those who won't eat two particular foods in combination in the same meal (and remember, those who don't mix meat with dairy will not want butter on vegetables). Then there are those who happily eat vegetables and anything aquatic, but won't touch food taken from a two- or four-footed creature. Others simply won't eat food if it isn't meat. And don't forget those who are allergic to nuts, strawberries, or shellfish.

When planning a wedding menu, keep in mind that the most common allergens are shellfish, nuts, strawberries, and egg whites.

Unless you know the specific dietary preference of every single guest attending your wedding, it's probably safe to assume you'll have at least one person dining with you who has particular tastes. How to accommodate everyone?

It's easier than you'd think – and the secret is to provide two or three entrées. Serve one vegetarian entrée, such as baked vegetable lasagne, and one entrée containing poultry. The vegetarian entrée will be perfect for the vegetarians, the pescatarians (those who'll eat fish but won't eat red meat or poultry), and those who won't mix meat and dairy. The poultry entrée can be eaten by all the carnivores and omnivores. If you want to, you can go a step further and offer a third, ***vegan*** entrée for anyone who doesn't eat dairy products at all, or who is looking for a low-calorie option.

DEFINITION

A **vegan** *– pronounced "VEE-gahn" – may also be called a strict vegetarian because he or she eats no type of animal product, regardless of whether the product was retrieved without killing the animal. Thus, a vegan eats no eggs, no honey, no cheese, no milk – indeed, no dairy of any kind.*

Something to suit *your* tastes

Okay, that's the guests catered for, but what if either of you – the bride and groom – prescribe to a particular diet? Should the reception be catered to reflect your tastes? Ultimately, the menu you decide on is your choice, but think about why you follow a particular diet.

■ **The food served at your wedding** *should be simple, not fussy. Catering for all tastes by serving dishes of meat, fish, and vegetables ensures no one will go hungry.*

Do you follow a low-calorie, low-fat diet to watch your weight? Do you avoid simple carbohydrates because you're a diabetic? Do you forgo shellfish for religious reasons? If your diet is health-based, it's easy to offer a few selections that support your choices, as well as providing some slightly less healthy dishes. Are you a vegetarian because you're concerned with animal rights and environmental causes? If your diet is based on conviction or religion, you can honor these beliefs by creating the entire menu around them. (As a precautionary measure, you might consider forgoing pork, even if you eat it, because it is shunned by a number of religious groups.)

Choose a vegetarian menu if you're vegetarian, a kosher menu if you're kosher, and so forth. Your reception is your chance to show off your tastes and beliefs – and the food you choose to serve is a wonderful and easy way to do this. There's no need to alert people that you'll be having a halal or vegan wedding – simply provide the best of those foods you'd like to offer and everyone will be happy.

The fewer entrée choices you provide, the lower your catering bill will be. Whittle your entrée choices down to two or three that can work for a wide range of people.

Finding a caterer

YOU KNOW WHAT FOOD you want at your wedding and even how you'd like it served; now all you need is someone to make it for you. Traditionally, this is where a caterer comes in. Wedding catering is big business nowadays, so it should be easy for you to get in touch with a number of these food professionals operating close to where you live.

■ **Phone several** *caterers and arrange to meet them to discuss their services.*

Your task is to find the professional who can do the job the most efficiently, with the best taste, for the least amount of money. To find her or him, there are a number of things you can do.

First, speak to married friends who you know were happy with the food provided at their reception. Use a wedding website to seek out caterers in your area. Next, ask at the local wedding boutique or florist for recommendations. And finally, if you have one, ask your bridal consultant. Once you've found a caterer you like, you need to raise the following points with them:

All wedding caterers should be licensed by the state in which they work and they must also have liability insurance – check their credentials.

- **Budget:** Have a rough idea of how much you're looking to pay for your reception. A good caterer is creative enough to work with whatever you can afford to spend.
- **Taste testing:** Can you taste the planned dishes? This is important – you don't want to end up serving two main dishes that you think taste horrible.
- **Style:** Do you and the caterer share similar tastes? If you're having an informal wedding, can he or she provide a finger buffet to suit the relaxed atmosphere?
- **Waitstaff:** Ask if your caterer provides servers – most do. You'll need roughly one server for every ten guests. Is it important to you what the servers will be wearing? Can you make wardrobe requests?
- **Table decorations:** Some caterers provide these as part of the service. Does yours? If so, will he or she work within your wedding theme?
- **Leftovers:** Most brides and grooms have little opportunity to eat at their own reception. Will your caterer make up a leftover basket for you both to eat later?
- **Flexibility:** If you want a special family dish made, will your caterer be willing to make it from your personal recipe? Likewise, if you have food preferences – vegetarian, or no beef, for example – will the caterer cheerfully accommodate you?

- **Guaranteed numbers:** Often caterers quote prices based upon a minimum number of guests – usually around 100 people. If you're inviting far fewer than this amount, will the caterer "penalize" you with an extra fee?
- **Wedding cake:** Will your caterer provide this? Some include a cake in their fee.
- **Tax and gratuities:** Are these included? Should you know about any other fees?
- **Serviceware:** Will your caterer provide tablecloths, napkins, dishes, glassware, and flatware? If so, can you view this serviceware prior to your wedding day?

Going it alone

Catering your own wedding – or having your family do it – is another alternative. The pros of this option are that it's inexpensive and you're guaranteed that the food will taste just like you want it to. Also, if you have any dietary restrictions or follow a certain eating plan, you will be able to tailor each dish to suit your needs.

The cons of D.I.Y catering are that what you save in money, you pay for in time – either your own or, if you're having family members cook for you, their time. Furthermore, you may not have the space or the equipment needed to cook for a large number of people. Lastly, most caterers supply waitstaff, linens, and other necessities, which you will have to arrange for yourself if you decide to make your own meal.

SAVING MONEY ON WEDDING FOOD

If you can't stomach the idea of catering your own wedding, and your mom refuses to do it for you, you can still save money using a professional. Here's how:

- Be aware that many caterers will try to sell you the most extravagant and, therefore, costly meal package.
- Do you really need ten types of hors d'oeuvres? Stick to four and make them vegetarian to save on costs. No one will feel slighted.
- Don't get sucked in to purchasing six courses. A salad, main meal, and the wedding cake for dessert is all the food you need.
- Some caterers may be willing to prepare certain courses, allowing you to furnish the others. If the idea of catering your entire party is a daunting one, perhaps you could manage preparing your own hors d'oeuvres and salad, and have a friend make your wedding cake. This way, the only preparation the caterer will need do is to make your main-course selections.
- If you don't want to go overboard on food expense, avoid seafood and beef, which will increase your costs. Instead, decide on a poultry and a vegetarian main course.

Beverage service

TO SOME, BEVERAGE SERVICE is more essential to the wedding reception than the food. It's certainly true that alcohol can add a little something to all weddings – not least in bringing everyone together to toast the bride and groom. But depending on how you handle the subject of beverages, the cost of drinks for the day could end up mirroring that of the food.

Different bar services

Just as there are different types of meal service, there are also several types of bar service. The following is a brief description of each:

- A full, open bar is the most extravagant of the options in that it offers just about every type of liquor available, as well as a selection of beers, wines, and non-alcoholic beverages – and at no cost to the guest. This means a guest can choose whisky rather than rum, or drink five whisky on the rocks in a row – and all for free. Not surprisingly, a full, open bar is warmly welcomed by guests but it's also the most risky option if you're worried about drunken behavior or people getting home safely. This kind of bar is always the most expensive option.
- A full bar simply means the bar stocks every type of alcohol available. However, unlike a full, open bar, it isn't necessarily free to guests.
- An open bar is a free bar. This means that the selection of drinks available may be limited solely to house-brand liquors, domestic beer, wine, and non-alcoholic beverages. That said, many open bars offer an extravagant range of beverages and are stocked with every kind of drink your guests might ask for. Here's a useful tip if you want to keep your beverage costs down while preventing any excessive drunken behavior: Keep the availability of hard liquor on offer to a minimum. This will generally ensure your bar costs stay low while keeping your guests merry but not too drunk.

Serving alcoholic beverages *at your reception will keep most guests happy, but be sure to provide non-alcoholic drinks too.*

Never underestimate the cost of serving alcohol at your wedding. If you include spirits behind your open bar, you could be faced with quite a hefty bill at the end of your wedding reception. Be prepared!

- A cash bar means that alcoholic drinks – other than the wine offered with dinner – are paid for by the drinkers. This popular option is used by those who are worried about tipsy guests or don't have the funds for a more lavish bar.

When alcohol is served at a wedding reception, there is always the remote chance that someone may have too much to drink and then drive – and end up in an accident. If you're offering alcohol, check your liability, as well as that of the caterer and the venue for damages in case this happens. You may also want the phone numbers of several car services to take guests home safely.

- A partial cash bar is a bar that offers certain drinks for free – usually beer, wine and non-alcoholic beverages. Mixed drinks and liquor are charged for.
- Then there are mixed style bars. Many couples opt to start the reception with an open bar, which continues while hors d'oeuvres are served. Once dinner begins, the open bar changes to a cash bar.

A do-it-yourself bar

Most sites, such as wedding halls and country clubs, have restrictions that prevent you – as wedding organizer – bringing in your own alcohol. If you're marrying at home or at a site that has no restrictions on what you bring in, you can save a considerable amount of money by supplying your own drinks.

- Set a liquor budget and stick to it. You can easily work with a smaller budget by using less expensive liquors, and wines from smaller, lesser-known wineries.
- Find a reputable wine and liquor store that you feel comfortable working with. Knowledgeable staff can help you select the right beverages according to your budget, your guests' tastes, and your menu.

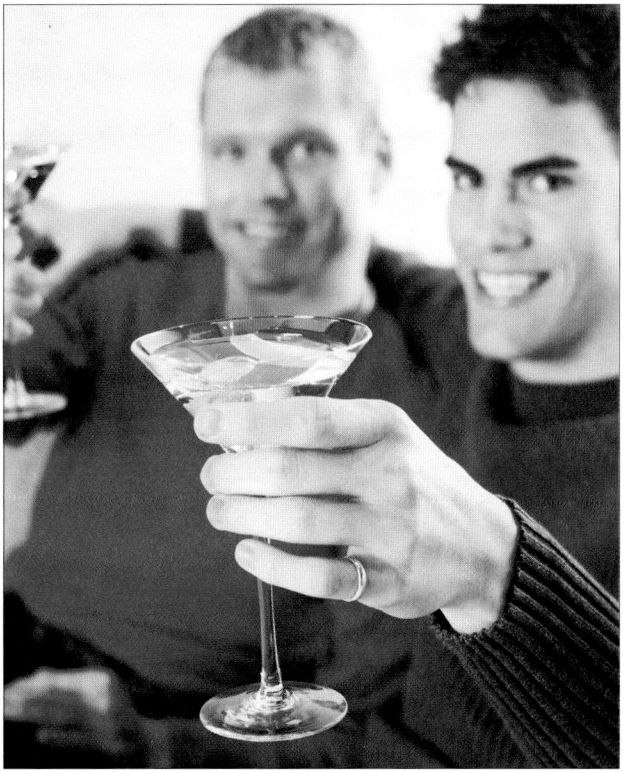

■ **Deciding on where** *you would like to hold your wedding reception also means deciding what kind of drinks you'll serve and how much they will cost you.*

- Does your chosen liquor store charge for delivery? Thankfully, many don't. Will they credit you for any unopened bottles of wine? And remember, many reception venues charge for corkage – this can be very costly so check beforehand.
- At many receptions you'll find champagne flutes already filled with bubbly, sitting on each table, ready for the first wedding toast. If you're having a champagne toast, find out if you, too, could arrange glasses of champagne to be waiting for you. Surprisingly, this is a good way of saving money. This is because the guests don't actually see the brand of champagne being poured – and so it needn't be an expensive one. If you need further encouragement to go with a less costly brand, remember: Most people just sip the champagne for the toast, then switch to wine or something else to drink with their meals.

Champagne at weddings *is a nice tradition, but serving cheaper, sparkling white wines is an option.*

On your wedding day, you will be the recipient of at least one toast – and probably many more. As the toastee, you do not stand. Instead, smile, raise your glass toward the toaster, then take a sip of your drink. You are not obliged to propose a toast in return.

- What quantities you should purchase depends on your guests' tastes in wine, beer, and liquor. For example, a very general guideline for 100 guests is: two cases of domestic beer; two cases of microbrewery beer; two cases of imported beer; two or three cases of lite beer; two cases of chardonnay; two cases of white zinfandel; two cases of cabernet sauvignon; one case of pinot noir; one case of merlot; and one to two cases of champagne. As for liquor, consider stocking up on the following: five liters of vodka; three liters of gin; two liters of rum; two liters of scotch; two liters of bourbon; 750ml of vermouth; and three liters of Kahlua. You may also want a bottle of a few different types of liqueurs.
- Remember, not every guest will want to drink alcohol. Some will be too young, while others may be avoiding the hard stuff because they're driving. Non-alcoholic provisions you'll need include: ice; one or more coolers to keep drinks cold; orange juice; cranberry juice; lemon juice; lime juice; soda water; tonic water; seltzer; lemons; limes; soda; diet soda; ginger ale; milk; maraschino cherries; olives; cocktail stirrers; straws; and glassware.

INTERNET

www.foreverwed1.com

Great do-it-yourself information on catering – and setting up bar – for your own wedding.

A toast!

You probably know what a toast is: A friendly salute given by one person to honor another person or persons. It is customary at weddings for the best man and the maid of honor – and often various parents, friends, and even the bride and groom themselves – to offer a toast. These short eulogies can include a little bit about how the couple met, a good wish for the duo's future, or an expression of friendship, love, or appreciation. Here's a blow-by-blow guide to the art of giving a toast.

Make sure that not only your glass but also all other glasses are filled before you propose a toast. It's fine to stand up, say you'd like to propose a toast, and motion to a waiter to begin filling glasses.

- Once you're ready to begin, raise your glass with your right hand, making sure that the glass is held straight from the shoulder.
- If you know beforehand that you will be offering a toast, write it out on a card in advance and bring it with you. Something to remember: Do not include inside jokes that half the audience won't understand, and stay away from anything that may hurt feelings or offend. Thus, no talk about the bride's large pool of admirers, or her early days as an underwear model. Likewise, avoid mentioning the groom's past womanizing or his struggle with alcohol.

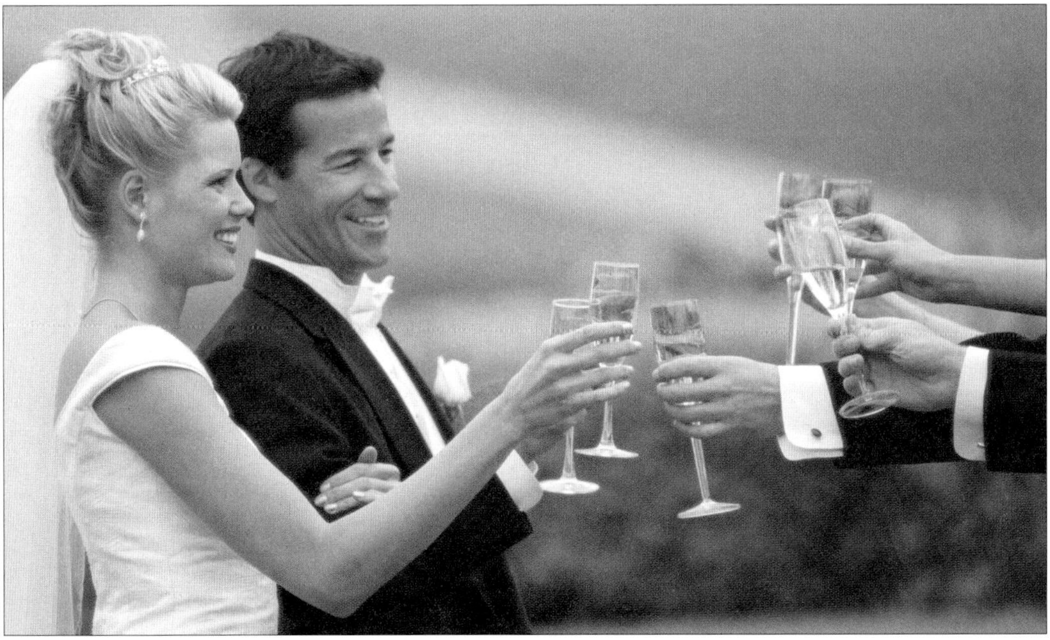

Raising a toast is a charming tradition. *If you're called upon to propose a toast to the bride and groom, grasp the opportunity to express how happy you are for them.*

- If the space is large or your voice is small, walk yourself over to the nearest microphone – probably the DJ's or the band's – and use it.
- Somewhere early on in your toast, inform the audience of your relationship with the toastee and how you came to know her or him.
- Refrain from making any negative comments about the toastee, no matter how subtle. I was recently at a wedding where the maid of honor – the bride's sister – relayed her surprise at the bride's choice of groom, especially since the guy "looked like Curly from The Three Stooges." There was a collective gasp, then an uncomfortable feeling as the guests studied their napkins.
- Avoid negativity in general. However well intentioned, it's not nice to say something like, "Here's to the bride and groom. With 50 percent of all marriages these days ending in divorce, let's hope their marriage escapes untouched."
- Be brief. Limit your speech to five minutes. If you talk for too much longer, you'll start to lose both the concentration and the patience of your audience.
- End your toast with a formal indication that you are coming to a close. You do this by saying, "Please join in a toast to my fabulous groom, Jack. To Jack!"

The best man is usually called upon to raise a toast, *and he'll have the rapt attention of every guest. Now's his chance to regale them with all those humorous anecdotes about the groom.*

- It is customary to clink glasses after the toast has been proposed, but before it is drunk. This tradition is an ancient one: It was believed that the clink of glasses frightened away any evil spirits who could harm the couple or upset the wedding ceremony.

■ **Alcohol needn't** *be a feature of your wedding. Serve a non-alcoholic punch.*

A dry reception

What, a wedding without alcohol? Is that possible? Well, yes, it is – and done more often than you might realize. The bride and groom may choose not to serve alcohol for any number of reasons, all personal, all valid.

Perhaps one partner is underage. Maybe the bride is a recovering alcoholic. The groom might have a health condition that prevents him from drinking. Perhaps the couple are having the reception at a church that forbids alcohol. Or maybe the bride and groom would simply rather spend their money on the food, or the honeymoon, or put it toward a house. The reason could even be because one of the guests has a problem with alcohol and neither the bride nor the groom wants to risk any bad behavior on their special day.

Can a wedding toast be performed without alcohol? Of course it can. If you want a festive, alcohol-free drink for the toast, consider sparkling white grape juice. Toasting etiquette, however, frowns on toasting with hot beverages or water.

If you, too, would prefer a dry reception, then there's no reason to feel apologetic about your wishes. You may hear a few grumbles from relatives, such as Uncle Ed, who wants a scotch on the rocks. But as long as you warn guests of your intentions some time in advance, there shouldn't be a problem.

Trivia...

Although champagne has been around for centuries as a non-bubbly white wine, the fizzy version we know was created in the late 1600s by a blind, French Benedictine monk named Dom Perignon. Upon tasting his discovery, Perignon exclaimed, "Brothers, come quick! I am tasting stars!"

Instead of serving liquor, beer, and champagne on your wedding day, offer your guests a variety of interesting non-alcoholic beverages. Serve these in addition to the standard sparkling water, sodas, tea, coffee, and so forth. Fun options include lemonade in the warmer months and mulled cider in the cooler months, while tea punches, juice punches, and fruit spritzers can be served at any time of year.

A piece of cake

LIKE EVERY OTHER ELEMENT of your wedding day, it's important – or, at least, very nice – to have a cake you love. Fortunately, from a cake standpoint, there has never been a better time to get married: You can have a traditional off-white tiered confection, a tower of brightly colored hearts or other shapes, a large sheet cake, a dessert shaped like a flower or some other sentimental item – really, you can have whatever your cake maker can pull off. So, think about how you want your cake to look and how you'd like it to taste, and keep reading.

INTERNET

www.weddingchannel.com

This site has terrific information on wedding cakes, including photographs of dozens of different wedding cakes, a cake quiz, and a cake budgeting tool.

What kind of cake?

As most bakers will tell you, your cake can be any flavor you want it to be. If your favorite cake is a white sponge cake, then so be it. If you love angel food, go for it. If you dream of devil's food, or mousse cake or spice cake, fine. You really can have whatever you want. But – and isn't there always a but? – the cake recipe you choose may influence what your finished product will look like, and vice versa.

Let me explain: A delicate chiffon cake may not be strong enough to support multiple tiers, heavy frosting, and weighty decorations. A dense fruitcake may weigh too much to stand on your mother's heirloom cake pillars. If your wedding is an outdoor summer affair, heat-sensitive desserts such as cheesecake, meringue, or ice cream cake aren't your best choices. The most all-around, easy-to-decorate, easy-to-stack, temperature-proof cake is the butter cake. This not too dense, not too delicate, not too moist, not too dry variety of cake can be flavored in a variety of delicious ways, such as with chocolate, lemon, liquor, vanilla, almond, spice, and so on.

■ **If you want a tiered fruitcake,** *but you are worried about it collapsing, you could place the middle-sized cake directly on top of the largest cake, and support just the top, lightest one on pillars.*

Types of cake style

Your wedding cake can be made in a variety of configurations, limited only by you and your partner's imaginations, the cake maker's skill, and the forces of gravity. Here are some of the more popular wedding cake ideas:

If you choose *a layered cake for your wedding, why not have different types of cake for each layer? Then, your guests get to choose between, say, fruitcake or butter cake.*

- **A sheet cake**: This is baked in a large, shallow, rectangular pan. The finished product looks like a "sheet" of cake, and is frosted and decorated on the top only. Few people use sheet cake as their "display cake," but it is incredibly common to have a sheet cake already cut, portioned onto plates, and ready to serve to the guests after the bride and groom have cut into their "display cake."
- **A stacked cake**: This is the most traditional option. It consists of three or more stacked layers – each layer smaller than the one underneath. Support poles can be hidden in the layers to prevent each level from sinking into the one below.
- **A tiered cake**: This is a multi-layered cake, with each layer separated by ***columns***, with open space between the layers.
- **Round cakes and round cake layers**: These are the most popular wedding option. They are also the easiest to frost and decorate, hence their esteemed position with bakers.
- **Square cakes**: These look cool, but they are more challenging than round layers to stack and frost. For this reason, many bakers charge more for square cakes – something to keep in mind if you're watching your budget.
- **Flower-shaped cakes, heart-shaped cakes, and other shapes**: These are fun to look at, but difficult to frost and stack, so they may be an expensive option.
- **A satellite cake**: A slightly more complicated layer cake that's great for anyone who wants width, height – and lots of cake. The base consists of several large cakes, each with another – and perhaps even another – cake supported above on columns. The finished effect is a bit like a pyramid. Perhaps surprisingly, it is actually easier for the baker, and thus a bit cheaper, to create than constructing a towering stacked or tiered cake. This is because a satellite cake is a sturdier construction.

DEFINITION

Columns, *or pillars as they are also known, are just that: Visible columns used to support layers of cake. Some people buy elaborate columns, which they then pass on to other family members for their wedding days.*

In some cultures, fruit and nut cakes are traditionally used for weddings. However, you may want to avoid anything with nuts unless you are absolutely certain that not a single one of your guests suffers from nut allergies.

Choosing your cake decoration

When professional pastry folk talk about decorating a cake, they are referring to anything from frosting on outward. Here are a few favorites:

- A basketweave pattern is a frequently used frosting pattern created by using a pastry bag to pipe frosting in a woven pattern.
- Buttercream icing is a rich, butter-based icing that is popular for its delicious taste. In fact, of all the icing treatments, buttercream is one of your tastiest options. It does have its downside: It doesn't give a smooth, impeccable finish, nor is it particularly heat-resistant, making it a poor choice for a warm day.
- Crystallized flowers are old-fashioned, pretty decorations made by coating edible flowers – such as violets, Johnny-jump-ups, and roses – in sugar.
- Cornelli, also called lace work, is a type of decorative icing that resembles lace.
- Dotted Swiss icing resembles Swiss fabric. It involves using a pastry bag to pipe small white dots onto a frosted cake.
- Embroidered icing, also called embroidery, uses a pastry bag to create fine-as-thread decorations that resemble needlework.

Flowers, when fresh, and of an edible type that have not been sprayed with pesticides, make gorgeous cake decorations. Furthermore, dressing a cake with real or fresh flowers takes less work than making one accessorized with icing – so you'll actually pay less for your beautiful creation.

- Fondant is a favorite wedding cake finish for its beautifully smooth, glossy appearance. It is, however, an acquired taste.
- Pastillage is similar to fondant, but dries to a sturdy, hard finish. Used for three-dimensional decorations.
- Marzipan is a smooth, pliable substance made of almond paste and sugar. It is commonly used to fashion decorative elements, but some bakers cover each cake layer in marzipan – an option that is as pretty as fondant, but better tasting.

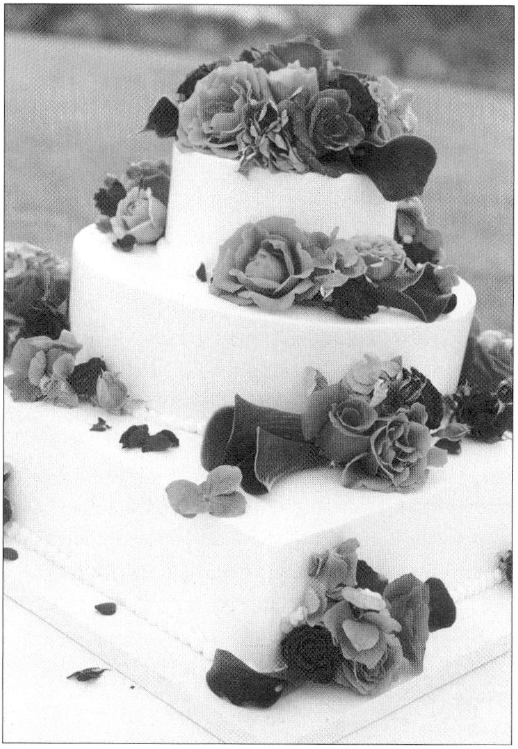

Flowers scattered *artistically over a layered cake make for a very dramatic look. You can use a mixture of flower buds, as well as petals, too.*

- Lattice work resembles a lattice fence – except it is created not with wood, but with icing, a pastry bag, and a skilled hand.
- Ganache is a super-rich icing that lends a lovely, sleek finish to cakes. It is made by melting together chocolate – bittersweet, semisweet, milk, or white – and cream, and then pouring the slightly cooled mixture onto the cake. As delicious as ganache is – and it tastes absolutely amazing – it is gooey stuff and it melts very easily. Even a fluorescent light is enough to send ganache running.
- Piping refers to any type of icing, but especially thin lines, used to decorate a cake. It is always done using a pastry bag.
- Plastic icing, also known as Australian fondant icing or molding paste, is a bit thicker than straight fondant, and can be molded into various flowers, leaves, and other decorative elements.
- Rosettes are decorations made of icing using a pastry bag. They are typically roses – hence the name – but can be any decorative "blob."
- Royal icing is a thin, egg white-based icing that dries to a hard, shiny, durable finish. Popular for flat decorations and ornamental writing.
- Spun sugar, also called angel's hair or pulled sugar, is a kind of brittle caramel fashioned into threads. Used solely as a decorative element.

Cake toppers, *which are the cherry on the wedding cake, are traditionally a figurine of the bride and groom.*

Several small cakes and other options

A large wedding cake isn't your only option. In fact, having several small cakes is an idea that has grown quickly in popularity. Many couples choose to have a small cake placed on each reception table. These smaller desserts can be identical to each other, or in different flavors, colors, or designs.

If you are planning to make your own cakes, baking and decorating several smaller cakes can be easier than constructing some nuptial fantasy for 100 or more guests. However, unless you allow the guests at each table to serve themselves, be prepared to send waitstaff to each table to do the honors. To eliminate the need for table service, some brides and grooms go a step further and place a tower of gorgeously decorated mini cakes – cupcakes, if you will – in the center of each table.

When interviewing bakers, be adamant about the quality of ingredients that will go into your cake. Many a couple has paid top dollar for a cake, only to find upon serving that the cake and frosting were made with margarine – not butter – which leaves a greasy feeling on the tongue.

If a wedding cake is not your thing, think about options such as "wedding" cheesecake, ice cream cake, croquembouche, savarin, baked Alaska, Paris brest, trifle, pavlova, summer pudding, fig pudding, or fruit tarts.

Groom's cake

A groom's cake – a smaller, less elaborately decorated confection than the wedding cake – began as a type of boozy fruitcake. Just how, why, and where it began, however, is a mystery. According to some sources, the groom's cake is a long-standing custom throughout the southern United States, where it began as a gift from the bride to her beloved. This explains why many groom's cakes are decorated in ways close his heart: You'll see cakes as musical instruments, cars, boats, sporting equipment, and so on. Other sources place the groom's cake in early England, where it sat alongside the wedding cake, and was sliced and placed in bags – one bag per wedding guest.

If you'd like to have a groom's cake, you've got several serving options: Offer a slice with the wedding cake (or as an alternative for anyone who prefers it), send slices home with guests, or put it on a buffet table and let guests help themselves.

No matter what story you accept, the groom's cake is a way to add another cake to your reception. Modern tastes being what they are, this fruitcake has evolved into any type of rich cake, such as chocolate mousse, bourbon cake, or rum cake.

CUTTING THE CAKE

There's a certain amount of protocol to cutting the wedding cake. If this is your first time slicing one, here's how it's done:

- The bride stands facing the cake, with her groom behind her. After she picks up the special cake knife, he wraps his arms around her and "helps" her by resting his hands on each of her wrists or forearms.
- The first slice, which is a kind of ceremonial slice, should be small – not much bigger than a mouthful – and should come from the cake's bottom layer.
- The bride feeds this piece of cake to her groom, then he moves so that he can cut a small piece to feed to her.
- After the bride and groom have performed the "ceremonial feeding," the cake is whisked into the kitchen to be sliced up and plated for the guests.

Finding a cake maker

FINDING SOMEONE TO MAKE your wedding cake is much like finding someone to make your reception meal, or create your floral arrangements: You want someone who is creative and highly skilled, but the person also has to be a reliable, detail-oriented professional. Moreover, this expert can't be so arrogant to charge an out-of-this-world amount for his or her work. If you're willing to do some research, you should be able to find just the person to help you – even if that person turns out to be a friend, family member, or yourself.

Professional cake maker

You know what you want in a wedding cake – or, at least you have an idea. What you don't know is who is going to transform your idea into delicious reality. If you are like many people, you may turn to a professional baker for help. This is a logical choice, considering these people make and decorate cakes for a living. To find someone, think about the following:

- Before you start to look, begin studying wedding magazines, gourmet food magazines, dessert cookbooks, and so on, to get ideas of what you might want in a wedding cake. Even better, create a "wedding cake wish book" that you can show cake makers.
- Have an idea of what flavor of cake you may want, such as carrot cake, chocolate cake, yellow cake, and so on.
- It helps the baker if you can provide him or her with color swatches of your wedding colors, as well as telling him or her what type of wedding flowers you will be using. If there is any specific element you want incorporated into your cake – maybe your mother's wedding cake topper, or your uncle's famous marzipan – tell the baker.
- Ask other brides and wedding professionals for referrals. You want someone who comes recommended.

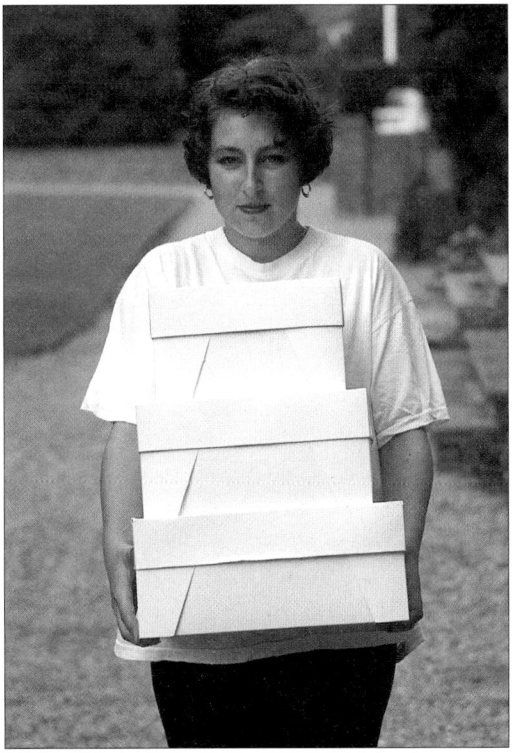

Many cake makers *deliver directly to your venue. This is a good option, so that you know your cake will be packed securely and transported safely.*

- Have a firm idea of how many people your cake must feed. If you haven't received RSVPs from all your guests, remember that it's far better to be stuck with extra cake (which you can distribute among family members and attendants) than not enough.
- Does the baker have references you can check?
- Does the baker offer a selection of cakes and frostings that sound enticing?
- Does the baker have a cake portfolio that you can look through to study the workmanship? Is he or she versatile, with good ideas?
- Do you feel comfortable with the baker? It's important to find someone who is both talented and nice, since you'll be spending a lot of time conversing with him or her.
- Will the baker allow you to sample a choice of cakes and frostings before you make up your mind?
- Have a set cake budget and ask if the baker will be willing to work within that budget.
- How much and how does the baker charge? While some bakeries charge a flat fee per cake, most charge per slice.

INTERNET

www.pastrywiz.com/wedding

Great information for anyone looking to make his or her own cake – or that of a friend.

Inform your baker about the likely weather conditions for your wedding. If you're having a backyard wedding in August, for instance, your baker should forgo heat-sensitive fillings, frosting, and decorations.

- Is delivery included in the cake's price? Many bakeries will not only deliver your cake but set it up at the reception. Find out if the baker will personally accompany the cake and make any emergency repairs to the frosting or decoration. Also worth asking: How will the cake be packaged for transport? How will it be handed to your caterer?
- Are cake table accessories included in the cake's price?
- What kind of deposit will you need to put down? Most bakers ask for anywhere from 25 to 50 percent of the cake's total cost.

Once your cake *is in place, the cake maker can do the final touches – such as placing the separate tiers of the cake on columns.*

- How far in advance must you order your cake? Some bakeries ask for as much as eight to ten weeks advance notice.
- Are there any surprise costs? Some bakeries charge extra for certain types of decorating techniques, different flavored tiers, or for using cream or fruit in the filling – it's best to know all the extra costs before you've made your final decision on your cake.
- Ask for a written proposal outlining all the points you and the baker have agreed upon.
- If you want to freeze the top layer of your cake for your first wedding anniversary or for your first child's christening cake, will your baker wrap it for you? Or better yet, will he or she be willing to make you a fresh cake at a reduced rate when your anniversary rolls around?

The alternative routes

If you don't feel you can afford a professional cake decorator, you've got alternatives. In Chapter 3 I mentioned two money-saving options: Hire a pastry school student to make your wedding cake, or use a dummy styrofoam cake for the display table and have your caterer serve pieces of already-plated sheet cake. If neither of these options appeals to you, here are two more: Make your own cake, or have a talented loved one do the honors.

If you do choose *to decorate your own cake, bear in mind that it can be tricky to achieve a perfect result. Practice on a small cake first.*

An easy compromise that will save you a bit of money and time is to order your wedding cake undecorated, then decorate it yourself, in your own, unique style.

The advantage to serving a homemade cake – in addition to the money saved – is you're virtually guaranteed something that tastes good. Many professional wedding cake bakers deliberately make the cake on the dry, sturdy side – all the better to stand up to vigorous decorating. As great as these creations may look, they can taste boring or even bad. With a homemade cake, you're more likely to get a creation that tastes wonderful.

The downside, however, is that if you or the assigned wedding cake creator aren't a handy cake decorator, you risk having a delicious cake that looks a bit, well, homey. This isn't a problem for many people. However, if you're obsessed with presentation, you might be disappointed with a home-decorated cake.

A great book for do-it-yourselfer cake makers is* The Cake Bible *by Rose Levy Beranbaum. Included is meticulous instruction in large-scale baking and decorating, as well as information on special occasion desserts.

The cake table

AS ITS NAME SUGGESTS, the cake table is where the wedding cake sits – preferably all by itself, with nothing but floral arrangements and a few bows surrounding it. There's a good chance you've never set up a cake table before, so here are a few pointers:

Trivia...

In the United States, it is common for the bride and groom to smear cake into each other's face during the ceremonial cake feeding. If you, as the bride, have spent a large chunk of change on your wedding day makeup, or are worried about sullying your gown, have a heart-felt chat with your partner before your wedding reception.

- Make sure to earmark a table just for your cake – and mark it in a very visible way. You don't want the table being "borrowed" to use as a food station. Furthermore, marking it clearly will ensure your baker, if he or she is delivering your cake, will know exactly where to place your treasured dessert.
- Your table will look best in a tablecloth that matches the linens of your guests' tables.
- Talk to your florist and your baker about decorating the cake table – both professionals traditionally help with this.
- Set up the table in a "photogenic" spot. You'll be taking a lot of pictures at the cake table and you don't want the kitchen, garbage area, or restrooms evident in your photographs!
- Do not clutter your cake table with other food items.
- A cake stand will elevate your cake, giving it a "bigger presence." If you can use a keepsake cake stand, fantastic. If you need to buy one, consider your décor, and your cake. Your baker may have ideas – ask him or her.
- Make sure the table is at a comfortable height, allowing you to cut your cake easily.

■ **Floral displays** *can give your cake table dramatic impact – which may be just what you want for those cake-cutting photos.*

A simple summary

- ✓ While dinner and lunch receptions are among the most popular types, you've got many other options to choose from, including breakfast, brunch, tea, cocktails, and dessert.
- ✓ Finding a caterer who respects your budget and your wishes is as important as finding one whose style matches your own.
- ✓ Catering your own wedding is the ultimate money saver.
- ✓ Alcohol can be a festive addition to your celebration – when used wisely. If you are worried about guests getting too drunk, an open bar may not be the best option for your reception.
- ✓ Stocking your own bar is a great way to save money and tailor your beverage selection to your guests' tastes.
- ✓ While alcohol is commonly served at weddings, it isn't obligatory: Dry weddings are increasing in popularity.
- ✓ If you're unsure of what kind of cake you want for your wedding, begin by looking at books, magazines, and in bakeries for ideas.
- ✓ Don't like cake? Have a wedding baked Alaska, savarin, pavlova, platter of cookies, or some other favorite dessert.
- ✓ The secret to finding a great cake-making professional? Know what you want, and then find someone who can deliver that.
- ✓ Do you have a cake-making friend? A handmade cake can add a lovely touch to your wedding – it'll save you money, too!
- ✓ If you'd like a sweet favor to send home with your guests – or if you'd like to indulge in two different cakes – a groom's cake is for you.
- ✓ Give your cake the showplace it deserves with a smartly decorated cake table.

Chapter 10

Setting the Stage

IF YOU'RE LIKE MANY ENGAGED FOLK, you'll find that one of the hardest parts of creating a wedding isn't choosing a great outfit, picking a nice menu, or even finalizing your vows – it's deciding on exactly what your ceremony and reception are going to look like. Fortunately, this is also one of the most fun areas of planning for your special day. It's a great chance to show off your personality by incorporating favorite flowers, plants, and other elements – from candles to art, ribbons to brocade drapes. Go as wild as you like – it's your day to treasure.

In this chapter...

- ✓ Picking the perfect accents
- ✓ Decorating for the ceremony
- ✓ Decorating for the reception

FINDING THE RIGHT FLORIST IS AN IMPORTANT PART OF CREATING YOUR DREAM WEDDING

Picking the perfect accents

YOUR WEDDING DAY IS GETTING CLOSER. When you envision the day itself, what do you see? I bet I can guess. In a word: perfection. Fortunately, perfection is a very achievable thing if you know what you're after. If you want your wedding to look as fantastic as possible, think about what you – as a couple – like, then incorporate these things into your wedding day décor. In this way you can design the look of both the ceremony and the reception.

In Chapter 2 I talked about creating a wedding theme. If you haven't already done this, you may want to consider doing so. Why? Because creating a theme for both your ceremony and your reception builds an esthetic link between the two events, creating continuity and visually pleasing order. (I probably don't need to tell you how much we humans like order, visual or otherwise.)

Using the seasons

Incorporating elements of the season – winter, spring, summer, or fall – into your wedding is not only charming but an easy and inexpensive way to decorate. Here are some ideas:

Consistency is essential in creating your own brand of perfection. As long as you are consistent in the materials you use and where you use them, you can buy the cheapest materials and flowers and still achieve a more polished result than you would by using expensive decorations in a random way.

Winter

- Decorate large areas of space with red velvet ribbons and winter greenery, such as pine boughs, holly, and mistletoe.
- Incorporate winter greenery into the bridal bouquet, all floral arrangements, and the table centerpiece.

■ **The rich colors** *of winter, here set off with gold, will lend a warm, sumptuous feel to your wedding décor.*

- Pine cones, amaryllis, Christmas flower cactus, and poinsettias are additional decorating ideas.
- An all-white wedding – including flowers – can be lovely when decorated with strand upon strand of tiny white lights.
- If yours is a December affair, use traditional Christmas colors, such as green and red. Blue and white are also lovely wedding colors, and are an especially appropriate choice for a Jewish ceremony.
- Consider wearing a rich red velvet or green velvet throw over your wedding dress.
- If it isn't a fire hazard, decorate the tables with candles.
- New Year's weddings can be decorated with snowflakes. Try also using black, white, and red colors to enhance the display.
- Valentine's Day weddings can feature ribbons and hearts in white, deep red, and pale pink.

Spring

- Spring is when bulb flowers – such as tulips, irises, crocuses, and daffodils – arise. Use one or more of these in the bridal bouquet, floral arrangement, and table centerpieces. For something different, use potted flowers. If you have enough these can do double-duty as wedding favors.
- Branches of tree blossom – apricot and cherry are especially pretty – make gorgeous and very sophisticated decorations. Use in the bridal bouquet (and pin pieces in the bride's and bridesmaids' hair), floral arrangements, and all table centerpieces.
- Lilacs are lovely for a spring wedding.
- For a May Day wedding, consider having a maypole and pastel ribbons.

Spring flowers *give an especially pretty and fresh touch to your wedding décor.*

Summer

- In many areas, wildflowers appear in early summer. Gather a large amount for your bridal bouquet, all floral arrangements, and table decorations.
- I was once at a summer wedding at which the only flowers used were enormous bunches of flowering rosemary, lavender, and thyme – in the decorations and floral arrangements, on the table, and in the bride's bouquet. It was unexpected – and exquisite. If you'd like to follow suit, use sturdy herbs that have gone to flower. More delicate ones, such as basil and mint, will wilt too quickly.

Do not choose an outdoor site before investigating what might be happening near it. Things to research: Loud motor and foot traffic, any already scheduled event, and whether or not the site officials are willing to do what they must to guarantee you near-serenity.

Fall

- Choose a venue that overlooks fall foliage. If it is early fall, and warm enough, consider having an outdoor wedding.
- Large branches, heavy with autumn leaves, can be used to decorate, while smaller leaf-laden switches can be stood in a vase and used as table arrangements.
- Consider incorporating autumnal shades into your decorating scheme: An ecru dress rather than white, and flowers, ribbons, linens, and other accessories in spiced reds, muted greens, deep oranges, and rich yellows.
- If your wedding is to be held in mid- to late fall, the fruits and vegetables of the harvest, such as pumpkins, pomegranates (a classic symbol of love), persimmons, and kumquats, can be incorporated into floral arrangements and table decorations.
- Ask the flower girl to strew well-chosen fall leaves instead of flower petals.
- Consider scheduling your wedding near an autumn holiday, such as Thanksgiving (for Canadians and Americans) or Guy Fawkes Day. Incorporate favorite holiday decorations in your ceremony and reception.
- One of my friends, who married on Halloween, had a masquerade party. It was great fun and required very little decorating work – the guests were decoration enough!

Unusual and decorative artificial lighting *can make a significant contribution to the atmosphere of your event, even if your wedding and reception will take place during the day time.*

SEASONAL FOODS AND DRINKS

Incorporate traditional seasonal foods into your reception menu, and use some of the prettier ones in the décor.

Puddings made *from seasonal fruits – a popular wedding choice.*

- Traditional winter foods include roasts, baked pastas, and sweets such as gingerbread, panettone, and rice pudding.
- Foods of spring are baby green salads, morel mushrooms, ramps, fiddlehead ferns, asparagus, artichokes, new potatoes, lemon (great in desserts and as lemonade), early strawberries, and rhubarb.
- The foods and drinks that are most associated with summer must include ice cream, wine cooler punch, and anything cooked on a grill. Seasonal items include berries, stone fruits, eggplant, melons, corn, tomatoes, peppers, and zucchini.
- For a fall wedding, ideas include squash or sweet potato bisque; pear, roasted beet, and gorgonzola salad; pecan or pumpkin tarts. Hard cider, pear brandy, and Beaujolais Nouveau are beverage ideas. Quinces, apples, cranberries, grapes, and various root vegetables are also common fall-harvested foods.

Who does the decorating?

If you have friends and family willing to pitch in and help you – or better still, do it for you – terrific. You'll save yourself money and have the sweet satisfaction of knowing that your loved ones helped contribute to your big day.

Your bouquet and those of your wedding party should match the flora you use to decorate the ceremony and reception, as should the petals your flower girl throws. It's visually jarring to see one type of flower used by the bridal party and a completely different type used for room decoration.

If no one in your life is particularly crafty or generous with their time, or you have the money to hire a professional, then do. There are professionals out there – nuptial decorators, if you will – who specialize in setting up chapel and reception sites. These folk will direct florists, caterers, and bakers, as well as physically arrange the space. If you are working with a wedding consultant, he or she may do this. If you are using a wedding hall, the decorating may be included in your site fee.

Decorating for the ceremony

DRESSING UP YOUR ceremony space isn't particularly difficult. That's because the main decorative element is you, your partner, and your wedding party – all of whom will be decked out in gorgeous clothing and carrying (or wearing) exquisite blooms. Everything else in the space will seem boring in comparison, but you still want the location to look great. I don't blame you.

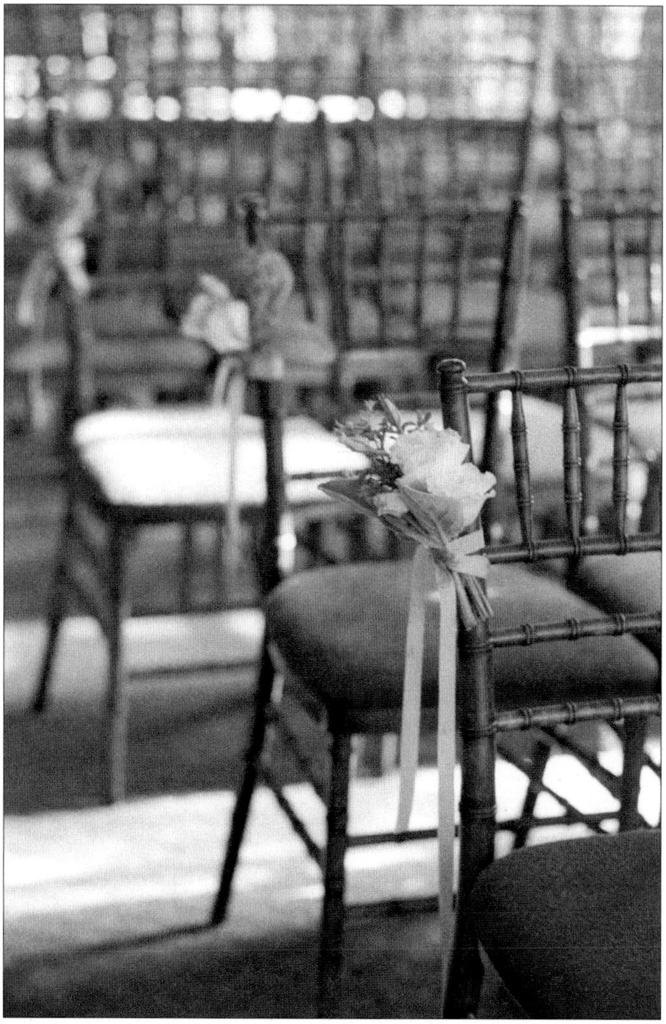

The easiest way to create a gorgeous environment is to visit the undecorated space beforehand – preferably with your florist, wedding consultant, or a friend with a good eye for decoration. Following the same path your guests will follow, study what they'll see as they enter the space. Perhaps there's a spot of peeling paint to the right of the altar that needs to be camouflaged with a potted plant or a large floral display. Are there worn spots along the pews' edges that could be hidden behind a garland or some ribbon? And what about the altar or huppah area? Is there any treatment that could enhance its appearance?

■ **Simple posies** *made from in-season blooms make charming decorations for chairs, pews, pillars, and so on. Bear in mind that flowers that shed pollen should not be used on chairs or where they may come into contact with people's clothes.*

How to hire a florist

■ **Choosing your** *favorite flowers will add the finishing touch to your wedding day.*

You can get flowers from local farmers, friends' gardens, an aunt's orchard, but if you are going to use a florist you will need to consider the following:

- Before even speaking to a florist, consider how much money you can devote to flowers and other vegetation. A florist's fees can cost up to 15 percent of your overall wedding budget. Don't worry if you can't afford a large sum; a good florist will be creative enough to make much from relatively little.
- If possible, have color swatches to show florists, as well as pictures of your wedding and reception site, and your wedding day outfits.
- Ask around. Which florist did your married friends use? Question the local bridal boutique. Can you go online to find talented florists in your area?
- Ask to see the florist's wedding portfolio. Do you like the designs? Is the person versatile? If you have the money, ask each florist you interview to create a centerpiece for you. This will give you an idea of each one's style.

Have a firm idea of what you like – and do not like. Keep a "wish folder" of pictures and notations that might help a florist help you.

- Provide a list of all wedding party members who will need flowers, as well as a general idea of how many tables and other areas will need floral or plant decorations.
- How much does the florist need as a deposit? Many want 25 to 50 percent down.
- Are there any hidden fees, such as delivery fees and state tax?
- How much advance notice does the florist need?
- Does the florist have his or her own "accessories," such as silver urns, polished stones, lanterns, ribbons, and so on? Or will he or she have to rent them and pass the cost on to you?
- Will the florist also be able to create arrangements for your other wedding events, such as showers and the rehearsal dinner?
- Will your florist deliver your flora the morning of the wedding, then stick around to help set up the plants? (It helps to have someone who can meet the florist at the site to ensure everything goes to plan.)
- Once you've committed to a florist, get everything – from what you are ordering to costs to delivery dates – in writing.

Decorating for the reception

GENERALLY, DECORATING THE reception site is more complicated than decorating your wedding site. Unless your wedding and reception sites are one and the same, the reception hall will have more space than the wedding chapel with more surfaces to accessorize. Remember that your guests will spend more time at the reception than they will at the wedding, so it is important to make it a pleasant environment.

To get a better idea of what your reception site may need, visit the undecorated room with your partner, wedding consultant, florist, or a friend (four eyes are better than two), and make notes: What do you see upon entering the space? Does it need to be spiffed up a bit? Are there unattractive or worn areas that possibly need to be camouflaged with potted trees or other decorations? Does the space have any design elements, such as arches, that you'd like to play up with flowers or garlands? How does the ceiling look – will it need to be spiffed up with tulles or hidden with dim lighting? Will the restrooms need a bit of decorative help? All these little details make a big impact.

Make sure floral centerpieces *do not obstruct your guests' view either of each other or of the dance floor.*

Decorating tables

Floral centerpieces are the obvious choice for decorating tables. Other nice options include using hurricane candles for a romantic glow, votive candles floating in silver bowls, framed pictures of the newlyweds, and displays of fruit or vegetables.

Take-home favors are strictly optional, and many couples forgo the expense of having them. But if you would like to give guests a trinket to remember the day by, make the item part of each place setting: Little decorative picture frames that hold the guest's name, small potted plants, antique-looking mirrors, or any other modest knick-knack that complements your décor.

INTERNET

www.superweddings.com/bridalcrafts.html

Here you'll find some great ideas for decorating your own reception.

Decorating other areas

Buffet stations and serving tables look pretty with a few flowers or some simple greenery. Like food tables, the bar is a busy place – you don't want to clutter it with too many plants, candles, flowers, photographs, or whatever else. A bouquet or plant behind the bar, or a garland above it, are simple, tasteful touches.

Don't feel you must limit yourself to the same decorations everyone else has. If you and your partner love sailing, teddy bears, horseback riding, for example, find ways to incorporate these interests into your décor.

While you don't want to hide the entertainers behind the flowers, you may want to hide the amps, cables, foot pedals, and other musical gear behind a low wall of plants. But since the dance floor must be open, you can't position planters where people can trip over them. Instead, try hanging garlands or lengths of tulle from the ceiling.

A simple summary

- ✓ Incorporate flowers, plants, framed photographs, candles, ribbons, and draped fabric into your decorating scheme.
- ✓ Create a cohesive decorating scheme by using the same elements in the bridal party arrangements, room decorations, and table displays.
- ✓ It doesn't matter who decorates your ceremony and reception sites – friends, a wedding consultant, or your florist. The important thing is creating a space you love.
- ✓ Remember that you and your wedding party are among the most elaborate decorations that the guests will see at the wedding ceremony. How you all look is what really matters.
- ✓ Using large floral displays and a selection of potted plants is a great way of hiding tired-looking or empty spaces.
- ✓ Because your guests will spend a large amount of time at the reception, be thoughtful and create a pleasing environment for them – and for you!

Chapter 11

A Picture's Worth a Thousand Words

As you'll find out, wedding photographs take on a different meaning at each stage of married life. If you're like many couples, you'll return from your honeymoon anxious for photographic proof of how gorgeous you looked in your outfits, what a great job you did choosing reception decorations, and how happy your friends looked for you. As the years pass by, every time you return to those photographs you'll relive that initial rush of just-wedded bliss. Truly, one of the greatest gifts you can give yourselves is your wedding pictures!

In this chapter...

- ✓ **All about wedding photography**
- ✓ **Videotaping the occasion**
- ✓ **A little more help for you**

All about wedding photography

MY HUSBAND AND I keep a small wedding album on our living room piano. The album's cover features a formal photograph of us, standing side by side, looking dazed and excited. On a nearby wall hangs a framed picture taken moments after saying "we do." In it we're laughing – my husband giggling and looking to the side, me with my head thrown back, eyes closed, mouth open wide.

Try to arrange a *photographer you know for your wedding day – he or she will get the best shots of you.*

Whenever new friends visit the house, the album and the picture are among the first things they comment on. Although I get much pleasure from sharing our wedding photos with others, their real value is more personal: They let me relive a very special moment from my past.

That is why photographs are important: As well as allowing you to share your wedding with others, these images serve to remind you of the love you have for each other, the commitment you both made, and the fun you had celebrating your love. This is one reason why so much importance is placed on wedding photography. The other reason is pure enjoyment: It's downright delightful to pore over pictures of yourselves looking so gorgeous.

Focusing on style

When people talk about "photography style" there are a few things they may mean:

- **Formal**: These are also called posed shots, because they are, well, posed. Think of the wedding photos you so often see of the bride standing alone, the groom standing alone, the bride with groom, the groom with best man, and so on. These photos can be taken indoors against a backdrop, or outside in front of pretty scenery or an attractive-looking wall.
- **Candid**: You probably already know what candid shots are. Candid photography is a great way to capture a wedding's spontaneous emotional moments.

Upping your photogenic quotient

Hate the way you look in photos? Sure, you could spend time wishing you looked different – or that you could afford plastic surgery. But it's easier and far more pleasant to accept your looks. Perhaps these tips will help:

- Re-read Chapter 4 to get your looks in camera-ready shape.
- Since skin glitches, dark circles, and extra pounds are common bridal complaints, practice a bit of advance prevention. In the weeks before the wedding, visit a dermatologist or esthetician. Eat well, get plenty of sleep, and find yourself a sensible way to shed a few pounds and tone up. Slow and steady is the only surefire way to coddle your looks – fast fixes may treat one area, but invariably throw another out of whack. For instance, the beef-and-grapefruit diet may help you drop ten pounds fast, but it could leave your skin a mess and your hair brittle and thinning.
- Be yourself. The fussier you make your hair, makeup, and neckline, the more likely they are to photograph "strangely."
- When posing outdoors, head for the shade. Bright sun casts shadows, emphasizes lines and blotches, and distorts facial features.
- Look at old photos and identify which poses always work for you, and which never fail to make you look like your rather interesting-looking Uncle Edgar. Remember those flattering poses at your wedding when the camera begins flashing. This is the time to turn on the style!
- If you need it, here's a slimming pose: Turn your hips at a right angle to the camera. Leave your shoulders squared forward. (This is called the "celebrity twist." I probably don't need to tell you why.)
- Relax and have fun. A woman who is calm and happy is always more beautiful than a woman who is uptight and self-concerned. This is one of those unexplainable but true adages that are easy to prove: Just go out into the street and look around.

Find your good side: *Few of us are symmetrical, so study yourself in a mirror to find your best angle.*

■ **A posed portrait:** *Just one form of wedding photography.*

- **Combination**: Combination photography can mean two things. The first is where a photographer takes both formal and candid shots – which really is your best option at a wedding. (Just think how boring your wedding album would be if it was made up entirely of formal shots!) Combination can also mean photographs that are posed to look candid, such as the bordering-on-overdone shot of the bride and groom – taken at a short distance from behind – standing together as a couple, hand-in-hand.
- **Straight shooting**: This form of photography means pictures are taken as they appear – with no backdrops, no special photo effects, no fuzzy background.
- **Creative composition**: Whether formal or candid, the photographer slightly manipulates the creative composition. Perhaps the background or foreground is made fuzzy, or it could be that a certain camera speed is used to create streaky lines of movement for a dance-floor shot.
- **Photostories**: Also called "wedding photo-journalism," this is more of an account of the big day. The photographer aims to create a "story" of the event by capturing emotional moments in chronological order, including the bride's anticipation as she gets ready, the groom's nervousness as he waits for his partner, and the emotional exchange of rings.

Trivia...

Ever wonder why the bride and groom take their formal photographs between the ceremony and reception – leaving their guests waiting for the newlyweds to appear? It has something to do with keeping the bride and groom apart until the actual ceremony: Back in the days of arranged marriages, the bride's family hid their daughter away until the last possible moment out of fear the groom might see her and change his mind. Things are different today though – many couples have the posed photos taken before the ceremony, thus avoiding any waiting around.

GET MORE SHOTS FOR YOUR MONEY

Here's a great way to augment any professional photography you're having done: Place several disposable cameras on each guest table and encourage attendees to take as many photos as they'd like. Appoint one or two of your attendants to collect the cameras for you at the end of the ceremony. When you return from your honeymoon, get all the film developed – you'll be surprised how terrific some of these candid shots will be!

How many pictures are enough?

I know happily married people who have only a dozen photographs of their wedding day, stuffed (lovingly) into a homemade scrapbook. I also know divorced couples who spent thousands on documenting their wedding and preserving the photos in elaborate, professionally prepared albums. There is no right or wrong number when it comes to deciding how many pictures to have taken of you. It's not having too few – or too many – wedding photographs that will make you a happily married couple. Simply buy the photos you can afford, being sure to include some of the following shots:

Don't assume your photographer will know the kind of shots you'd like! Instead, create a list of the must-take pictures you and your partner really want. The more specific you can be the easier your photographer's job.

- Getting ready. This is especially nice if the photograph includes the bride and her mother, maid of honor, or attendants. However, if your photographer is unable to be with you before the ceremony, ask a bridesmaid to take a few shots.
- Various attendants and guests walking down the aisle.
- The groom waiting at the altar.
- The bride walking down the aisle.
- The couple exchanging vows.
- Rings being exchanged.
- The kiss!
- Formally posed full length and three-quarter length shots of the bride, the groom, and the newly married couple.
- Close-up of the bride's and groom's intertwined hands.
- Post-ceremony shots of the bride with her maid of honor, and of the bride with her attendants.
- Post-ceremony shots of the groom with his best man, and with his attendants.
- The couple's arrival at the reception.
- Various guests.
- The receiving line.
- Shots of the numerous toasts given.
- Photographs of the couple cutting the cake, and feeding it to each other.
- Shots of various dances.
- Photos of garter tossing, bouquet tossing, and confetti tossing.
- The newlyweds' departure.

It's not only the official photographer *who takes good shots at weddings. The sheer number of guests guarantees plenty more special photos.*

Videotaping the occasion

SHOULD YOU VIDEOTAPE YOUR WEDDING? While many couples feel that a stack of photographs is the only record they need of their wedding day, there are those for whom an event is not an event without a videographic reminder. It's up to you whether you have the day filmed or not. To help you decide, here are some pros and cons:

INTERNET

www.weva.com

Get information about wedding videography – and videographers – from the Wedding and Event Videographers Association's website.

THE PROS

- Videography offers great documentation of the big day.
- Video can pick up nuances and action that photography alone simply isn't able to.
- Using video, you can record the vows, various toasts, and other visual–audible moments.
- Through editing, voiceovers, guest interviews, and any courtship photos you supply to your videographer, he or she can create a documentary-style film of your relationship with your partner, up to and including your wedding day.

Once your photographs have been developed and you have your videotape in hand, take steps to preserve them for the decades to come. Keep them away from light, heat, and humidity. To further protect photos, safeguard them in albums made of polyethylene, polypropylene, or polyester.

THE CONS

- Videography is an added expense.
- It's one more detail to worry about, one more person to hire.
- Having someone chase you around with a video camera can feel intrusive.
- Vanity. It's harder to look good on tape than it is in photographs. You can't constantly pose in such a way as to make yourself appear more attractive!

■ **Check with your wedding officiant** *to see if it's okay for you to videotape the actual ceremony. Some wedding venues won't permit filming.*

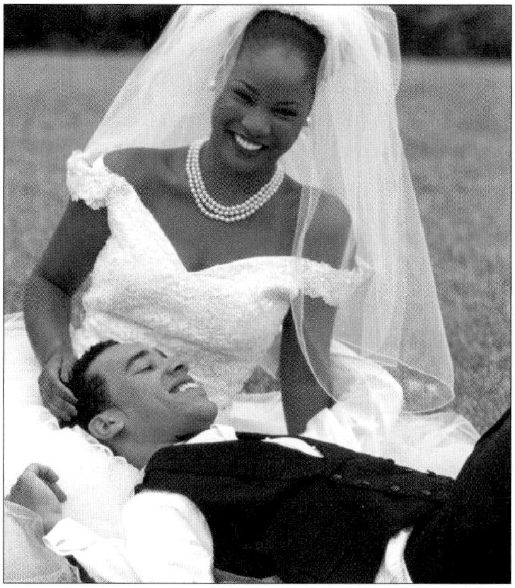

A little more help for you

AS ANY WEDDING PHOTOGRAPHER will tell you, wedding photography is an art, a skill, and a science. Here's what you need to know in order to find a photographer – and, if you wish, a videographer – who is skilled in both the artistry and the science of capturing special moments on film:

- Ask for references. Like any of the other professionals helping to create your wedding, the person who records your special day should come with glowing recommendations. Ask your friends, go online and look for local picks, chat up a nearby wedding boutique owner, question your florist, caterer, and wedding consultant – in short, research, research, research.
- Take a look at the previous work of the photographer or videographer you're proposing to hire. Do you like it? Was he or she able to capture "the unique essence" of each couple, or do all his or her samples look the same?
- Do you actually like the photographer or videographer as a person? Even a professional model will tell you that she is more comfortable – and thus more photogenic – when working with someone she has a rapport with.

Look at a photographer's *previous work. It will give you an idea of how skilled they are and help you to develop your own ideas.*

Think about costs: How long will your photographer be expected to spend at your wedding? How many photos will you want taken? And what type and quality of photo album will you want to order from her or him?

- Make up a budget. Unless you count professional photographers among your friends, or you have a cousin who videos events for a living, you'll need to spend money on a professional. To ensure you get the best photographs possible, many experts suggest you should earmark 10 percent of your wedding budget to photography – and up to 15 percent if you'd also like your event videotaped.

Asking the nitty gritty

You've found your wedding photographer. Now to ask the really important questions:

- Is the photographer or videographer available the day and hour of your wedding ceremony and reception? How about the preparation time before the reception?
- How far in advance does the person require you to commit to him or her? What kind of deposit is required? Check all sums.
- Will the photographer or videographer carry a backup camera, in case of equipment failure? It does happen, you know.
- Does he or she work with an assistant? Some brides feel more comfortable having the photographer calling the shots, while others like the idea of having an assistant who can take simultaneous shots from other angles.

■ **Many brides like** *to have a few shots of themselves getting ready for their big day.*

At some point shortly after your ceremony, sit down with your partner and identify each wedding photograph. Place each shot in order of when and where it was taken. To avoid damaging the prints, use a 6b drawing pencil to mark the back of the photo.

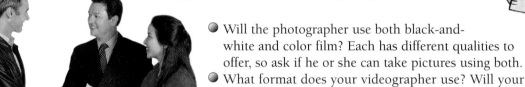

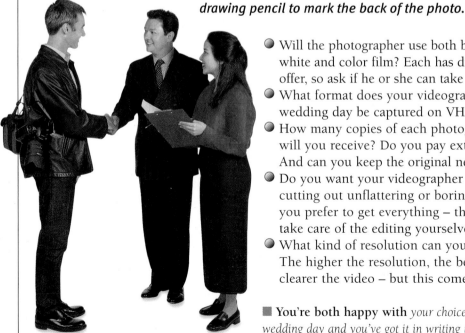

- Will the photographer use both black-and-white and color film? Each has different qualities to offer, so ask if he or she can take pictures using both.
- What format does your videographer use? Will your wedding day be captured on VHS tape, DVD, or CD?
- How many copies of each photograph, or videotape, will you receive? Do you pay extra for more copies? And can you keep the original negative or master tape?
- Do you want your videographer to edit the tape, cutting out unflattering or boring footage? Or would you prefer to get everything – the bad and good – and take care of the editing yourselves?
- What kind of resolution can your videographer offer? The higher the resolution, the better the quality and clearer the video – but this comes at a cost.

■ **You're both happy with** *your choice of photographer for your wedding day and you've got it in writing that he'll be there.*

- What guarantees can your videographer give you regarding sound quality? Will microphones be needed at the altar and for reception toasts?
- How many hours will your videographer spend editing? Many professionals need upwards of 30 hours. Beware: Time equals money.
- Get the following in writing: How many rolls of color film and black-and-white film to be shot; type of film; cost per additional roll if needed; complete package details including number of ***proofs*** you will receive; when you can pick up the proofs; how long you can study the proofs before getting back to the photographer with your picks; when you'll receive your chosen pictures; total cost; reorder cost; and cancellation and refund policy. If you're using a videographer, you'll also need to ask how many tapes the videographer plans on using, and how many cameras he or she uses.
- Have the following ready to give your photographer and videographer: You and your partner's names and various contact numbers; the correct date and time of your event; how many hours you will need him or her; directions to the event – or events, if your ceremony and reception are at different venues; special parking instructions; special lighting instructions; and a contact person (make this a best man or wedding consultant) at the venue in case the photographer needs to come early and set up.

DEFINITION

In photography speak, **proofs** *are small copies of a photograph, made especially for you to examine. If you like what you see, you can order them as regular-sized photographs. A sheet filled with different proofs is called a contact sheet.*

A simple summary

✓ Decide on the different styles of photography you'd like at your wedding. Is it formal? Would you like some candid shots? How about a photostory?

✓ Decide how many pictures of your wedding day you would like. It can be a costly process, but it's worth paying a little more rather than risk having too few memories of your special day.

✓ Want to look great in your wedding pictures or video? Hire a photographer or videographer who is not only talented but someone you like.

✓ Ask the questions listed in this chapter. You're not an expert on photography – the person you're paying is. Grill them for any bits of information or advice that will make your photos perfect.

Chapter 12

Sweet Melodies

WE PLAY NUPTIAL MUSIC AT WEDDINGS for the same reasons we have decorations, eat food, and wear wedding day attire: To create a comfortable ambiance, and to craft an atmosphere that celebrates the bride's and groom's personalities and their feelings for each other. The music people choose for their ceremonies and receptions is usually selected purely for personal reasons, be those based on tradition, entertainment, or something else entirely. True, you don't need music to get married. But I'm sure you'll agree that a selection of carefully chosen tunes can certainly add that something extra to the festivities.

In this chapter...

- ✓ Nuptial music: the basics
- ✓ What type of music?
- ✓ Hiring the musicians

Nuptial music: the basics

MUSIC PLAYS AN INTEGRAL PART in most wedding ceremonies and receptions. In fact, music is a wedding day tradition the world over. From the duh-duh-da-dum of the "Bridal March" to the sentimental tune chosen for the newlyweds' first dance, music touches our emotions and can really capture the moment. For these reasons, plan to spend upwards of 10 percent of your wedding budget on musicians.

This figure isn't, however, set in stone. As you'll read in this chapter, you've lots of options, and not all of them are costly. Better yet, for many people the pricier choices aren't necessarily the better ones.

■ **The sound of a choir** *will fill your wedding venue, creating an unforgettable atmosphere.*

The ceremony

Typical wedding music is soft and melodious, used both as a backdrop and to highlight specific moments of the ceremony. While pianists or organists are the most traditional choices, many couples opt for a singer or choir, a harpsichordist, or a small ensemble of strings, guitars or woodwinds, to create the sounds they want.

Drastic changes in musical style are jarring! Not only should your choice of tunes complement your decorating and floral scheme but the music you play should remain relatively consistent throughout the day. Another way to think of this: If you begin your ceremony with a Spanish guitar trio playing classical music, you shouldn't then break out the heavy-metal guitars for your reception.

A custom-made CD with your choice of music is another idea. Whatever format you decide on, the following moments are the occasions you'll want accompanied by specially chosen music:

- **Prelude**: The music played while guests are seated.
- **Processional**: Songs played as the members of your wedding party take their places.
- **Bridal processional**: The tune playing as the bride walks down the aisle.

- **Interlude**: The music played during the actual ceremony.
- **Recessional**: The tune performed as the newlyweds walk up the aisle and out of the chapel – think of it as a kind of grand finale.

The reception

While the music played at the actual wedding creates a solemn backdrop to the ceremony, the music played at the reception should capture the mood of celebration, bringing out lively emotions. Here are a few key moments you'll need to choose special songs for:

- **The first dance**: The newlyweds' first dance as a married couple. This is traditionally performed to a tune that has special significance to the bride and groom. While this dance is often the first highlight of the reception, it's becoming more popular for newly married couples not to dance together until after the cake has been cut.

Let's dance! *After the formality of the ceremony, it's time to let your hair down.*

If you're getting married, or even having a reception, in a house of worship, check to see what instruments – and what types of music – are permitted in the building. Some denominations have restrictions that may conflict with your choice, which could mean making changes to your music or even to your venue.

- **The father-daughter dance**: This generally takes place after the bride and groom's first dance, and the tune is usually something that carries sentiments dear to them.
- **The mother-son dance**: Usually the third "official" dance, this also requires a tune guaranteed to tug on the heartstrings.
- **Cutting the cake**: Suitable choices of music to accompany this event are gentle pieces that won't compete with the big moment.
- **The last dance**: The last song of the night is traditionally the same tune as was played during the couple's first dance.

Trivia...

Think of weddings and it's likely you'll think of one tune. What we call the "Bridal March," or "Wedding March," is actually a piece of music from Felix Mendelssohn's A Midsummer Night's Dream. *Its popularity as a wedding tune began during the mid-19th century, when couples first started using the piece as processional music.*

What type of music?

IF YOU'RE LIKE MANY COUPLES, you may choose an organist or pianist for your ceremony and a wedding band or DJ for your reception. While there's nothing at all wrong with these choices, as you'll see in this section, these types of performers aren't your only options:

- **An organist**: Organ music is both grand and moving, making it a terrific choice for the wedding ceremony. However, there is a negative side to this kind of music: Because of the sheer size of the instrument, you're limited to venues that already have an organ in place, such as chapels.

If the reception is being held in a restaurant or bar, ask the proprietor if dancing is allowed. Some establishments must hold a special permit for dancing to take place. If you find that your reception venue doesn't allow dancing, you don't need to forgo music, just the dancing.

- **A pianist**: Perfect for wedding ceremonies, being versatile enough to play classical music as well as a wide range of modern pieces. A good piano player will know enough tunes to be able to provide entertainment at the reception, too – either alone, or teamed up with other instruments. Be aware, however, that if your reception space is large and your guests are noisy, piano music may be hard to hear.
- **A harpist**: Harp music is light, ethereal, and spiritual sounding – making it a perfect accompaniment for your vows! It can work beautifully for an intimate gathering, but its gentle sound may get lost in a large reception venue, and it may be hard to dance to.
- **A choir**: What could be lovelier than a group of sweet-sounding, harmonious voices serenading you on your special day? This is a novel alternative to the standard organ or piano music heard at most wedding ceremonies. Bear in mind, however, that a choir may not be versatile enough – or easy enough to dance to – for your reception entertainment.
- **A singer**: A lovely voice, either solo or accompanied by musical instruments, is another worthy option.

Why not accompany *the bride's tossing of the bouquet with some upbeat music?*

- **A wedding band**: One of the most common choices for reception music, a wedding band is typically a pop-style group of three to six people, featuring a singer, guitars, bass guitar, drums, sometimes an electric keyboard, and some type of horn.
- **The DJ option**: The majority of brides and grooms today use disc jockeys at their receptions. A DJ is cheaper than the common wedding band, he or she offers a greater musical range than a band, and most DJs are willing to help introduce specific wedding party members and make other wedding announcements.
- **A light-jazz combo**: A cool option for any wedding. While a light-jazz group may not play you a rollicking Beatles' medley, neither will it risk offending certain sections of your guest list.

The chance to dance *may be what your guests are after, so make sure the music reflects this.*

A simple way of saving money is to hire the same musician or group of musicians for both the ceremony and the reception.

- **A string quartet:** A string quartet lends an air of elegance to any type of wedding and is a particularly good choice for formal affairs.
- **A small "big band" orchestra:** The big band sound, popular in the 1940s, is characterized by sloping notes and lots of horns. Different and great fun.

Keeping the sounds sharp

If you've ever attended a formal wedding, you know how easy it is to unwittingly "de-formalize" the event by playing pop music. Rap, techno, country, metal, acid, golden oldies, garage, grunge, mod, punk – all can lend a certain informality to what might otherwise be a slightly swankier affair. Should you be worried about this, your best bet is to go with something a little more classy, like a string quartet, harpsichordist, woodwind ensemble, classical guitarists, or a DJ who specializes in classical, swing era, big band, and other melodious music styles.

Hiring the musicians

WHETHER YOU'VE OPTED for an organist or a singer for your ceremony, a mariachi band or a DJ for your reception, you need to be aware of what kind of performers are turning up at your wedding:

- You must know exactly what you want – from the type of music, to the duration you'd like the musicians to play. It's easier to weed out inappropriate choices when you have an idea of the sounds you would like.
- For musical references, ask other brides, question your local wedding professionals (including consultants, bridal boutique owners, and florists), and search online.
- Is it possible to listen to a demo of the music? Most musicians and DJs will happily send you a CD or tape of their work to make sure it's the right kind of thing for you.

Looking for a string quartet or a flute-piano duo to play at your reception? Contact the music department at your local university. You'll often find students who are willing to play at weddings.

- Check out the performers' live sound. Some will send you a videotape, invite you to an "audition open house" (where they play for a number of possible clients), or invite you to one of their gigs. All three are excellent ways to sample their music.
- Is the band or DJ available on your wedding and reception date? Many wedding musicians are booked a year or more in advance, especially for peak marriage times, such as the summer or Saturday afternoons. Make sure you find out – and get an assurance that they will attend.

Make sure *your choice of musician suits both your and your partner's tastes.*

Before booking musical entertainment, find out if your wedding reception venue has any restrictions. Certain establishments have laws that forbid music played above a certain decibel. Other venues aren't set up for extensive use of electrical instruments.

- Is the band or DJ willing to make announcements, publicly introduce people, and direct guests to their tables for lunch? This can be an enormous help. So try to find a professional who is prepared to do all this – then present him or her with a plan outlining what you need done and when.
- What will the band or DJ be wearing? If yours is an ultra-formal affair, will you need to have them dress accordingly? And will this be at your expense?

You may have heard of music brokers. These "middle men" work as agents of sorts, hooking up wedding musicians and DJs with those who need them. If you don't mind spending a little extra money, a music broker can save you time and effort.

- How much of his or her fee does the entertainer require as a deposit? Many musicians and DJs want as much as 50 percent up front.
- Get it in writing! It's important to have a contract that outlines everything you and the entertainer have agreed to. You can't afford any mistakes on your wedding day.

Just as you listen to *your favorite music with a critical ear, do so also when choosing a wedding DJ, band, or singer.*

Karaoke – welcome at your wedding?

Karaoke is a popular evening activity in many clubs and bars. Large numbers of people, usually in various stages of inebriation, converge on these establishments and, singly or in small groups, "sing" along to recorded music. As appalling as this can sound – and it often is – there are legions of people who take karaoke very seriously. They enter contests, practice in front of mirrors, and plan entire evenings out around it. Perhaps you yourself are keen on karaoke and would like to include it at your reception?

DEFINITION

Karaoke, *taken from the Japanese words "empty" and "orchestra," is a type of musical entertainment. A person stands in front of an audience with a microphone and sings along to various popular songs, which have been specially recorded with only the tune's instrumental portion.*

My thoughts? If you love karaoke, go ahead and do it. Simply find yourself a DJ with karaoke equipment (this may raise his or her fee considerably), and give him or her a list of songs you'd like included. Make sure you avoid any tunes with overtly naughty content, and also be certain to include a few "golden oldies" for any of the more senior relatives who'd like to get up and sing.

Some last-minute thoughts

If you're undecided about going with a karaoke reception, then let me give you a few things you should really think about first:

Karaoke gives you and *your guests the chance to be stars for the night – or until you're booed off stage!*

- If yours is a formal wedding, karaoke will add a decidedly casual feel to the proceedings. Is this the vibe you want?
- Place tables with older folks at them as far away from the karaoke machine as possible. Tipsy people seem especially fond of karaoke, and their boisterousness could easily ruffle more mature feathers.
- Limit karaoke to a specific time period. It's inappropriate to perform songs during the first dance, meals, cake cutting, and other special moments.
- It's hard to dance to a karaoke singer. If it's important that guests dance at your reception, you may want to forgo it.
- Give your DJ instructions on how you would like her or him to control any bad behavior. If you've ever watched inebriated people doing karaoke, you will know that shouting, making up sexually offensive or hurtful lyrics, or getting physically rowdy, can be common practice. If any intoxicated guests get out of control when singing, instruct your DJ to lower the volume, or stop the music.

If you do decide to feature karaoke, be very explicit about the songs you DO NOT want included as sing-along options so as not to offend any guests. Barring any tunes you know to be overtly offensive is a good start.

- Avoid using an unmanned karaoke machine. I once attended a wedding where it was a thinly veiled secret that the bride had pressured the groom into proposing. Perhaps the new husband was getting back at his bride as he began to sing a karaoke version of *You've Lost that Loving Feeling* (in itself a poor wedding choice). It became immediately clear he was creating his own, unflattering lyrics about his partner. His groomsmen, tipsy on champagne and mixed drinks, then started to join in with their own mean-spirited lyrics. The bride's family, having paid tens of thousands of dollars for the wedding, could only sit and listen helplessly as their new son-in-law badmouthed their daughter (the bride had already left the room in tears). Finally, a guest found and pulled the machine's plug.

Trivia...

Karaoke's origins are uncertain, though it's commonly believed the practice began in Kobe, Japan, in the early 1970s. Historians debate whether karaoke has its roots in the sing-along bars popular in Japan at the time, or if it was the invention of a specific bar owner.

Non-musical entertainment

Depending on the type of wedding you're having, you may want to hire non-musical entertainment in addition to any musicians. This is especially true if you're having a themed wedding. For instance, a renaissance wedding theme could be enhanced by jugglers, magicians, and madrigal singers. Even if you aren't having a themed wedding, there are plenty of fun entertainment options to investigate, including hiring a dance instructor to get the guests on their feet.

Children can be the most welcome of guests at weddings, but also the most difficult to keep amused. If it fits in with your theme, a children's area with balloon artists, jugglers, magicians, or clowns is a smart way to keep them happily occupied and safe, while you adults enjoy your reception.

Hiring non-musical performers *for your wedding is an innovative and memorable way of entertaining guests.*

A simple summary

- ✓ There is no wrong or right choice of music for a ceremony and a reception. Choose the music and musicians who best reflect your personality.
- ✓ It's worth seeing a live performance before hiring a band, musician, or DJ.
- ✓ Keep your ceremony and reception music similar in style – and make sure they complement your wedding's overall style.
- ✓ Consider all your guests when choosing music – and avoid using songs that could offend some listeners.
- ✓ Love karaoke? Follow a few commonsense guidelines to decide whether or not to feature it at your wedding.
- ✓ Non-musical entertainers can add fun to theme weddings and are a great way to keep your younger guests occupied.

Chapter 13

Coming and Going in Style

WEDDINGS AND TRANSPORTATION – two words not often used in the same sentence, unless the talk has turned to the infamous getaway car, decorated with shoes, cans, streamers, and other doo-dads. Yes, we all know how vital is the fashion in which you depart from your wedding, disappearing off into the distance – into the unknown – to begin your new lives together. But how you arrive at your wedding is equally important, as this chapter reveals. Buckle up now...

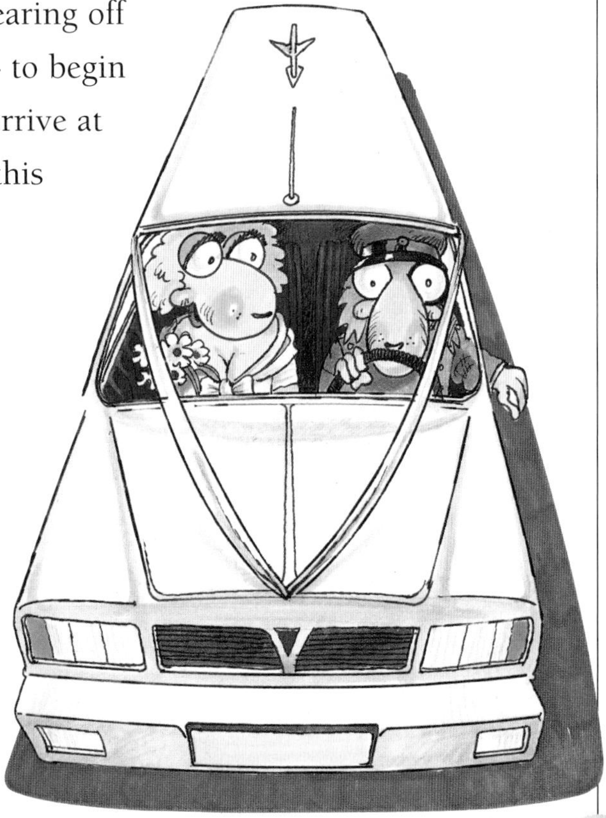

In this chapter...

- ✓ **Getting to the church on time**
- ✓ **Guest transport**
- ✓ **A quick getaway**

Getting to the church on time

WITH SO MUCH to think about before your wedding, deciding how you'll be getting to the ceremony is probably the last thing on your mind. But, it's a detail that must be attended to. Also, you should remember that if your reception is at a different site from the ceremony, you'll need to book transportation to make your way there too. It's all in the detail!

Time to go! *The journey to your ceremony should leave you relaxed and ready to wed.*

Private cars

Ever since automobiles first hit the road, they've been used to ferry people – including brides and grooms – to and from weddings. This utilitarian option is always appropriate – and it frees up money for you to spend elsewhere.

Fancy traveling to your wedding in something a little different? Check around for luxury car rentals. You might find that renting a unique vehicle for a few hours is cheaper than hiring a limo.

If you, as the bride, are traveling to the ceremony with your maid of honor, bridesmaids, mom, or sisters, as well as your dad, consider letting one of them drive you.

Rental cars

Do you dream of arriving at your ceremony in a vintage Thunderbird? How about a 70s-era Corvette? Unless someone in your family collects cars, renting is the easiest – and perhaps only – way to be chauffeured in high style. There's one catch though: Since brides and grooms don't – at least not traditionally – drive themselves to the wedding, you'll need someone to do the honors for you. In the past, this was the duty of the maid of honor or the best man, though any special person who's happy to drive will do.

Limousines

A limo is one of the most popular ways to travel to your own wedding. Not only are you ensured a stylish ride but you can invite your maid of honor, bridesmaids, mother, and even the photographer to join you and your father, giving the journey a party atmosphere. Many limos come stocked with champagne, allowing you to have a "good luck" toast before the ceremony. Because there is more than one type of limo, I have listed the options available to you below:

One of the newest trends in wedding photography is the "in transit" photo. If your wedding photographer isn't able to travel with you en route, get your bridesmaids to take some pictures of you during your journey.

A little luxury: *a glass of champagne is one of the perks of riding in a limousine.*

- **Town car**: 2–4 passengers
- **Limo**: 6 passengers
- **Stretch limo**: 8–10 passengers
- **Super stretch limo**: 10–12 passengers
- **Extreme stretch limo**: 15 or more passengers. Be aware that this last option isn't always the sanest wedding day choice. Not only does an extreme stretch limo look a bit cheesy, but on occasion these cars have been known to actually snap in the middle when hitting a bump in the road!
- **Novelty limo**: For those looking to travel in style, a novelty limo may be a little too déclassé to consider. Novelty limos can be any make of car – SUVs, Humvees, Broncos, you name it – that have been stretched (literally) into a limousine.
- **Amenities**: Many limousines, regardless of how many people they seat, come with amenities. Some of these are optional, but if you're prepared to pay for them you can have a stocked bar, a bartender, a snack center, sunroof, television, stereo, hot tub, game center, and so on. I'd counsel you to ignore these options – well, perhaps the stocked bar and sunroof could be nice – and save yourself a considerable sum.

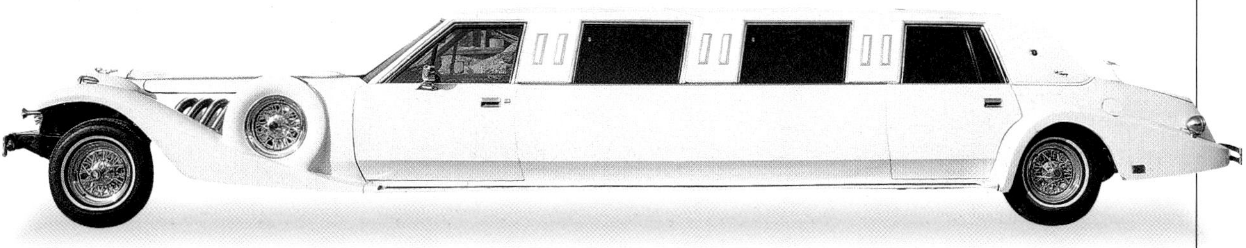

Finding a limousine *that's right for you isn't going to be a problem. There are hundreds of models to choose from, each with its own character and amenities.*

Other options

You don't want your dad to drive you, limousines bore you, and you don't feel like renting a fancy car. No worries – here are a few more ideas:

- **Boat**: If your wedding or reception site is located on a river or lake, you – and other wedding members – can travel via a canoe or row boat. Someone else will do the paddling, of course. Or maybe a small ferry or other motorized boat appeals?
- **Horse-drawn carriage**: This much-used option is romantic, but can be hard on the horse if you are getting married in hot or humid weather, or if the animal must navigate through busy traffic. You don't want to arrive late, do you?
- **Horseback**: If you're a proficient equestrian and your wedding is taking place on a beach, in a meadow, or in another area of countryside, arriving and leaving by horseback is romantic and could be a lot of fun.

When choosing transportation to your wedding, think about your hairdo. An open-air vehicle could muss up a coif that took hours to create. If you love the idea of traveling via horseback or by jet skis, consider using one of these methods for your getaway.

- **Trolley**: If your town has streetcars, call the chamber of commerce or a city authority and ask if these are available for hire. This way, you and your entire wedding party can arrive at the ceremony in style!
- **Hot-air balloon**: Though a hot-air balloon can't take you exactly where you want to go, it is a fun choice for a pre- or post-wedding ride, especially for weddings that take place in rural locations. In fact, in some areas of the United States, hot-air wedding rides are very popular.
- **Helicopter**: This novel option is a very extravagant way to come or go. You'll need to make sure there is a helipad near your wedding site.

How you make your way *to your ceremony is up to you. A horse-drawn carriage is romantic, a limo is flashy, while a helicopter ride is unforgettable.*

However you travel to your wedding ceremony, it will be an exciting occasion in itself. It's a chance for the bride to have one last giggle with her bridesmaids and attendants prior to entering the ceremony. Likewise, before saying "I do," the groom can enjoy the ride in the classic Cadillac he's always coveted.

Take into account your wedding outfit when choosing transportation. You'll want to avoid wrinkling your gown or smashing your headdress. Try putting your outfit on and practicing getting in and out of the car.

Trivia...

Ever wondered why we decorate the getaway car with shoes and cans? Tradition states that the noise that results from doing this will frighten away any malevolent spirit, allowing the couple safe passage from the wedding to the honeymoon.

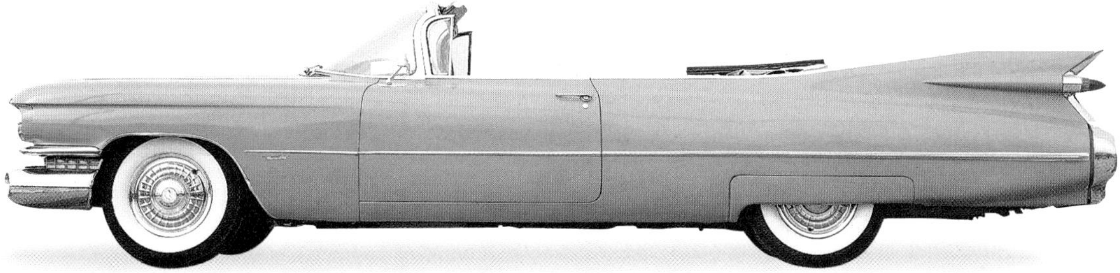

Rental cars are a very popular way *of being chauffeured to your wedding. Just pick the model and color you'd like, then enjoy the experience of turning up to the ceremony in your dream car.*

THE WEDDING PROCESSION

In the days of horse-drawn carriages a wedding procession was the only way to travel to the ceremony (and, of course, carriages are still used today). The wedding procession consists of three or more carriages that align themselves in the following order: the bride's mother and maid of honor in the first coach; the bridal attendants in the second; and the bride and her father in the third. The groom, groomsmen, other wedding party attendants, and the groom's family make their own way to the church – preferably arriving at least 30 minutes before the bride and her folk. After the ceremony has finished, if it's necessary to drive on to a reception site, then the seating arrangements change: the bride and groom in one coach; the bride's parents in another; and the attendants and maid of honor in the third.

Guest transport

GUESTS ARE PLAYERS in your wedding day drama, witnesses to your special occasion. A long time in advance of the ceremony you can help these treasured people share your big day in several ways: Provide directions that help them travel to your ceremony in the most efficient way possible; arrange for group transport if necessary; and ensure there is adequate parking.

Providing directions

How will your guests find your ceremony and reception? With the expert directions you'll be sending them, of course. Any written instructions can be included with the invitations, or mailed separately at a later date – this last option serves as a terrific "save the date" reminder. You'll want to be sure you include a map of the general area, and specific street plans. It's also considerate to go a step further and include driving instructions for a number of different routes – not all attendees will be traveling from the same starting point.

■ **Remember,** *your guests might not know the route to the ceremony. Equip them with directions.*

If you are providing guests with driving directions to your wedding, don't forget to include any parking information.

Lastly, don't forget bus and train information, as well as the name and number of at least one taxi service that guests can contact should they need a ride from the station to the wedding site. All this planning saves any last-minute mishaps.

Parking options

Parking can be a huge deal if your site doesn't have much of it – or if there are more cars than spaces available to accommodate them. For this reason, scope out your site's parking situation in advance. If it is meager, you've got a few options: Hire a **valet** parking service (if the site doesn't include this) to fit all vehicles in; rent car space from a neighboring business; direct guests to a nearby pay lot; encourage attendees to carpool; or arrange for a few minivans or a small bus to pick people up at a pre-arranged site then return folks at a set time.

DEFINITION

A **valet** *parks guests' cars for them and fetches the vehicles when they leave. Plan on one valet for every 100–110 guests. Similar to valets are parking attendants, who point out parking spaces to guests and help safeguard parked cars.*

A quick getaway

BECAUSE HIRING A SPECIAL CAR – or trolley, or carriage, or whatever – for the wedding is a large expense, many couples make do with getting a lift to the ceremony with friends or family and then hire a limousine or other vehicle for their getaway. A getaway vehicle is especially fun if you aren't leaving immediately for your honeymoon: You, your partner, and your wedding attendants can cruise around town, drinking champagne, waving at passersby, and simply relaxing in each other's company. Having someone else do the driving is also smart if you, your partner, or attendants have been drinking.

Transportation: how to hire

It doesn't matter how many cars – or other modes of transport – you need to hire for your big day, organizing your ride to the ceremony can be daunting. I hope these tips will make the process more pleasant:

- Decide what you'll need transportation for. The ride to the wedding? The journey to the reception? What about reaching the airport after the reception?

Congratulations, husband and wife! *With the wedding proceedings over, it's time for you both to hit the open road and enjoy one more spin in your fantasy car.*

- If you are choosing a chauffeured option, would you like your driver to wait for you between rides? This guarantees you flexibility, since you don't have to wait for appointed pick-up times. However, this is more expensive than hiring a driver only for specific rides.
- How many guests do you need transportation for? Do these people need to travel together? And do they have to be in a specific number of vehicles – consider parking restrictions.
- Do some online research and ask for references from married friends and local wedding professionals. Not only do you want a company that is reputable, responsible and fair, you want drivers to be calm, kind and personable. You don't want to be stuck with a grouchy driver who's constantly cursing in heavy traffic.

INTERNET

www.mapquest.com

A terrific tool that can be used for locations throughout the world. A guest plugs in his or her starting point and final destination, then the site creates a detailed map.

Reserve your getaway car as early as possible – especially if your big day is in the late spring, which is prime high-school prom time, or during the summer, when you'll have competition for vehicles from other couples.

- In what condition are the company's cars (or whatever other type of transportation)? Don't be afraid to visit the premises and take a look at the vehicles. Look for recently made cars that are in pristine condition. Why pay hundreds of dollars only to arrive at your wedding in a jalopy?
- Does the company have a flat fee or does it charge by the hour? If the latter, is there a minimum and maximum time limit? And what about tipping? Is it already included in the stated price? If not, look to add 15 percent – or 20 percent if the service is truly phenomenal – to the bottom line.
- Are you required to pay a deposit? Most companies will ask for a sum up front.

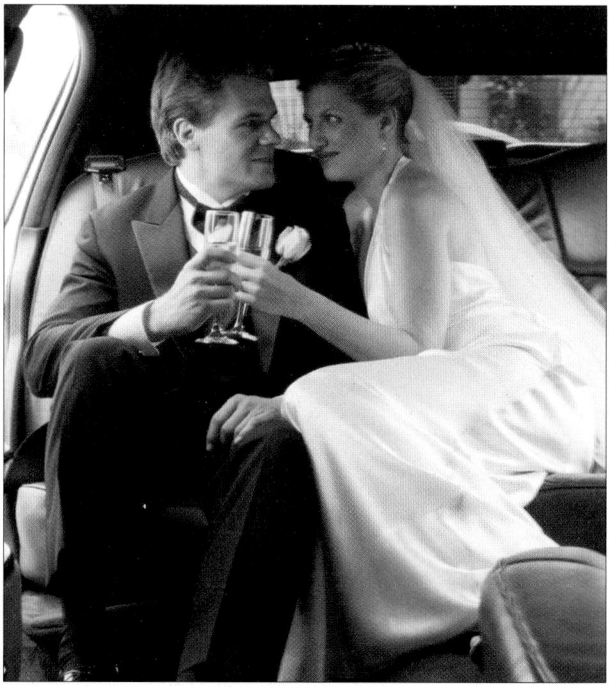

A luxurious interior *is an essential factor to consider when deciding on what kind of car to hire on your big day. This is a great chance to relax together.*

- If you are offered a selection, be sure to specify which vehicle – or vehicles – you would like for your wedding. You don't want to book a special cream-colored stretch limo, only for a black town car to show up.
- If you are choosing a chauffeured option, does the driver know the area? You don't want to spend your wedding day being a backseat driver.
- Many companies provide wedding packages. These come complete with complimentary champagne, some candy or chocolate-dipped strawberries, perhaps a rose, and – in some cases – even a red carpet.
- Do you care how the chauffeur is dressed? If so, ask what he or she will be wearing when they pick you up.
- Make sure your contract includes the type and size of vehicle, the pick-up and drop-off times and locations, and any other specific instructions.

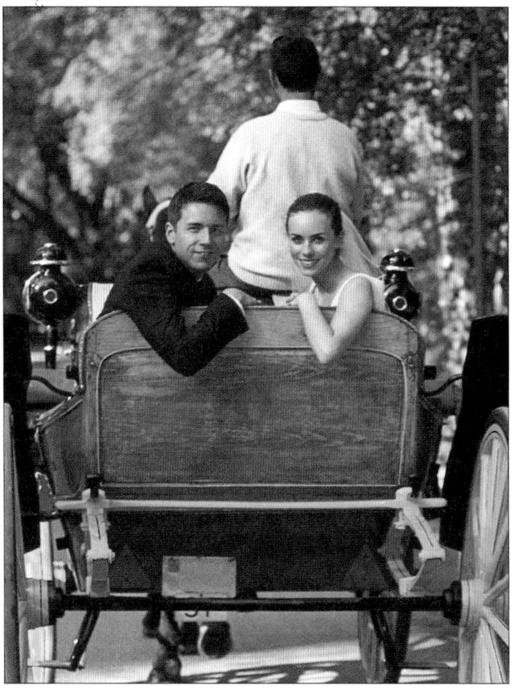

Enjoy yourselves. *Let someone else do the driving (or riding!) as you take it all in.*

A simple summary

✓ Feel like a queen for a day – travel to your wedding in something other than your own car.

✓ If you're choosing a limousine, decide how many people you want to ride with you.

✓ Limos aren't your only option – think about flying, sailing, or riding to your wedding site!

✓ Giving your guests maps and clear directions helps ensure you'll not have any latecomers.

✓ Parking can be a huge wedding day issue. If your site has scant parking, remedy the situation before the big day.

✓ Do some thorough research before hiring transportation.

Part Four

You're Nearly There!

Congratulations: You've finished planning your ceremony and reception. Now it's time to attend to all those niggly official details. Once these are done, get ready to celebrate with a pre-wedding soiree – there's a whole range of different parties you can throw. That said, keep a clear head as you'll want to be prepared to handle any pre-wedding freakouts – you don't want a manic mother-in-law ruining your day!

Chapter 14
Official Details

Chapter 15
Pre-wedding Soirees

Chapter 16
Pre-wedding Freakouts

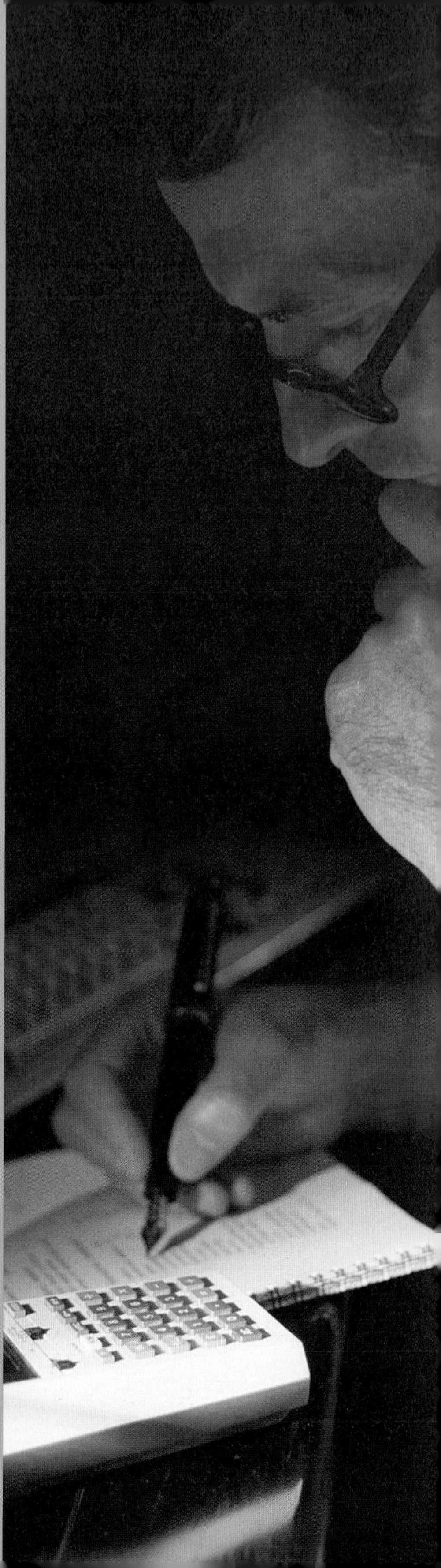

Chapter 14

Official Details

THERE'S A LOT MORE to getting hitched than planning a wedding. There are also the small, non-wedding details that are essential to getting and being married. I'm talking about arranging pre-marital counseling, blood tests, a marriage license, financial matters, and even deciding whether or not either – or both – of you should change your surname. True, choosing a wedding dress or planning a honeymoon is probably a lot more fun than dealing with any of this stuff, but it's these issues that will have a long-term effect on your married life together.

In this chapter...

- ✓ Pre-marital counseling
- ✓ Getting a marriage license
- ✓ Monetary matters
- ✓ Your last names

ADDRESSING THE LESS GLAMOROUS WEDDING DETAILS IS A CHORE – BUT A NECESSARY ONE

Pre-marital counseling

PRE-MARITAL COUNSELING is a type of therapy that many couples attend during their engagement period. Its purpose is to help you learn how to communicate in an open, fair, considerate way so that you're more likely to stay happily married. In addition to teaching communication skills, many therapists also prepare newlyweds for just-married trouble spots, such as adjusting to joint financial management and dealing with in-laws.

Pre-marital counseling can give you the skills needed to enjoy your marriage. But if the counseling – be it run by a therapist or a religious leader – makes you uncomfortable, don't hesitate to lodge a complaint and find a new counselor.

Many municipalities in the United States require you to undergo some type of therapy – usually a "marriage skills class" taught by a licensed therapist – in order to qualify for a marriage license. In addition, there are certain faiths that demand that you have some form of pre-nuptial therapy from a priest, rabbi, or whichever religious authority is appropriate. Both partners are required to attend, even if one partner isn't of the faith. Be aware that most religious-based therapy is just that: religion-based, so in addition to general relationship help you'll receive a generous dose of ideology too.

Being married can be difficult. The first year of marriage is particularly challenging, so many couples who aren't required to undergo counseling choose instead to attend private or group pre-wedding sessions. Think of it this way: You're spending thousands of dollars on wedding outfits, entertainment, and flowers, all of which provide only a few hours of pleasure. Spending a small sum on improving the long-term health of your relationship is an investment that will pay off every day of your marriage.

Having to attend *pre-marital counseling sessions isn't everyone's idea of fun, but it could benefit you as a couple. It helps you learn more about each other and brings you even closer.*

Getting a marriage license

OBTAINING A MARRIAGE LICENSE may be the easiest thing you do from now until after your wedding. Simply contact the clerk or other city authority for the city in which your ceremony will take place. He or she will tell you exactly how far in advance of the wedding you must apply and what you need to bring with you. Most areas require at least some of the following:

- Both partners must be present.
- You must be of legal age – or have a guardian's permission. The legal age differs from area to area, ranging from 14 to 18. Some areas will waive the age requirement if the bride has a signed notice from her doctor stating that she is pregnant.
- Your blood test results (if required).

While many areas issue a marriage license on the spot, others take between a day and a week to process your application. Be sure to ask about this before applying!

Make certain you *know precisely what you must have with you when you apply for a marriage license.*

- Birth certificate.
- Driver's license.
- Passport.
- Social Security Card.
- Proof of your current address. This can be either a utility or phone bill sent to your home address.
- Proof of "singleness." If you've been married before, you'll need to bring paperwork with you showing that your previous marriage ended in death, divorce, or annulment. Be aware that some areas enforce a waiting period between marriages; the period of time differs from one area to another.
- Cash to pay for the license. The precise amount differs from place to place.
- Your wedding date and address of the ceremony location.
- The name, address, and phone number of the person or persons performing your ceremony. (This is not required in all areas.)

With your license, you'll get something called a certificate of marriage. This must be signed and filed with the correct officials – usually within a few days of your wedding – by the officiant who marries you.

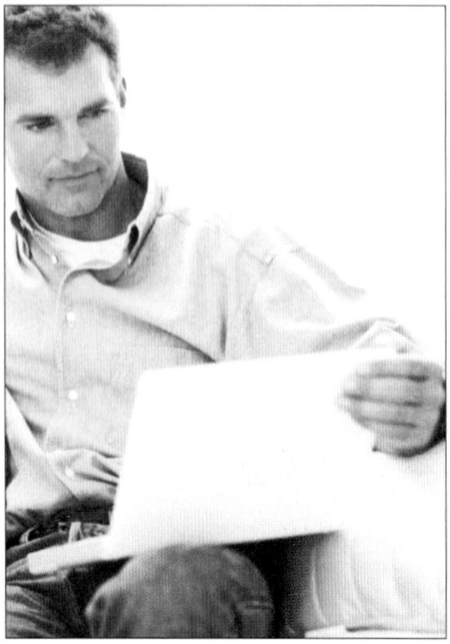

■ **Use the internet** *and any other sources that may help you in obtaining your marriage license.*

Anything else?

To find out whether it is necessary for you to have premarital counseling, or a blood test – or whatever else – in order to obtain a marriage license, contact your county or city clerk. Or simply log on to your computer: Requirements are often detailed online at your city's official website. If you're not marrying in your hometown, you must submit to the requirements of the city where you're planning to wed. Inquiries regarding the validity of a marriage abroad should be directed to the attorney general of the state in which you both live.

INTERNET

www.vitalrec.com/ index.html

This really useful site contains information about where to obtain vital records (such as birth, death, and marriage certificates) from each state, territory, and county of the United States.

BLOOD TESTS – WHAT YOU NEED TO KNOW

A blood test is another location-dependent marriage requirement: Some areas demand it; others don't. If you are marrying in a place that calls for a blood test, call the city clerk for the locations of certified testing labs that you can visit, or make an appointment with your doctor. He or she will perform the test, then fill out a special form, which you must present when you apply for your marriage license. The purpose of this blood test? It's to make sure you don't have an unknown communicable disease, or a genetic condition that could affect any potential offspring.

Blood tests differ depending on where you live, but the most commonly identified conditions are syphilis, rubella, and sickle-cell anemia.

The results of your blood test are valid for only a short time – how short a time depends on the locale. For this reason, it's important to apply for your marriage license before your test results expire. This time limit ensures that you have developed no new medical condition between the time of your blood test and the time you apply for a marriage license.

Monetary matters

YOU'VE PROBABLY HEARD that what married couples fight about most is money. Merging your life with another person's means merging your spending and saving habits with his or her spending and saving habits. Unfortunately, these do not always blend as easily as you would both like.

■ **Never let money** *worries come between you – they can always be resolved.*

Whatever your own attitude toward financial management, the chances are that your partner's will be different. One person's thrift is another's stinginess; one person's easy-going approach to money and spending is another's wasteful extravagance.

Because finance can be such a highly charged topic, it's important to start talking about it and get comfortable with it long before you wed.

Prenuptial agreements

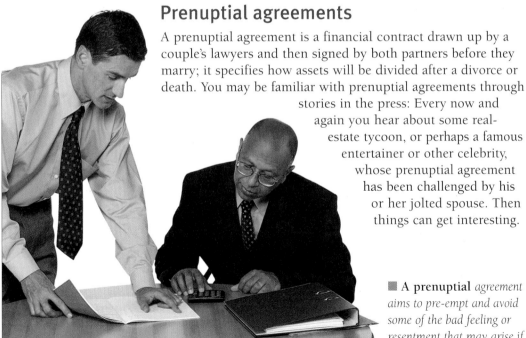

A prenuptial agreement is a financial contract drawn up by a couple's lawyers and then signed by both partners before they marry; it specifies how assets will be divided after a divorce or death. You may be familiar with prenuptial agreements through stories in the press: Every now and again you hear about some real-estate tycoon, or perhaps a famous entertainer or other celebrity, whose prenuptial agreement has been challenged by his or her jolted spouse. Then things can get interesting.

■ **A prenuptial** *agreement aims to pre-empt and avoid some of the bad feeling or resentment that may arise if a marriage ends in divorce.*

Do you need a prenuptial agreement?

Because these contracts plan for divorce before the wedding even takes place, they are not only unromantic but can be offensive to many people. For that reason, prenuptial agreements aren't for everyone.

Who is best served by a prenuptial agreement? Anyone bringing a sizeable sum of money into a marriage may want to be sure of keeping this money if the relationship doesn't last. People who stand to inherit a large sum at some point while married may want to ensure the money doesn't leave with an ex-spouse. And those in high-salary professions may not feel inclined to share their wealth with an ex-partner.

Other reasons for drawing up a prenuptial agreement include protecting yourself against the problems brought about by a spouse who is irresponsible with money, and ensuring that you don't inherit your spouse's debts in the event of divorce.

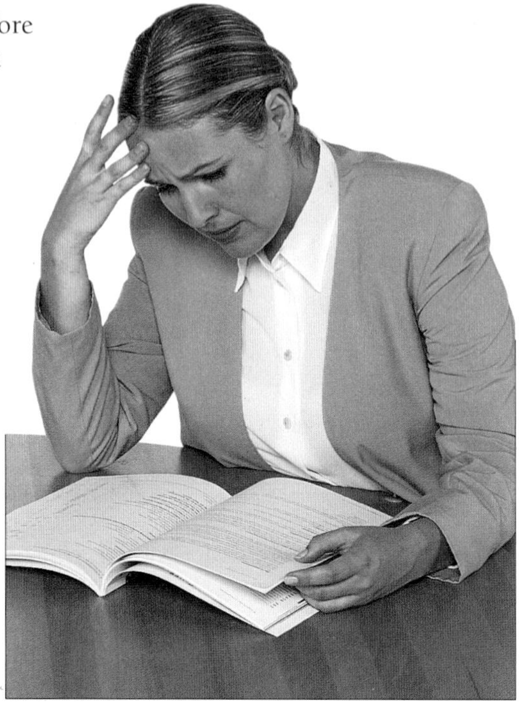

A prenuptial agreement *is hardly romantic, but it is very practical. And the process of drawing up the agreement can in itself help to spotlight – and so enable you to avoid – potential areas of discord.*

A word on tax filing

Regardless of where you live in this world, there's a good chance you have to pay taxes. But did you know that the way you pay taxes – and even how much – changes after you are married? In most places, your marital status on December 31 determines whether you are considered married for that year.

Do not forget to inform all financial institutions, as well as anyone you've worked for in the last year, of any post-marriage address or name change.

After marriage your salary can be combined with your spouse's, moving you into a different income level. Furthermore, depending on your situation – perhaps you've bought a new home, started a business, or had a child – your exemptions may change after marriage. It's important to learn about your new tax situation well in advance of the tax filing date.

Sharing resources

In Chapter 3 I suggested opening a joint wedding account, which you can use to save and pay for your wedding expenses. If you have done this, you will already have a **joint account** that you can easily continue to maintain once you are married.

DEFINITION

*A **joint account** is a shared account – checking or savings – in both your name and your spouse's name. The two of you pool money to be used on shared expenses, such as rent, utilities, entertainment, food, and so forth.*

Managing joint accounts

There are several ways of using joint accounts to organize your money:

- Checking, savings, and investment accounts can all be shared. If you have decided to share all your resources equally you can opt to have only joint accounts.
- The "yours, mine, and ours" method. While there are people who don't feel married unless they combine all their finances, others like to retain a modicum of financial independence by maintaining individual accounts. Some couples therefore have joint checking, savings, and investment accounts while at the same time maintaining their own separate ones.

The beauty of a joint account is that it can enhance your feeling of "coupleness." There is something about sharing your resources that binds you in a way that few other things can quite match.

- Assuming that you and your partner have joint finances plus your own independent accounts, how do you decide who should deposit what into the joint accounts? There are a few options. You can both place an equal amount of money in each joint account each month. Or one spouse can contribute to the joint checking account while the other deposits money in the joint savings; all monetary gifts can go into the joint investment fund. Another wise idea is to agree that you will each contribute a certain percentage of your paychecks into the joint accounts; this is especially useful when there is great disparity in earnings between the spouses, because the higher-paid spouse will deposit more than the lower-paid partner.

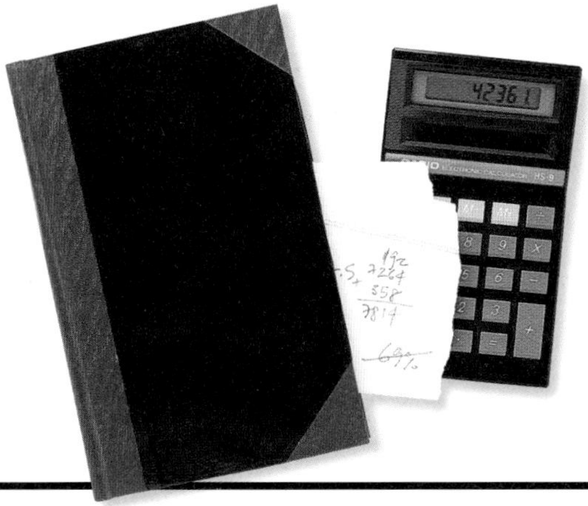

If you are setting up *joint accounts in addition to your own separate ones, you and your partner must decide what you can each realistically contribute to your shared resources.*

Your last names

WAY BACK, WHEN humans lived in small groups, or villages, people had just one name: their first. Then, as the planet's population grew, several people in each area might have had the same first name. So, for centuries, identically named people were distinguished by where they lived, or by a physical characteristic, or by whatever they did for a living. Thus, John Hill, John Gray, or John Smith.

Name changes aren't *always necessary when getting married.*

Surnames were not necessarily passed from one generation to the next. So, if John Hill's son moved away to live near a brook he might have become known by the surname "Brook," or "Waters." Mr. Gray's quick-footed daughter might have been referred to as "Swift." If John Smith's son worked in a mill he might have been called "Miller." With time, royalty and nobility settled on fixed last names, and by the 1400s most of Britain used established surnames. However, the Scandinavians didn't adopt fixed surnames until the 1860s, while Iceland used a flexible system for last names – and still does even today.

INTERNET

www.enamechange.com

www.changeyourname.co.uk

If you or your partner – or both of you – plan on changing your name, you'll find an abundance of help on-line. Americans of both genders may want to check out enamechange.com. Changeyourname.co.uk offers the same service to brides and grooms in the UK.

Must the bride give up her surname?

Ever since fixed surnames started to become the norm, some brides have replaced their last names with their husband's last names. You may have already guessed the reason for this: Women were thought of as property. By calling a married woman by her husband's surname, society was defining her as her "master's" appendage. But what about today? Are brides still expected to give up their last names for their husband's? Not at all. In fact, a growing number of women, offended at the origins of the bridal name change, are choosing to keep their birth names after marriage.

Is there ever a reason to change your surname? Yes: If swapping your name for your husband's is what you want to do. In many circles, adopting the husband's name is certainly the socially accepted choice.

There are other reasons why you might decide to stick with the name you were born with:

- It denotes your ethnic identity, which can be lost if you trade your name for one of a different ethnicity. For instance, if you were born as a Chen, and you marry a man named Smith, taking his last name could erase the Chinese identity from your name.
- You like your last name, and you don't care for your husband's surname.
- You feel too emotionally attached to your own family's name to want to part with it.
- You don't want to go through the hassle of changing your name.
- You've already accumulated impressive educational and professional accomplishments under your own surname, and you feel that there might be confusion in your professional life if you changed names.

Brides and grooms: name options

It may be that both you and your partner strongly agree about whether or not you should change your name. In other cases, where you need to come to some compromise, there are a number of options:

- Both partners use their own last names. Should any children come along, they can have their mother's last name, their father's last name, or both names hyphenated. Be aware that it is not uncommon for children to have their mother's surname rather than their father's. (My own son carries my last name.) Hyphenated surnames are growing in popularity.

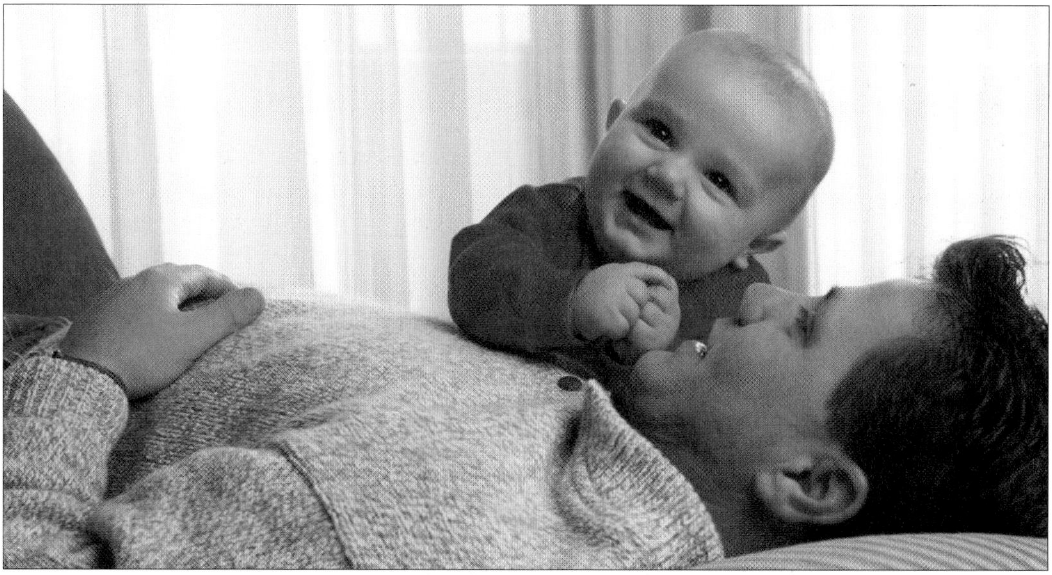

■ **If you and your partner** *decide to stick with your own names, you have several options as to what surname your children will bear. It's worth talking about this in advance to avoid any misunderstandings.*

- Bride uses her own name professionally, her husband's name socially. An option for women who like the idea of trading their name for their husband's but who've accomplished much professionally under their own name.
- Bride takes groom's last name. The most conventional choice.

As the bride, if you want to go on using the name you were born with, be prepared for resistance. You may get negative comments from your mother-in-law, your husband-to-be, and perhaps even from envious women in your own family who went the traditional route. Don't feel bad about your choice! It's your name, your decision!

- Groom takes bride's last name and drops his own. While this isn't commonplace, it isn't extremely rare, either. If a man wants to adopt his bride's surname, he can go through the same name-changing procedures she would traditionally go through.
- Bride adds her groom's last name after her own. This is traditional, yet also modern, and still a very popular choice for many couples.
- Bride adds her groom's last name to her own, joining the names together with a hyphen. The hyphen is the most conventional way of joining names together.

If you decide to invent or adopt an entirely new name, you should choose something that you will not constantly have to spell out for people.

- Both bride and groom use both names, hyphenated or otherwise. This practise is adopted by an increasing number of couples who want to feel the sense of "togetherness" of having a shared last name, but who don't want to lose their own individual names. Note: This won't work for all surnames.

To avoid the problem *of deciding which of your names to adopt, you can choose a completely new surname. Some couples derive a surname from the name of a favorite place.*

- A last name combo. The couple creates a new last name from both their surnames. Thus, Smith and Swensen might become Smithsen, Guitterez and Hutchings might become Guiterings. While this option isn't common among the general population, it is encountered in certain "artier" enclaves.

If you decide to use both last names, make sure they sound good together. For instance, Liz Chalk and Mike Cheese might like to ponder something else!

- An entirely new surname. A special location, activity, person, or something else that has deep meaning for you might be usable as a last name. For example, a couple whose favorite place on Earth is the red desert of Sedona might find this a suitable option.

Trivia...

In some Middle Eastern Muslim countries, such as Yemen, Iran, and Syria, brides keep their surnames. In Spain and most South American countries, women combine their own and their husband's names – but only the woman's part of the name is passed to the children. And in Iceland, it's common for women to keep their birth names and pass these on to their children.

A simple summary

✓ While pre-marital counseling isn't required of everyone, it's a great way to develop your relationship-strengthening skills.

✓ When applying for a marriage license, be sure to apply in the city you'll be getting married in.

✓ Taxes may be different for you as a married person. Don't forget to notify any appropriate financial institutions – and anyone you've worked for during the last year – of your new married status.

✓ If you like the idea of joining funds, then consider setting up a joint checking, savings, or investment account.

✓ Don't feel pressured to give up your surname if you don't want to! You must live with your decision, so you make it.

✓ If you and your husband would like to share the same surname, but you don't want to take on his last name, you've got plenty of other options.

Chapter 15

Pre-wedding Soirees

SURE, YOUR ENGAGEMENT PERIOD is hard work – you've got so much to do. But the time before your wedding is also a social one, filled with friends, family, and fun. Oh, and plenty of parties, including an engagement party, a shower, various nights out, the rehearsal dinner, and even more. Of course, how many of these parties you and your partner can attend depends on how you are getting married, your budget, and your desires. But there's no denying you have plenty of entertaining opportunities available. So take advantage of the festivities and enjoy yourselves!

In this chapter...

- ✓ The engagement party
- ✓ Showers
- ✓ Throwing bachelor and bachelorette bashes
- ✓ The rehearsal dinner

The engagement party

A PARTY IS A LOVELY WAY to celebrate your engagement. Traditionally, the engagement party was hosted by the bride's family with or without help from the groom's family. Today it can also be thrown by friends of the wedding couple or by the bride and groom themselves, and is typically held in someone's home or in a restaurant. Furthermore, the festivities can take the form of a cocktail party, afternoon tea, backyard barbecue, casual potluck, brunch, formal dinner, informal luncheon, or a picnic.

Different ways to throw your engagement party

If you host the affair, you can tailor the event to suit your guest list. You can also throw a surprise party. This fashionable option involves inviting family and friends, then astonishing them all with news of your engagement. Of course, a surprise party takes some advance planning – and the ability to keep quiet about your engagement until the event comes around.

There isn't a specific or best time to hold your engagement party, but these celebrations often work well as evening events. If, however, you want to make it a more informal occasion, perhaps with lots of children attending, then feel free to host it on a Saturday afternoon in the comfort of your own backyard.

Engagement parties are *a fun way to announce and celebrate what is going to be the most important day in your lives.*

If you decide to go ahead and hold your engagement party at your place, it's a good idea to have it catered, thus leaving you, your family, and your friends free to enjoy yourselves. Be prepared and allow at least two months to book the caterers. A simple tip to remember is that the bigger the party (and therefore the greater the number of people attending), the more notice you need to give. Also consider the type of entertainment you want to provide: Will a friend playing a few party CDs suffice or is it worth looking to bring in a DJ?

Finally, if somebody else arranges your engagement party then be sure to thank him or her with a nice note and a little something – a gift certificate for dinner at their favorite restaurant is always a good idea.

Standard etiquette states that anyone invited to your engagement party must also be invited to your wedding. Think carefully before sending out any invitations.

A couple in County Durham, England, are still waiting to walk up the aisle, 34 years after getting engaged. Rod Burtt got engaged to his fiancée, Judith Kent, in 1969 – before man landed on the moon. The 62-year-old proposed on 21 June and the announcement went into the Forthcoming Marriages section of the Daily Telegraph. *Mr. Burtt said: "I've never believed in rushing into important decisions, especially things that are going to affect your whole life."*

It's party time!

Here are some tips to make your engagement party especially eventful:

- Decorate the party site with mementos from your courtship days. Include photographs from your youth – they'll raise a laugh!
- Set the party date well in advance of other pre-wedding events, such as showers and rehearsal dinners. The earlier the better.
- Invite both the bride's and groom's families. An engagement party is an ideal way for the two sides to get to know each other better.

The guests attending *your engagement party will find it charming to look through photo albums and relive your childhoods with you both.*

- Wonder where you'll find the time to plan a party? Get help. Accept assistance from whoever offers. Hire caterers and do whatever you can to lighten your load. Remember, engagement parties are supposed to be fun, so make sure you enjoy it!

Showers

■ **Giving gifts** *to the bride-to-be at her shower is a way of helping the engaged couple set up house.*

WE HUMANS HAVE been getting married for thousands of years but the wedding shower is a relatively recent custom. Thought to have originated in Holland some time during the 19th century, the bridal shower as we know it began when a young Dutch woman fell in love with a poor miller. Her father, angry at her daughter's choice in groom, disowned the woman, leaving her without the customary dowry needed to set up a home. When the townspeople learned of the bride's predicament, they decided to "shower" her with gifts of linens, dishes, and other helpful items.

Showers today

The bridal shower has since evolved into a small luncheon held at the home of a relative or the maid of honor. The bride sits at the head of the table and can be literally showered by gifts, chosen to help her set up her new home. Attended by female friends and family, the bridal shower of old focused on more than just gifts: It was a time for married guests to share their wisdom with the bride and help allay fears. In fact, it was at their bridal shower that many women of past generations learned exactly what went on in the marital bed.

Your maid of honor may ask you for a list of the friends you'd like to be at your shower. Be sure that these people are also invited to the wedding!

■ **The bridal shower** *is a time for the bride to socialize and enjoy herself before the wedding.*

The conventional bridal shower

For many modern brides, the bridal shower is a much anticipated part of being engaged. And why not? This all-female affair offers a chance to be showered with gifts, as well as spend time with friends and family. Unfortunately, if you happen to be the bride, you have no role in planning this soiree: It is organized by your attendants. However, that doesn't mean it has to be a complete surprise. Most traditional-style bridal showers follow the same format:

Trivia...

Before the bridal shower concept was born, bridesmaids used to organize a get-together with the bride in order to strengthen friendships, talk through any fears the bride may have about marriage, and help plan the wedding.

- At some point within four months of the wedding, you meet female family and friends at a home or restaurant for brunch, lunch, tea, or dinner. One of the bridesmaids stands at the door, acting as an official greeter.

A small gift sent within two weeks of your bridal shower is a lovely way to thank those responsible for organizing the event.

- You then mingle over hors d'oeuvres.
- Next up are the formal introductions.
- Then you play a shower game or two. Don't know what a shower game is? Visit a wedding website and take a look for yourself.
- It's time to eat.
- Why not play another shower game?
- Gift-opening time. One of your bridal attendants will collect the gift cards for you, so you know who to send thank-you notes to.

Bride-groom showers

One of the hottest trends in pre-nuptial parties is the co-ed wedding shower. Like a traditional bridal shower, but with your groom and his friends in attendance, the co-ed shower is an especially fun way to share wedding excitement with the men in your life.

Food plays an important part *in your bridal shower – sharing a meal brings you all closer.*

The co-ed wedding shower is almost identical to the conventional, all-female variety, except – because men are attending – it is less girly. Yes, you read that right: *less girly*. Generally, bridal showers are excessively delicate, with the commonplace pastel decorations, the serving of a light luncheon or tea menu, and the cute games played by attendees.

Like the conventional variety, the co-ed shower is planned by your attendants, though they can – and should – ask the groomsmen for help. For a more gender-neutral soiree, ask your attendants to consider dinner, replace the shower games with plenty of chat time, and be sure that the gifts reflect both your and the groom's interests. This way you can guarantee that everyone eats well, gets to know one another, and – who knows? – that single friend might just meet someone!

INTERNET

www.ultimateshower.com

This site features ideas for shower themes, meals, games, as well as historical information on showers. And there are plenty of shower doo-dads available to buy.

CO-ED? CONVINCE ME!

A co-ed wedding shower! What will my stodgy Aunt Bertha say? Won't my groom and his friends find the whole occasion odd? And can I also enjoy a conventional bridal shower? Relax. Your aunt will do just fine. Trust me. I've been at co-ed showers with great-grandmas and great-aunts, and these older ladies enjoyed themselves just as much as anyone else. If you're worried, then seat all the women of a certain generation together. The guys will also enjoy themselves. You'd be surprised how much fun men can have opening gifts – especially if some of the presents include electronic gadgetry. One final point – a single wedding shower is the most you can reasonably expect your attendants to organize. Now if your co-workers arrange an office shower, that's an entirely different matter...

The aunts' table. *Co-ed bridal showers are a chance to bring different generations together.*

Throwing bachelor and bachelorette bashes

THE FIRST BACHELOR PARTIES took place as bachelor dinners, given in honor of the groom the night before his wedding. Historians disagree as to whether the custom has its origins in Greece or Rome, but it's generally placed within the first five centuries A.D. At some point between then and now, these dinners turned into the boozy, overtly sexual parties we so often hear about today. Time has further shaped the bachelor party by giving it a feminine spin-off, hence the modern-day bachelorette party, the female equivalent of the boys' big night out. It's only fair.

A bachelor party in full swing. *Bachelorette parties are now also growing in popularity.*

The bachelor party

Bachelor parties sometimes receive a lot of flak, and often with good reason: Strip bars, lap dancers, prostitutes, and mobs of bachelors descending on Las Vegas to sample the city's licentious sexual entertainment industry hardly do these parties any favors. This kind of disregard – some might even say disrespect – for the bride makes today's bachelor parties highly controversial. Many brides dread them, having heard what goes on. First off, dear bride, don't feel jealous or "old fashioned" for being troubled by these conventional bachelor parties. Believe me, if all the brides of the world enjoyed a similar night of carousing before saying "I do," the grooms of the world would be positively horrified. Second, you aren't alone in your feelings about bachelor parties: they're a major reason why brides break it off with their grooms.

Trivia...

Bachelor parties are also known as stag parties, while bachelorette parties are also called hen parties.

Some women don't mind what their future husbands do at their bachelor parties. If you, however, are bothered by what you've heard goes on, express your feelings to him. Realize, too, that – against his wishes – his friends may exert great pressure on him to follow along with their plans.

A mutual solution

So what to do? Realize that yes, there are men who think a guy deserves a night of debauchery before settling down with one person. Also, know that the very people who push hardest for inviting a prostitute to the groom's festivities are not grooms, but their friends. An easy way for you both to avoid dealing with the fallout caused by sex-based bachelor parties is to suggest a less offensive mode of entertainment. An increasing number of guys are opting to celebrate with their friends by doing one of the following:

- A day of golf, skiing, hang gliding, or other favorite activity.
- A day at the races, catching a ball game, or other sporting event.
- Dinner and a comedy club.
- Going to see a favorite band.
- A night at a local casino's gaming tables – always a popular choice.

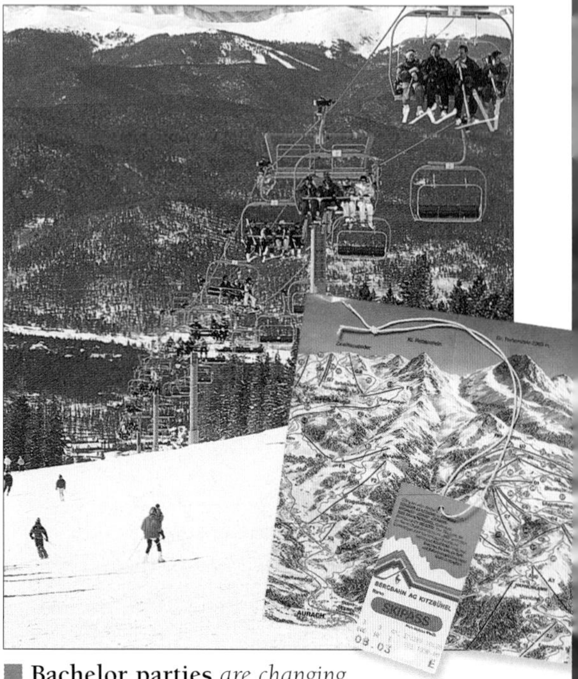

Bachelor parties *are changing. Boozy nights in strip bars are gradually making way for more sociable kinds of activity.*

The bachelorette party

The bachelorette party has only relatively recently been recognized as a social occasion. It was concocted in response to the bachelor party's excess because, after all, what's good for the goose is good for the gander, right? Thrown by the bridesmaids or the bride herself, the festivities are less inclusive than the wedding shower: For this party, moms, grandmas, and aunts are not invited, nor is anyone related to the groom.

Be consistent in your moral standards! It's hardly fair to give your groom a dressing down before he goes off to his bachelor party, only for you to head out with the girls on your bachelorette party and get up to mischief that oversteps the mark! Think about each other's feelings and you'll both be okay.

The bachelorette party isn't as raunchy as the traditional male version – though some bachelorettes do hire male strippers or visit male strip or co-ed sex clubs. Dinners, cocktail cruises, and concert outings seem more common ideas. What else is there to a bachelorette's do? Party activities include a few risqué games, such as pasting a bride's shirt with candy and asking random males to nibble off the sweets, or playing "pin the phallus" on an enlarged photograph – taken just for this purpose – of the naked groom.

The combined his-her party

One of the best – and most popular – ways to share a bachelor and bachelorette party is the combined his-her party. More and more couples are pooling their friends and going out for a night of cocktails, dinner, a comedy club or concert, pub hopping, and then dancing. The great thing about this kind of party is you and your intended get to release tension together. Plus, your attendants and any other friends you've invited get to socialize en masse, which is often more fun than going out with a gang of people who are all the same sex. So, if you and your partner are interested in having a bachelor-bachelorette bash, consider rounding up all of your favorite friends, renting a flashy limousine, making reservations for dinner, buying concert tickets, and then hitting the town.

Combined his-her parties *open up a variety of alternative ways to go out and celebrate. What's more, you get the chance to enjoy the evening with your beloved.*

IN SICKNESS AND IN HEALTH

Any bachelor, bachelorette, or bachelor-bachelorette parties should take place well in advance of the wedding. True, in the old days, these parties were held the night before the ceremony, but the old ways aren't always the best. When you reach the altar, you don't want your groom to bolt down the aisle and toward the bathroom because he is reeling from the night before – nor do *you* want to be the one feeling sick. This does happen. A friend of mine was abandoned in front of the church when her groom dashed out of the side door. For 15 minutes the wedding guests were treated to the sounds of him retching onto the church lawn.

The rehearsal dinner

THE REHEARSAL DINNER is an intimate – or somewhat so – meal that takes place after the wedding rehearsal. Typically joining the bride and groom are the wedding party attendants, both sets of parents, the officiant, and any significant others. Out-of-town guests can also be invited. The invitations, by the way, need not be formal. There are those who like to send out formally printed notes complete with maps and driving directions to the meal's location, but a phone call or e-mail will suffice.

If you and your partner haven't already given your attendants their thank-you gifts, the rehearsal dinner is the time to do so.

Though it is often called a rehearsal "dinner," the meal can be anything from a brunch to a lunch to cocktails. It can be held at the groom's parents' home – the traditional choice – or at a restaurant. The only requirement is this: If your rehearsal meal takes place the day before your ceremony, it must end early so you and the wedding party can rest-up for the big occasion.

Other parties you throw

As if there aren't enough wedding parties to get through, here are a few more. Fortunately, all are optional, and none require formal invitations; an e-mail or phone call are absolutely acceptable. Pick and choose – or ignore – at will:

- **The attendants' cocktail party**: If the bridal attendants and groomsmen don't already know each other, then a cocktail party is a really fun way of acquainting everyone. If they do know each other, a cocktail party is still enjoyable and lets everyone share each other's company. Hosted by the bride and groom, the attendants' cocktail party should be held within two months of your wedding. Invite everyone over to your place, or direct folks to your favorite nightspot.

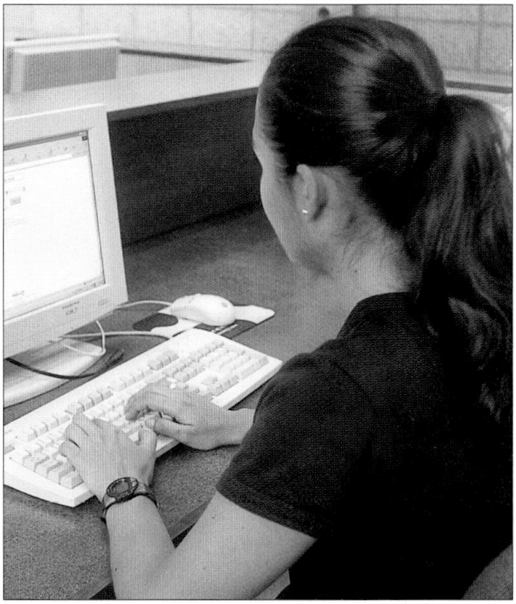

A lot of expense and planning *went into your wedding invitations. Keep any invitations to parties simple and inexpensive – an e-mail will do.*

- **The bridesmaids' luncheon**: Hosted by the bride, and thrown at some point in the weeks leading up to the wedding, a bridesmaids' luncheon is a fun way to hang out with your girlfriends. It needn't be fancy: Take-out in your living room, a picnic in a local park, or a table at a favorite restaurant.
- **The day-after brunch**: If you and your partner aren't rushing off to your honeymoon, you may want to consider hosting a day-after brunch. This intimate gathering – the newlyweds, attendants, and parents only – allows the wedding's key players to sit back and rehash the wedding point-by-point in a convivial and comfortable atmosphere. It can take place in someone's home or at a cozy restaurant.
- **The "thank-you parents" meal**: During the weeks leading up to the wedding, or the weeks following your honeymoon, many couples have a small brunch with their parents to thank them for their financial and emotional support. Consider inviting both sets of parents over to your home – this will give you a chance to use those new dishes you received.

■ **There's a whole host** *of party options available before and after your wedding day.*

A simple summary

✓ An engagement party is a formal, festive way to announce your commitment to each other.

✓ Your bridal attendants are responsible for throwing you a bridal shower. Be sure to thank them all for the hard work and expense they invested in you!

✓ Let the guys in on your night. Consider having a co-ed wedding shower. You'll meet double the friends and so double your fun!

✓ Bachelor parties are no longer for men only – and no, strippers are not a requirement.

✓ The rehearsal dinner lets the wedding participants unwind before the big day.

✓ Love parties? Then go beyond the engagement party, shower, bachelorette party, and rehearsal dinner by enjoying an attendant's cocktail party, a day-after brunch, and plenty more options.

Chapter 16

Pre-wedding Freakouts

THE TIME SPENT PLANNING YOUR WEDDING is a highly charged period – not only for you and your partner but also for both sets of parents, the siblings, the relatives, and anyone else close to you. And when the pressure starts to get to people, they behave in inexplicable ways: Your best friends suddenly make snide comments about your intended; your fiancé's brother utters the words "marriage equals death," and so on. As bothersome as this can be, you must realize that it's normal for people to react to other people's weddings like this. You'll survive this pre-marriage hoo-ha. This chapter tells you how.

In this chapter...

- ✓ A case of cold feet
- ✓ Canceling the wedding
- ✓ Dealing with nasty-makers

A case of cold feet

"HAVE COLD FEET" is to be so uncertain about a situation that you'd like to retreat. It doesn't matter that the origin of the expression is unclear – if your wedding date is near, chances are you know exactly how it is to have cold feet. Don't feel guilty or ashamed about your emotions; having cold feet doesn't necessarily mean that getting married is a bad idea.

Thinking of canceling? *Ask yourself whether you simply have pre-wedding jitters or bigger, more serious doubts.*

Having second thoughts about getting married is completely normal. Consider what an enormous life change marriage is: Wouldn't it be odd if you were not scared? But how do you distinguish between normal pre-nuptial jitters and serious misgivings? Simply ask yourself the following questions. Your answers will help you to decide whether your doubts are common premarital fears or a sign of something more serious:

- Think of yourself ten years from now. Do you see yourself with your current partner? Is it easy or hard for you to picture growing old together?
- If your fiancé disappeared tomorrow, would you feel grief? Or relief?

POSTPONING YOUR WEDDING

If there is a death in your family, or some other unforeseen disaster or terrible event, you may have to postpone your wedding. Start by scheduling a new date and calling all vendors and the manager of the wedding location. Then telephone all your guests with the news. Follow up with a printed card that reads something like this: "Owing to a death in the family, Mr. James John and Ms. Cynthia Hall announce that the marriage of their daughter, Lara John-Hall, has been postponed until July 4, 2004." Note that if your original venue is already booked for the revised date you will have to find a new location for your wedding. If this is the case, add the new site's name to the card, with directions.

- Can you commit yourself completely to this one person for the rest of your life? Be honest. This isn't a decision to make lightly.
- Can you commit yourself completely to this person knowing that in time he will age and look different from how he looks now, that he may grow intellectually in a different direction from you, that he may become sick and need care, or become poor and need your financial assistance?

If you are having serious doubts about getting married, do yourself, your fiancé, and your guests a favor: Right away see a counselor who can help you sort out your feelings. Only once you understand your feelings should you cancel the wedding.

- Are you madly, completely, and unequivocally in love?
- Are you realistic about who your partner is and what a relationship can provide? No one person or relationship can give you everything you want.
- Do you agree on key issues, such as what part of the country to live in and whether or not to have a child?
- Are you both free of addictions that can cloud your thinking and weaken your judgment? If you aren't, then you both need to address this.
- Is this a rebound relationship? In other words, did either you or your partner go straight from a previous long-term relationship to the one you're in now?

Marriage should be considered a lifetime commitment. *Imagine yourself with your partner in 10, 20, 30 or more years. If you can't do this, ask yourself whether you are doing the right thing.*

Canceling the wedding

AS I'VE MENTIONED, regardless of how much you love your fiancé, or how excited you are to be getting married, it is normal to have marriage doubts. For some people, however, these are more than simple doubts – they are serious indications that the wedding shouldn't happen. It doesn't really matter what the reason is. It may be that you love the idea of a wedding, but don't care too much for the groom. Maybe you've suddenly fallen in love with someone else. Perhaps the groom has wandering eyes or has emotionally or physically abused you, or is a criminal, or has a gambling or drinking or drug problem.

Trivia...

In the United States, 500,000 engagements are called off each year.

Whatever the circumstances, what's important is that you cancel the ceremony as quickly and neatly as you can. So just how do you cancel a wedding? This list might help:

- Tell your fiancé. He should be the first to hear your news.
- What about the ring? Modern etiquette states that if the groom's behavior – womanizing, a substance-abuse problem, and so on – is to blame, the bride gets to keep the ring. If the bride's reasons are more personal, she should return the ring. Any heirloom jewelry should go back to the family of origin.
- Tell your family. This is going to be hard, especially if your parents were fond of your partner, or are anxious about you staying single the rest of your life. But ultimately, they should support you.

■ **It can be very** *difficult to admit that you have changed your mind, but it is only fair to tell your partner before discussing it with anyone else.*

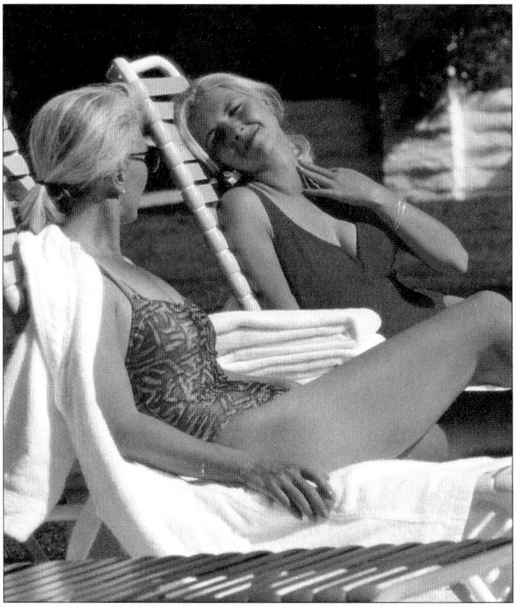

■ **If you cannot get a refund** *on the costs of the honeymoon, treat the trip as an ordinary holiday and go with a friend.*

- Assign a friend or family member to contact all guests and announce the wedding's cancellation. If the wedding is just days away, this should be done by telephone to give people the most possible notice. The telephone can also be used if invitations have not yet been sent. If invitations have been sent, and there is adequate time, a simple note can be mailed out. Commonly used wording is: "Mr. John Smith and Ms. Brown-Smith announce that the marriage of their daughter, Cecilia Brown-Smith, will not take place." A reason should not be given.

Be aware that the person who calls off the wedding is – at least from an etiquette standpoint – obliged to pay the jilted partner any deposit money he or she loses.

- Call the caterers, florist, and any other professionals with the news. Some may return a portion of your deposit, though many won't. If you have a sister, cousin, or friend getting married, perhaps she can use these vendors' services by having your deposits transferred into her name. Or, ask how long these businesses will keep your deposits "active." Perhaps the next time you get engaged you can use their services.
- Return any gifts you have received – even the monogrammed ones. It's the right thing to do. If you've used any of the gifts, buy the giver a comparable item to compensate.
- You don't have to tell anyone your reasons for canceling, unless you want to.
- If you can't get a refund on your honeymoon trip, consider going with a friend or family member.

Don't forget to inform the officiant who would have conducted your ceremony. This should be done as soon as possible.

INTERNET

www.theregoesthebride.com

For anyone thinking about calling it off, this site offers commiseration. In addition to the many personal "calling it off" and "being left at the altar" stories, you'll find resources on getting through the ordeal, as well as kind words from the site's founder, Rachel Safier, author of There Goes the Bride.

Dealing with nasty-makers

THERE'S SOMETHING ABOUT WEDDINGS that brings out the worst in some folks: Your future in-laws, perhaps also your mother, probably your fiancé's party-boy buddy, and certainly your freshly divorced cousin. Unpleasantness may manifest itself in small comments or subtle interference – or it can be blatant misconduct. I hope everyone in your life behaves beautifully. But if they don't, let this section assist you.

Family dysfunction

I had lunch the other day with two friends, one of whom was recently married. Of course, talk turned toward weddings, especially the crazy behavior of my friend's mother. Despite the fact that my friend was paying for her own wedding, her mother wanted artistic control over the entire ceremony and reception. Furthermore, the mother was furious with my friend's choice in bridesmaids' gowns. So furious, in fact, that my friend's mom called all the bridesmaids and tried to get them to revolt in hopes her daughter would choose other dresses for her attendants.

Respectfully remind both sets of parents that it's important for you and your partner to be allowed to "grow as a team" by planning nuptial details on your own.

As my friend jokingly says, for many parents weddings are about exerting control over you one last time before you fly the nest. By honestly acknowledging this fact to your parents you can do much to loosen their grip on your wedding plans. Sure, involve them in things, but don't let them take over.

When your wedding *plans are causing friction between friends or members of the family, try to keep your cool – losing your temper will only make things worse.*

Thankfully, most of us will not have to deal with this degree of crazymaking from our own family. Most brides, however, do have to tolerate some acting up from family members who have strong opinions about marriage and weddings. Below are some of the most common forms of misconduct, with a few suggestions for how you might handle each scenario:

- "How dare you rob me of my chance to plan your wedding!" If your mother is of a certain generation, be prepared to hear her say something like, "My mother planned my wedding, so I'm planning yours." You're right, this does sound ridiculous. And yes, you're also right that what your grandmother did should have no bearing on your big day. Tell your mother that you love her, and how appreciative you are of all the sacrifices she made to raise you. However, you absolutely should not give up control of your wedding – even if your mom is helping to pay for it. Involve your mother with those areas you're willing to compromise on. Otherwise, quietly – without sharing details – take care of the planning yourself, or let your fiancé or wedding planner do the work.

You can help to defuse many tricky situations by acknowledging that the person expressing a strong opinion has a valid point of view – even if you don't agree with it. Try to be firm without being disparaging or destructive.

- Your sister thinks marriage is a patriarchal scam designed to subjugate women, an idea she doesn't refrain from sharing with your squirming partner. I throw this one in here not because I think your sister is wrong – marriage did originally come about as your sister says – but because I've dealt with this one, as have a few of my friends. In my case, my sister had me and my beloved in her car. We were about 15 minutes into a moderately long drive when she began – and never ended. In fact, she was still ranting when we'd reached our destination, exited the car, and were seated at the restaurant we'd been traveling to. You can remind your sister that marriage today isn't about ownership, but partnership, which is what we kept repeating to my sister. Not that she listened. But still, we remained kind (if not a bit bemused) and finally – after ten years – she apologized for her behavior.
- Your other sister is angry that you and your stupid wedding are getting all the attention! This is a difficult one. Your first instinct will probably be to throttle your sister – or at least tell her how pathetic she is – but showering her with your attention may work better. If she's jealous because she has no romantic prospects herself, remind her that her turn will come (but without being patronizing, which will serve only to infuriate her more).

INTERNET

www.hitched.co.uk

This UK-based site covers everything from bridal fashion to wedding speeches, engagement issues to honeymoons. It also features helpful links and vendors throughout the UK, USA, and other countries.

- Your brother hates your partner. He may be protective, with only your best interests in mind, but there could be some jealousy there, also. Why not sit down with the doubting Thomas and let him explain exactly why you shouldn't marry your partner. Thank him for his concern and, in turn, tell him all the reasons you're going to go ahead with the ceremony. Don't forget to warn your brother to behave himself around your fiancé – or else!
- Your freshly divorced cousin won't stop telling you why marriage won't work. Nor will she quiet down on the subject of men – just how terrible they are. Sympathy is your best bet. Listen to her without bringing up your own situation, which could feel particularly affronting to her right now. If all else fails, you could arrange a night out with her and your marriage-hating sister!

Friction with the in-laws

Problems with your future in-laws are as common as problems with one's own family. Since you may not feel as comfortable with your in-laws as you do with your own family, in-law problems are often harder to deal with. Fortunately, you have a secret weapon: Your partner. He is essential in keeping control of his family. It doesn't matter whether your mother-in-law is making unreasonable demands on your guest list or your sister-in-law has personally offended you, tell your partner how you feel, and what you'd like him to do to remedy the situation. If he balks – perhaps he's a self-described mama's boy, or simply hates confrontations – remind him how important his support is to your shared future.

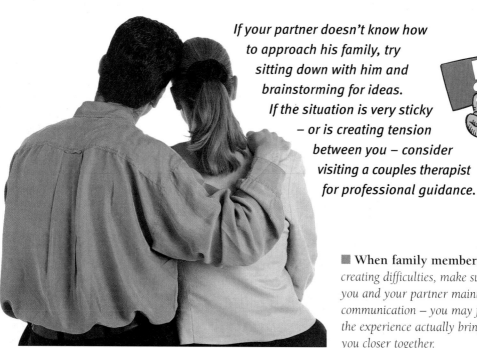

If your partner doesn't know how to approach his family, try sitting down with him and brainstorming for ideas. If the situation is very sticky – or is creating tension between you – consider visiting a couples therapist for professional guidance.

■ **When family members** *are creating difficulties, make sure that you and your partner maintain communication – you may find the experience actually brings you closer together.*

The bride's friends

As if crazy family members weren't enough, you may also run into some less-than-sane behavior from your girlfriends:

- One-upmanship. You'll probably recognize this when you see it, but here's a juicy example and one method of dealing with it: "Oh, you're going to the Bahamas on your honeymoon? Thurston and I went to Fiji. In fact, we rented an entire private island with our own staff of 57 for an entire month. How long did you say you were going for? Five days? That's a shame." When faced with this, smile your biggest smile, tilt your head and say, "How nice for you." Resting a hand on her forearm as you say it is an optional, but very effective, touch.

When threatened by someone's success – or simply when jealous – some people try to make themselves look and feel better by competing. Understanding this makes it easier for you to ignore bad behavior.

- What did you say? Whether she's commenting on your dress or giving you a backhanded compliment on your choice of wedding cake, your friend can't resist making hurtful remarks. Instead of letting her get away with the meanness – which will ultimately leave you seething – simply look at her and sweetly ask, "What do you mean by that?" You may also try, "I'm confused why you said that." Such apparent innocence on your part will make her feel foolish. Do this once or twice and I guarantee the lady in question will keep her comments to herself.

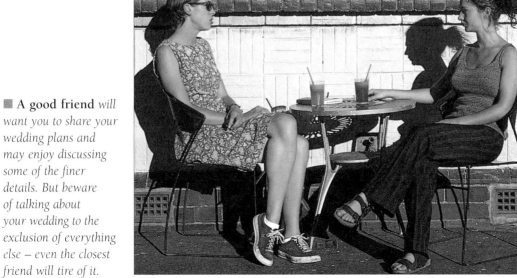

A good friend *will want you to share your wedding plans and may enjoy discussing some of the finer details. But beware of talking about your wedding to the exclusion of everything else – even the closest friend will tire of it.*

- When you talk about your wedding plans, your pal changes the subject. A good friend will love hearing your great news; someone who becomes quiet, withdrawn, or diverts attention to another topic may be envious of your happiness. Providing you're not boring her with too much wedding talk, point out her wandering attention and ask if there's a reason she doesn't want to share your news.
- "Shut up already!" Do you talk incessantly about your beloved, the dress, the caterer, your beloved, the honeymoon, the registry, your beloved...? If so, don't be surprised if someone tells you to give it a rest. And rightly so. As happy as we are for the brides of the world, listening to them prattle on and on about themselves can become tiresome.

The groom's friends

Tell me if this sounds familiar: Soon after your partner proposes, his friends begin to get weird, distant, obnoxious. They take to calling you "the old ***ball and chain***," get more aggressive about arranging boys-only pub nights, and may even try to introduce your partner to other women or persuade him to visit the local topless club. It's hard not to take this personally but, in truth, none of this behavior has anything to do with you as a person. It has to do with you as someone who is replacing them in their buddy's esteem. Try the following suggestions for dealing with these troublemakers:

DEFINITION

The derogatory expression **ball and chain** *originated in England. It compares the ball and chain that prisoners used to wear with a spouse – most notably, a wife.*

- Invite them to have their next night out at your apartment. Invite a few girlfriends over – perhaps the ones you're having trouble with – and have a dinner party. Close contact with you may be the jolt they need to stop treating you like an opponent.

Let your fiancé *hang out with his friends during your engagement period. This is a wise move on your part – respect their pal time with your fiancé now and they'll respect your couple time.*

- Talk to your partner about what's going on. When faced with your observations, your partner will do one of two things: Tell you you're imagining everything (more on this in a moment) or agree with you and promise to chat with his friends.
- So your fiancé says you're exaggerating or even imagining his friend's behavior? Why not go straight to the source – the annoying guys – and have a talk? While some relationship experts may not agree with this, others will: Two pals of mine were given this advice by couples' counselors.
- If a friend is being particularly offensive, ask your fiancé whether the guy is really important to him. When my husband proposed, one of his friends began trying to ply my husband with random women. My husband always turned him down, but I became so insulted that I finally told my husband that this guy was not allowed at our wedding, and that I never wanted to hear his voice or his name mentioned again. Fortunately my husband agreed and decided it wasn't worth continuing a "friendship" with someone who had such low morals.

Trivia...

The idea that a wife is a negative influence is an age-old one, and many of the terms "affectionately" applied to the female spouse are derogatory. One example is the London Cockney rhyming slang: "trouble and strife."

A simple summary

✓ Don't feel bad for having doubts – they're normal. Really!

✓ Examine mixed feelings closely. Are they normal jitters or a sign that you shouldn't go through with the marriage?

✓ Calling off a wedding is ultimately kinder than going through the ceremony and later divorcing.

✓ Honesty, courage, and a touch of obstinacy are needed when dealing with family members.

✓ In-laws can be notoriously difficult to manage. Save yourself some grief and have your partner deal with his family.

✓ Your happiness can turn people green with envy. Rather than ignoring friends' bad feelings, confront them straight on.

✓ Don't be shy about confronting your fiancé's obnoxious friends. If they're true friends, you'll be able to put your differences behind you. You don't want your fiancé to have divided loyalties.

PART FIVE

Your Wedding Day

YOUR SPECIAL DAY IS here, and you can enjoy the fruits of your hard work and exquisite planning. But unless you've done this before you may be a bit confused about how the whole wedding thing works. Who should accompany you down the aisle? Will you have any "couple time" during the reception? How are you going to feel being married? Relax. As you'll find out, there is no one way to perform your nuptial duties, just as there's no one way you must feel.

Chapter 17
The Actual Ceremony

Chapter 18
Party Time: The Reception

Chapter 19
We're Married! Now What?

Chapter 17

The Actual Ceremony

IF YOU'RE LIKE MANY BRIDES, the start of the wedding ceremony is the first inkling that life is about to change forever. True, you've probably been enmeshed in wedding details for months, but planning an event isn't quite the same as actually being there. Or at least that was my nuptial experience. Once that processional music started up and I took my first shaky steps down the aisle, no amount of planning could have prepared me for the exhilarating mix of love and fear that overcame me. I bet it will be the same for you too.

In this chapter...

- ✓ Practice makes perfect
- ✓ Personalize your vows
- ✓ Walking down the aisle
- ✓ After the ceremony

THE BIGGEST DAY OF YOUR LIVES HAS FINALLY ARRIVED – WELCOME TO YOUR WEDDING!

Practice makes perfect

THE WEDDING REHEARSAL takes place at some point before the ceremony – anywhere from two days prior to the night before. What exactly happens at a rehearsal? Pretty much the same things that happen at a wedding, except without an audience. The following will give you an idea of what to expect:

- Who attends the rehearsal? The engaged couple, the attendants, both sets of parents, and the officiant. If you'll be having any special readings or entertainment, those people should be present too, as should the pianist, organist, musicians, or DJ responsible for providing the ceremony music. If you are using a wedding consultant, he or she will also attend.
- Ideally, the rehearsal will take place at the site where you'll actually be marrying. However, this is often not possible, and many couples are obliged to rehearse in another space.

If you're booking a ceremony site some time in advance, try also to rent it for your wedding rehearsal. Not everyone rehearses at their wedding site, but doing so allows you to become familiar with the location, and this will help to give you confidence and ultimately will make for a smoother-running ceremony.

- Make sure everyone knows the date, time, and location of the rehearsal. If you feel it is necessary, send out separate invitations for the rehearsal.
- You will practice your ceremony in chronological order, from walking down the aisle to exchanging your vows to exiting the church or other ceremony venue.
- Attendants will be coached. This includes helping ring bearers, train carriers, and flower girls memorize their roles. Ushers will be directed on how to seat guests, including who to seat where.

No, you don't rehearse in your wedding gown. Just wear ordinary clothes – you want to save your dress for the big day – although some women find it helpful to wear shoes similar in type to the ones they will wear on the day so that they can get an idea of what it feels like to walk down the aisle.

- Plan on running through the entire ceremony at least twice. If anyone stumbles, you'll need to practice more. Be aware that reciting vows often gives people trouble so you may need to spend most of the rehearsing time practicing this aspect of the ceremony. It's a nerves thing.
- After rehearsal, it's customary to enjoy each other's company at a rehearsal meal.

THE ORDER OF THINGS

Most weddings follow the format below – though you're welcome (and encouraged!) to do things your own way:

- The groom, groomsmen, and officiant take their places.
- Guests enter and are seated.
- Bridal attendants enter, walk down the aisle, and take their places at the altar.
- The bride enters, either alone, or accompanied by one or two people, such as her mother and father.
- The officiant announces the purpose of the gathering, gives the name of the bride and groom, and welcomes the guests.
- Depending on the type of ceremony you've chosen – and your officiant's personality – this is the spot in the program where he or she ruminates on what marriage is, perhaps saying something about both you and your partner, and giving guidance on how to succeed as a couple.
- If you have scheduled someone to read a poem (or something else) or perform a musical number (or another piece of entertainment), now is his or her time in the spotlight.
- The introduction to the vows. Here, the officiant explains to you and your groom, as well as everyone else in the room, the significance of the vows you are going to exchange.
- Vows. Here's where you and your partner – prompted by your officiant – publicly commit to one another, while slipping the wedding rings on. After this point in the ceremony, you are officially married.
- The kiss! After the officiant announces that you are "husband and wife," he or she invites you to kiss. Incidentally, you and your groom should discuss this kiss – and even practice it – before your turn at the altar. This will prevent any awkwardness that could arise from different kissing styles – for example, if one of you is going for a long, wet, kiss while the other is preparing for something more modest. Your best bet is something between the two.
- Time to leave. You and your new spouse exit arm-in-arm, followed by your attendants, parents, and then the guests.

Hey, husband and wife! *Enjoy the sweetest kiss to consolidate your newly married status.*

Personalize your vows

YOUR VOWS ARE AN IMPORTANT PART of your wedding ceremony – in fact they are the most important part, since reciting them is what makes you married. Making these special words unique to you is easy. The typical marriage vow goes something like the following: "I, [your name], take you, [your partner's name], for my lawful wife/husband, to have and to hold, from this day forward, for better, for worse, for richer, for poorer, in sickness and health, until death do us part."

INTERNET

www.brilliantwedding pages.com/couples/ weddingvows.asp

Brilliant Wedding Pages has several articles devoted to helping you create your own vows. Have fun!

Your wedding vows are as important to your partner as they are to you, so don't forget to get his input. It is best to work on the vows together – this way you'll ensure the final results are meaningful to both of you.

To personalize your vows, simply take the standard version of the wedding reading and begin playing around. Maybe you don't like the bit about "lawful wife." Change it to "loyal soulmate." If you want to add something in there about emotionally supporting each other no matter what, then pencil it in, or whatever else you feel expresses what you want to say. While you don't want to make your vows overly long – most are kept to under five sentences – you want to include what's important to you and your relationship. Just remember to read your vows aloud a few times to make sure they sound okay, and don't forget to ask your officiant to look them over and offer his or her own suggestions.

■ **Many couples personalize** *traditional marriage vows, perhaps adding a couple more verses or changing words to create something more personal.*

Walking down the aisle

FEWER AND FEWER BRIDES are opting to have their fathers walk them down the aisle and "give them" to their grooms. Yes, it's still done, so if you'd like to follow this age-old custom, no one will raise an eyebrow. If you'd like to do something different, however, these are some of your options:

- Go it alone. The most dramatic way to get yourself down the aisle, going solo ensures all eyes will be on you and only you. This option is commonly preferred by independent-minded brides, by people getting married for the second time, and by older brides.
- Have your mother accompany you. This charming option is gaining popularity, probably because it is a thoughtful way to acknowledge the woman who gave birth to you and has done so much for you.

Trivia...

Wondering why, in traditional weddings, fathers give away their daughters? If you haven't guessed, the practice harks back to the time when women were considered property to be passed from one man to another.

If you choose to walk down the aisle alone, your parents can either sit with other family members or stand with your attendants. Whatever they decide, your partner's folks should do the same.

- Have both parents walk with you. A terrific way to acknowledge your feelings for your mom and dad, this option has none of the "ownership" associations that being accompanied solely by your father does. Don't, however, ask both parents to accompany you if they are divorced and have a stormy relationship.
- Have your grandmother, your grandparents, or a grandparent and a parent, escort you. Or your favorite great aunt. Or anyone else who holds a special place in your heart.

■ **If you are confident** *enough to walk down the aisle alone with all eyes on you, do it!*

After the ceremony

YOU'VE EXCHANGED RINGS, you've kissed, you've been proclaimed husband and wife. The recessional music is playing and your guests are starting to fidget. Now what do you do? Many newlyweds spend the time immediately after the ceremony having official photographs taken. But you don't have to – it's up to you.

A picture made in heaven. *Decide when you and your partner want the official photos taken.*

If you are having photographs taken, you, your new spouse, and the wedding party will meet after the ceremony to pose for pictures. However, many couples prefer to spend this short time alone with each other – walking the grounds or sitting somewhere private. Others gather close friends and family for a thank-you toast.

You're married now! *Spend the time before the reception as you wish – there are no rules. A special moment together might be just what you both need.*

Do whatever you like. Don't worry about your guests. If you're holding your reception at a different venue, it will take them a while to make their way there. During this time, you and your spouse can pose for pictures at your leisure, safe in the knowledge that your guests will be enjoying cocktails and a few appetizers while waiting for you to arrive. So make your way to the reception, arrive to a chorus of cheers, and enjoy it all!

Your guests will *be more than happy to socialize while you newlyweds deal with the photographer and other necessities. Just keep the bar stocked and the appetizers coming!*

A simple summary

✓ Make the most of the wedding rehearsal – it's the one opportunity you have to make sure your ceremony runs smoothly.

✓ Creating vows that are special to your relationship is surprisingly easy, but make sure you let the officiant know your plans.

✓ The bride doesn't have to be given away by her father. Walk down the aisle with your mother, with both parents, or by yourself.

✓ The period directly after the ceremony is for you and your partner to use as you'd like. Don't feel pressured.

✓ Wedding photography can go on for hours – if you let it. Make sure the photographer knows your wishes and sticks to them.

✓ Enjoy your reception to the maximum. It's time to let your hair down, have a drink, and party the whole night through!

Chapter 18

Party Time: The Reception

CONGRATULATIONS! You've made it through the ceremony and are now ready to rejoice in your new married status. That's where the reception comes in. Traditionally viewed as a celebration to follow the ceremony, the reception gives newlyweds, wedding attendants, and family and friends a chance to observe this very important occasion in a festive way. The reception also provides an opportunity for you and your husband to congratulate each other on months of successful wedding planning, while allowing you to compose yourselves after what may have been an emotional wedding ceremony.

In this chapter...

- ✓ **Play by play: What happens when**
- ✓ **Reception rituals**

TIME TO CELEBRATE AND MAKE A TOAST TO YOUR FUTURE HAPPINESS!

Play by play: What happens when

THERE ARE NO RULES about how a reception must be structured. Spend the entire time dining with your loved ones or arrange the party around various scheduled activities – it's your choice. Below, you'll find a common lineup used by many couples – but once again, do things your way. It's your reception, after all!

Don't allow your reception to go on for more than five hours – there's a limit to your own and your guests' stamina. Most receptions last from two-and-a-half to four hours, with five hours being the limit.

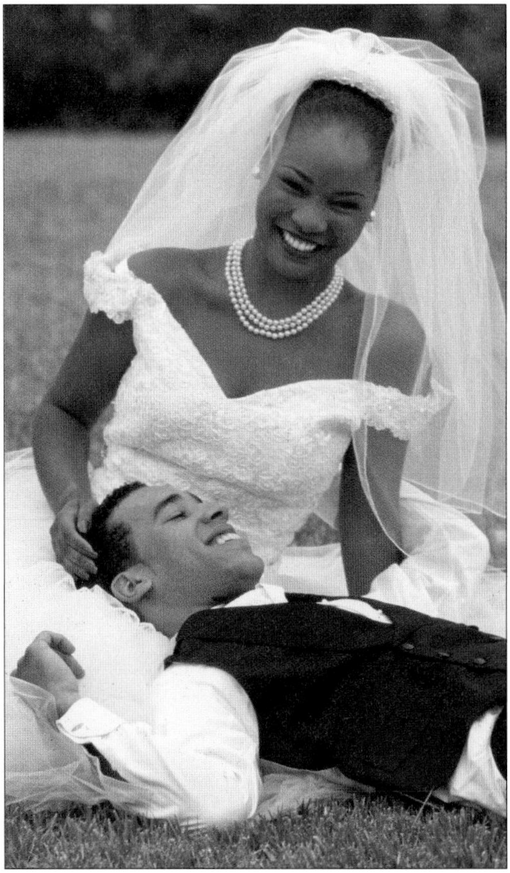

Here come the guests

After your wedding ceremony, your guests will make their way to your reception. So what does everyone do once they reach the reception site? A cocktail hour is a time-honored way to occupy guests while you have your pictures taken or steal a moment with your new hubby. Drinks are often served not in the actual reception room, but in an adjacent area.

The receiving line

A receiving line is exactly what it sounds like it is: The mother of the bride, father of the bride, mother of the groom, father of the groom, and the bride and groom themselves – in that order – stand in line somewhere in the reception hall. In some instances, the maid of honor and best man are also included in the receiving line right after the bride's parents.

■ **The cocktail hour** *is a great way to welcome guests to your reception while you newlyweds have your photos taken and enjoy a moment together.*

After the cocktail hour, the guests shuffle into the reception room for the official beginning of the reception. After forming a long line, guests inch their way past the wedding folk, offering good wishes to the parents and newlyweds.

Even if you opt not to go for the receiving line, be sure to greet all your guests formally at some stage. The more casual greet-them-as-you-see-them approach will inevitably mean some friends get missed out.

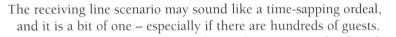

The receiving line scenario may sound like a time-sapping ordeal, and it is a bit of one – especially if there are hundreds of guests. This explains why many couples don't have a receiving line. Instead, a number of brides and grooms opt to visit each table when all the guests are comfortably seated in the main reception area, thus finding a way to talk with everyone – at least for a little while – and thank them individually for coming.

Some couples choose *to greet their guests formally outside the entrance to the reception site.*

Seating your guests

If you were hosting a dinner party, where to seat everyone wouldn't be such a big issue. But this is a wedding reception, and seating is an enormously important factor. So important, in fact, that there are computer software programs devoted solely to creating a wedding seating chart. Seating needn't be a hassle if you remember these few commonsense suggestions:

How does everyone know where they're supposed to sit? An easy way is to visibly number each table, then place a floor plan (available from the site manager) and an alphabetical list of guests at the entrance to the reception site. Guests look up their name and see which table number they are assigned.

- Many couples place name cards at each seat and then let guests find their places themselves. If you go with this option, make sure the cards are easy to read.
- Try to place relatives together.
- Divorced parents – divorced anyone, really – should be placed as far away from their exes as possible.

- Guests who don't get along should not be placed at the same table. This seems obvious, but many brides and grooms – hoping to make quick work of a seating chart – put antagonists at the same table assuming that they will behave at their friend's wedding. This isn't always true.
- The bride and groom should be seated with attendants and their significant others.
- Give each set of parents its own table, and let them fill it as they'd like. The officiant, if he or she plans to stay for the reception, normally sits with one set of parents – usually the set who knows him or her better.
- Make a "singles table."
- Place tables with younger people closest to the dance floor, and those with older people furthest away so as not deafen them with loud music.
- If you are hosting elderly or handicapped guests, be sure to place them at an easily accessible table.

INTERNET

www.weddingbasics.com /reception/seating.asp

Wedding Basics offers advice on every aspect of wedding planning, including the dreaded seating arrangement!

Your seating plan will be among the last tasks you attend to, so don't get flustered. This is because you may not know exactly who will be coming until just before the reception.

- Just as you would at a party, try to create tables with people who have similar interests – or at least complementary personalities.
- Children should be seated with their parents. Seat teenagers wherever you think is appropriate – perhaps not at a table of the more senior guests.

The length of *the mealtime varies, depending on whether toasts are given before, during, or after.*

Dinner is served

It's easy to let time slip away from you, especially when you're the center of attention. Yet, you don't want your reception to drag on longer than it should. Not only will you be billed for any time over the agreed amount but an overly long reception keeps you from being alone with your new spouse. So, if you're serving a sit-down meal at your reception – be it breakfast, brunch, lunch, tea, dinner, or dessert – get guests fed no later than the second hour of your reception. Allow approximately one hour for the main meal.

Reception rituals

LIKE THE WEDDING, the reception features numerous activities that originated centuries ago. These reception rituals generally take place between the time the food has been served and when the guests have finished eating. For anyone who has eschewed the traditional receiving line, it is during this same window of time that you should visit each table to greet guests.

Toasts

In Chapter 9 I talked a bit about toasts – both giving and receiving them. These mini tributes generally take place at some point in or around the mealtime: Some couples choose to have filled flutes of champagne sitting on the table when guests sit down, ready for pre-dinner toasting. Others have waiters serve champagne for toasts at the end of the meal. Still others prefer to augment their meal with toasts, thus summoning the champagne somewhere during the meal. As always with these kinds of wedding decisions, it's your choice.

It's been my observation that once guests have some food in their bellies and have had the chance to chat with other guests, they loosen up. Thus toasts given during the meal have a fun way of multiplying: The best man gets up, followed by the maid of honor, and the father of the bride, then the groom, then a sister, and a great uncle, and so forth.

You may wish *to link arms in a traditional lover's toast, but be warned that it's trickier than it looks and often ends with a dry-cleaning bill.*

Makes you feel like dancing

The first official dances – the bride and groom, the bride and her father, the groom and his mother, and other familial permutations – typically take place after the first course has been cleared away and everyone's awaiting the second course. You may feel a little self-conscious when it's your turn to dance, but no one is expecting Fred Astaire and Ginger Rogers. Just take a deep breath, relax, and enjoy this magical moment together.

■ **The first dance** *signals not only your love for each other but also that the night is about to really get going.*

THE TWELVE MONTHS OF MARRIAGE

The Victorians were a superstitious lot, especially when it came to matters of the heart. Here's what they believed about wedding dates:

- **January**: Wed in January's hoar and rhyme, widowed you'll be before your time.
- **February**: Married in February's sleepy weather, life you will dread in time together.
- **March**: Married when March winds shrill and roar, your home will be on a distant shore.
- **April**: Married beneath April's changing skies, a chequered path before you lies.
- **May**: When May blossom's flit, strangers around your board will sit.
- **June**: In the month of roses June, life after marriage will be a honeymoon.
- **July**: In July with flowers ablaze, bittersweet memories on for days.
- **August**: Married in August's heat and drowse, lover and friend is your chosen spouse.
- **September**: Married in September's golden glow, smooth and serene your life will go.
- **October**: Married when leaves in October glow, toil and hardship is what you'll know.
- **November**: In veils of November mist, fortune your wedding ring has kissed.
- **December**: Married in days of December cheer, love star shines brighter year after year.

After these dances, attendants and guests are usually welcome to step onto the dance floor. Not everyone eats – or dances – at the same speed, which means that there may be people up and dancing while others are still enjoying their meals. This is both expected and perfectly acceptable.

Cutting the cake

After the main meal, there is yet another customary event: The wedding cake is cut. This is one of those key wedding rituals and something that I addressed in Chapter 9. But when exactly to serve the cake is something I'll talk about right now: Immediately after dinner – at least within the first three-and-a-half hours of a four-hour wedding. All dancing traditionally stops at this point, and doesn't resume until after the cake has been served.

Set up a gift table – to be guarded by an attendant or family member – somewhere within the reception room. This makes it convenient for guests to leave their generous offerings.

A delightful idea is to accompany the cake cutting with a little music. The sound of violins and flutes – played in a semi-circle around the bride and groom – can make the occasion even more romantic.

■ **Whatever method you** *use to cut the cake, the ritual symbolizes the closeness of bride and groom.*

■ **Confetti** *or rice is flung at the newlyweds as they leave the party.*

The toss

Not every bride wants to throw her bouquet, nor does every bride want her groom to pull her garter off and throw it to a group of waiting men. However, if you are interested in participating in one or both of these activities, they should take place during the reception's final half hour. Either bouquet or garter can be tossed first, though the bouquet is more often the first to be flung.

During the reception, some guests will give you envelopes with cash or a check. Hand these over to your maid of honor, mother, or another trusted person, for safekeeping.

How it works: The bridesmaids and other single female guests form a line. The bride stands opposite this line with her back facing the guests, and then tosses her bouquet over her head. Superstition has it that whoever catches the bouquet will be the next girl to marry.

Trivia...

Long, long ago, guests threw grains of wheat at the newlyweds as they left the reception. Wheat was a fertility symbol and it was believed that pelting the bride and groom with grains would increase their fertility. At some point in history, rice replaced wheat. Today, birdseed or biodegradable confetti are used by eco-concious couples.

■ **Changing out of** *your wedding dress is fine if you're honeymoon-bound straight after the reception.*

The garter toss is a bit racier, and involves the groom sitting on a chair, balancing his bride on his lap. A throng of single men line up opposite the bride and groom. The groom then reaches under the bride's dress, pulls off the garter, and flings it into the crowd of single men. The guy who catches the garter will be the next one to marry – or so the story says.

On your way

If you'll be tossing a bouquet or garter, the band or DJ will play for another 20 to 30 minutes, allowing guests to fit in one or two more dances before departing. The wedding attendants will use this time to distribute small bags of rice, birdseed, or confetti to guests, to be thrown at you and your groom on your way out.

If you'll be leaving the reception for your honeymoon, then it's accepted practice to duck out of the hall for a moment and change into your traveling clothes. (It's worth asking if there is a private room or restroom that you and your groom can use for this purpose.)

Finally, all the guests will follow you out of the reception hall, shouting farewells and showering you with whatever they've been given to toss. Meanwhile, your parents and attendants will help you both by tipping those people who need to be tipped, paying anyone who requires their money, and gathering all your gifts and personal belongings to take home.

Waving goodbye to *the bride and groom as they depart is always a celebratory moment.*

A simple summary

✓ There's more than one way to arrange your reception. The only requirement is to create an event that pleases you.

✓ Creating a smart seating plan doesn't have to be difficult. Simply use your common sense!

✓ Toasting generally occurs at mealtime. The toasts may be proposed before, during, or after the main meal.

✓ Feel like dancing? Wait until the dishes from the first course are being cleared away.

✓ If you choose to toss your bouquet and garter, be sure to wait until the last half hour of the reception.

✓ At the end of the wedding, be prepared to go. Don't worry – your parents and attendants will gather up your gifts for you.

Chapter 19

We're Married! Now What?

HOW DO YOU FEEL? A little dizzy? Perfectly natural considering what you've just gone through. Fortunately, now is the time to relax and look forward to your first night together as husband and wife – a prelude to your honeymoon. Oh yes, the honeymoon. Don't worry, you'll have a great time and return home happy and ready to take on the world together.

In this chapter...

- ✓ Your first night as husband and wife
- ✓ The morning after: Oh my God, I'm married!
- ✓ Have a happy honeymoon
- ✓ Scheduling your departure
- ✓ How long should we go for?
- ✓ Time to relax and enjoy
- ✓ Easing into marriage

"CONGRATULATIONS DARLING! WE'VE FINALLY TIED THE KNOT!"

Your first night as husband and wife

*THERE IS MUCH HOOPLA about your first night as a married person. Most of the interest revolves around whether you decide to **consummate** the union or not. In olden times, people were so obsessed with this part of the marriage that in some countries town officials were allowed to observe the couple in the act. In other cultures, the couple's used sheets were hung out for public viewing.*

DEFINITION

When used in relation to one's wedding night, **consummate** *means to "make complete" through sexual intercourse. At one time – and still among certain religions – consummation was so important that an unconsummated marriage could be annulled.*

Thankfully, things have changed. While sex remains an important and pleasurable part of your first married night together, it isn't everything. Other factors, such as simply relaxing as a couple and enjoying some private time, are much more vital. You deserve this reward as newlyweds. Not only have you successfully completed months and months of arduous planning, you've endured a physically and emotionally exhausting day, and completed an important life step: Joining your life with another person's. This is certainly worth a couple of private toasts – with your own bottle of champagne – to celebrate the first night of the rest of your lives together.

Time for you *to be together: Your first night as newlyweds will be fun!*

Leaving directly for a honeymoon: how to stay calm

Though many modern couples decide to wait a day or two before departing for their honeymoon, leaving straight from the reception is tradition. True, rushing straight from the festivities can be stressful, but there are ways to make the transition easier:

- Give yourself enough time to travel from the reception to the airport, train station, or wherever else you'll be heading. Timewise, your safest option is a morning or early afternoon wedding and reception, followed by a mid- to late evening flight. If you're committed to having an evening reception, consider waiting until the next day to leave for your honeymoon.

- Book a car to take you straight from the reception to the airport, train station, or wherever else you'll be departing from. Don't forget to ask if the driver knows his or her way to your destination. To be safe, schedule the car to arrive at your reception an hour before the event ends. At this point in the festivities, have your maid of honor or best man check to see if the car has arrived. If it hasn't, ask one of them to call and inquire about its whereabouts.
- If you can't afford to pay for car service, or if it's going to be easier to have a friend or relative take you, make sure this person has directions to your destination. This will save any last-minute scares.

Will one of your reception guests or an attendant be driving you to the airport? Do not let him or her drink and drive!

- Have your packed bags stashed at the reception hall. Make sure, before you leave the house, that you have your traveling clothing, any necessary medication, and all necessary traveling papers.
- After the bouquet and garter tossing, change into your traveling clothes and rejoin the festivities for a few moments before leaving.
- Arrange to have your parents, maid of honor, or some other trusted person take your wedding gown, gifts, and other belongings home for you.

Have you made hotel reservations?

If you aren't leaving for your honeymoon and want to make your first married night special, I have a suggestion: Book the best suite you can in the most luxurious hotel in your area. In fact, go the extra mile and ask if the hotel has a wedding suite – many do. Even those that don't may treat you with extra care because you are newlyweds. One night is usually sufficient, though two nights could also be nice. Before paying for your room, however, ask the booking agent the following questions:

■ **It doesn't matter** *what kind of car you arrange to take you from your reception. A few added decorations give that just-married feel to things.*

Trivia...

In England in the distant past, when the bride first visited her family's home as a married woman, it was customary to place a piece of saved wedding cake on a plate and then throw this out the window. If the plate broke she could expect a happy future with her husband. If the plate remained intact, she could expect a stormy marriage. And if the plate happened to fall on someone's head? Well, that wasn't an option associated with one kind of luck or another!

- Will you be able to use the hotel room before your wedding to get ready and to relax with your attendants?
- Does the room have a wet bar, or at least a small fridge, where you can stash a bottle or two of champagne?
- What's the hotel's checkout time? Important to know if your wedding is an afternoon or evening one – or if you plan to spend the after-wedding hours celebrating with your attendants and don't get to bed until early morning. Many hotels have ridiculously early checkout times. You don't want to be awoken by an angry maid who is intent on bullying you out of the room.
- If out-of-town guests or attendants will also be staying at the same hotel, what will their checkout time be? Some hotels have later checkout times for newlyweds than they do for everyone else. When I got married, my husband and I stayed in a hotel that didn't expect us to leave until mid-afternoon. However, my sister and parents – who were staying in the same hotel – were kicked out at 9 a.m. Because they had nowhere to go, they showed up at our room. Not only had we just got to sleep a couple of hours earlier (we had an evening wedding and had done some celebrating afterward), but we wanted our privacy! Needless to say, we weren't very happy with the hotel for creating this situation!

INTERNET

www.bridestuff.com/newlyweds/

A series of articles to help you make it smoothly through your first married year together.

A special night at home

Let's say you aren't taking a honeymoon immediately after the wedding. And let's assume that you don't want to or can't afford to book a hotel suite for the night. Is there still a way to make your first married night special? Of course! You and your new spouse will probably be so exhilarated that your first night together is guaranteed to be special – no matter what you do or where you are. But yes, there are ways to add to the night's unique proceedings:

Spending your wedding night at home? Have some delivery menus handy in case you don't have the energy – or the desire – to make your own food.

You're spending your *first married night at home? Then treat yourselves to the finest foods.*

- Hire a cleaner to go through your house from top to bottom. It's so much easier to relax and create a romantic setting if you aren't distracted by sticky floors, dusty bookshelves, or overflowing trash bins. If possible, have your home cleaned the day before your wedding.
- Clean out your refrigerator and freezer, wiping down the insides and outsides, clearing away those items that are less than fresh, and making room in the freezer for your cake's top tier (should you be keeping this for your first anniversary). Stock up on champagne, organic tea and coffee, tropical fruit juices, breakfast foods, and other tasty treats.
- Clean and organize your kitchen cupboards, adding a selection of exotic goodies to enjoy later.
- Create a "romance basket" with scented candles, essential oils, lotions, bath bubbles, condoms (or other birth control alternatives), and whatever else tickles your fancy. Leave this basket by the bed.
- Put fresh linens on the bed. If you can afford to, consider buying new sheets and pillowslips for your special night. A set of new towels and a couple of plush robes are also a nice touch.
- Have some mood music ready – make sure you arrange a stack of CDs, cassettes, or records, waiting near the stereo.
- Add a few pieces of new lingerie to your underwear drawer. Likewise, why not slip a few pairs of new boxers (or briefs) in your partner's drawer.
- Buy flowers! These don't need to be expensive – there are plenty of charming, inexpensive blooms available. Plan to place a bouquet in your bedroom, and one in the living area. Additional bouquets are strictly optional.

■ **Flowers, candles, and** *other luxuries will make your wedding night at home extra special.*

■ **Wherever you share** *your first night together as newlyweds, make the setting as romantic as possible. You'll both want to remember this as a magical evening.*

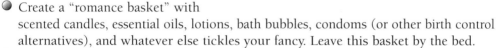

INTERNET

www.organicweddings.com/wedding_ideas/newlyweds.html

Organicweddings.com is a great site for anyone planning a wedding. It also has wonderful articles for newlyweds, covering everything from adjusting your finances to entertaining.

The morning after: Oh my God, I'm married!

FOR A FULL YEAR after I was married, I couldn't get myself to say the word "husband." I loved the new man in my life dearly, but I simply wasn't able to get used to the fact that I actually had a spouse. I'd keep repeating his name to myself – "Richard is my husband! Richard is my husband!" – to hammer this fantastic news into my head. Believe me, amazing as an experience as getting married is, the whole thing can take a while to register.

If you didn't undergo nuptial therapy before marriage, consider attending a session or two now. Couples counseling is simply a great resource for helping you create a strong, happy marriage.

After a decade of trying to figure this out, I still don't know my reasons. What I do know is I'm not the only woman out there who has felt like this. Many women have trouble using the "h" word; others get depressed after their weddings; some begin to feel cagey; and then there are those who keep losing their wedding rings. No, these women aren't mad, nor are they unloving. It's just that adjusting to the *idea* of being married can be as hard for some women as the day-to-day exchanges of marriage.

Awakening and realizing *you're married. Trying to explain the sensation may not be easy for a while – you're the same old you, he's the same him, but you're now husband and wife.*

If that comes as a surprise, you'll also be interested to know that the confusion can appear the moment you finish your vows, and can reappear sporadically at various times throughout your first few married years. Fortunately, it's usually nothing to worry about. Furthermore, it can be helped with the following marriage-strengthening tips:

- Acknowledge your crazy feelings. Chances are your new spouse is going through an adjustment period of his own. Talking about your feelings will give you both a chance to feel closer and offer you a sense of relief.
- Talk to your married friends and relatives about their newlywed experiences. Hearing what other women have gone through can give you a sense of perspective about your own feelings.
- Make an effort to spend regular time together. It's easy for newlyweds to slip into a whirlwind of socializing with friends, work, and other obligations.
- Set boundaries early on in the relationship. His mother expects you to visit every single Sunday? Your best (single) friend still calls you in the middle of the night to rehash her dates? While your families and friends are important, your first priorities are now each other. Find a kind way to tell your mother-in-law that Sundays are "couple time" and explain to your friend that her middle-of-the-night calls pull you away from your warm bed – and your new husband.
- Be honest about how much "together time" and how much "me time" you both need. It's easy, early on in the marriage, to give up nights out with girlfriends, or solo Saturdays at the movies. If you're someone who needs some time away from your partner, speak up! Better to be honest than to become restricted by your new roles.

When something's wrong

It's common to feel confused early on in your marriage – it's both your brain's and your heart's way of adapting to wedded life. However, any disconcerting emotions you experience may signal something more serious. If you develop any of the following behaviors, see a professional therapist:

- Uncontrollable crying, especially if you find weeping is a daily occurrence.
- Depression.
- The inability to be honest with your partner about your feelings or, for that matter, anything else.
- Discomfort with your situation or with your partner.
- Feeling misunderstood or belittled by your partner.
- Feeling trapped, stuck, or unable to work toward goals that you had been excited about before your marriage.

Have a happy honeymoon

OF ALL THE NUPTIAL PLANNING you and your partner must do before your wedding, creating your honeymoon is probably the most fun. Deciding on the ultimate getaway provides you both with the chance to visit a dream destination, to explore together, and to share your passions. Do the research now and make your honeymoon more than just a vacation.

Use your honeymoon *to combine travel with interests – do vineyards strike your fancy?*

Go to the library and check out travel books, watch travel documentaries, poke around online, thumb through travel magazines, ask your friends, and send away for brochures. My point is, collect as much information as you can – then collect some more! You don't want to limit your choices simply because you're unaware of what's out there. Your honeymoon is a time to open your horizons and have some fun.

Personal preferences

Most people have strong feelings about what a vacation is – and what it isn't. My husband, for instance, doesn't want to see anything but sunshine and a beach during a vacation, so it's no surprise that his favorite destinations are in the Caribbean and Mexico. You may love food and wine, making the vineyards of California, France, Italy, Australia, South Africa, or South America, more your style. Knowing what you and your partner like – and what you dislike – is important: You don't want to book a trip that either of you is less than happy with.

INTERNET

www.embassyworld.com

Planning to go abroad for your honeymoon? Find out what travel documents your destination country requires, as well as where embassies are located and other important need-to-know information.

You may know what sounds like a good time to you, but perhaps you are clueless as to what your partner would find fun. After perusing your travel options, why not give your beloved a pen and paper and ask him to make two lists: One cataloguing what he wants in a honeymoon, and the other stating what he couldn't possibly tolerate in a trip. Do the same yourself. Compare entries, but don't despair if your ideas of fun are wildly different. You'll just have to compromise. Fortunately, this is usually easy. If you want the beach and he wants "culture," perhaps you could go to, say, Jamaica, and while you enjoy the beach, he can study the art and music scene in Kingston.

Some destination ideas

Just about any place can be a honeymoon destination, from a little inn a couple of towns away from yours, to the South Pole explorers' station, to a safari tent in Africa. These ideas will help you:

■ **A beach honeymoon** *is probably the most popular destination choice for newlywed couples, allowing them time to unwind on the coast.*

- If you can't afford something slightly extravagant, a vacation nearby might be for you. Perhaps you live only a few hours from a great skiing locale, picturesque beaches, a famous health spa, a theme park, or a national park.
- Road trips are a fun way to see a great deal of country, and they are ideal for those who are both adventurous and keen to wander. But be warned: There are great distances involved in this option, so you must both like to drive.
- Which foreign countries are nearby? Often, the shorter distance you travel, the less money you spend on air fares – saving money for when you arrive.
- Ever considered a cruise? Cruises are arranged for various lengths of time, from the long weekend to nearly a month. Moreover, you can choose from a variety of routes, including the Mediterranean, the Caribbean, or an intercontinental crossing – typically across the Atlantic or Pacific.
- If you like the outdoors then camping, white river rafting, hang gliding, hiking, and other activities can be a fun way to spend your honeymoon.

■ **Choose a honeymoon destination** *that you'll both be happy with. An activity vacation provides a refreshing alternative to the typical sand-and-sun option.*

- If you and your partner are foodies, consider a cooking-school vacation. "Destination schools," as they are sometimes called, are typically found in food-famous locales, such as Tuscany, Provence, California's wine country, and Veracruz. And if you then happened to tire of all that culinary activity, some schools organize other equally interesting days out, such as bike tours of the area.

Don't book a foreign honeymoon without first checking out the area's weather patterns. Is there a rainy season? A hurricane season? A brutally hot couple of months? Make sure the climate will suit your personal preferences.

- A learning vacation of any kind. Art appreciation, foreign languages, horseback riding – you name the activity and there's an excellent chance that there is a school dedicated to teaching it. Many of these combine the best of a luxury vacation with classroom instruction and local tours, making for a fun, educational honeymoon.
- An all-inclusive resort. Usually located in sunny, Caribbean locations, many of these resorts specialize in couples, meaning you won't be vacationing with singles or families. Everything – from drinks to meals to service tips – is included in one price, so you don't have to carry your wallet with you. If this concept interests you, do some research – some inclusive resorts are more inclusive than others.

What can we afford?

A common question you'll have asked each other since you first got engaged, but don't send yourselves into debt over a honeymoon. Here are a few pointers for shaving costs:

- Consider the season. Almost every vacation destination on Earth has a peak season, during which the price of traveling and lodging rises considerably. This season is determined in part by the weather, but also by other factors, such as national holidays, popular vacation times, and so forth. So do your homework.

Make up a packet of "important stuff" to take with you on your honeymoon. Include your credit card numbers, as well as the credit company phone numbers. Also include photocopies of your passport, visa, and plane tickets. Keep these in the hotel safe.

Using a globe *to learn about the geography of different countries will give you an idea of climates.*

- Traveling during the more convenient hours of the day – mainly late morning to mid-afternoon – generally costs more than leaving in the early morning or during the evening. If you're flexible, you could save a lot of money.
- Ask about packages. Some travel agents have packages that include air fares, car rental, and lodging for less than you'd pay for these elements separately.
- Do you have a friend or relative who lives in a city you're interested in visiting? Perhaps they need someone to housesit for them while they are out of town. This could be an easy, cheap, and rewarding way to have a budget honeymoon.
- Go domestic. If there's an area of the country you'd like to see, consider doing it on your honeymoon. If it's within driving distance, you can design a romantic road trip.

BOOKING SMARTS

Be organized *when planning your honeymoon.*

By now you are probably an expert in booking things far in advance. Just as you did with the wedding and reception, your honeymoon should also be planned and confirmed as far in advance as possible. Some experts claim that even an entire year ahead isn't too early to do so! Here are some other useful booking tips:

- Take an inventory of any frequent flier mileage you and your spouse might have accumulated. Family members may also be willing to donate any miles to you to help your honeymoon go that little bit further. You can put this mileage toward airline tickets, seat upgrades, car rentals, or hotel rooms.
- Keep all travel brochures, reservation paperwork, frequent flier information, and other travel documents in one place – perhaps a large envelope.
- Consider using a travel agent. He or she will be able to get you seats, rooms, tickets, and upgrades that wouldn't otherwise be available. Moreover, a good travel professional can help plan your trip, advising you on the best sites to see, places to eat, and even the most appropriate times to take your trip.
- If you are reserving your hotel room, be specific about your requirements. For example, say if you'd like a quiet room overlooking the ocean or garden. If you're having no luck with the booking agent, why not mention that you'll be on your honeymoon. This works wonders on softening up some people!
- Once you've decided where you want to go, find out if you'll need vaccinations or any other health requirements – and how far in advance these must be done. Don't leave these things to the last minute.
- If you will be honeymooning in an area where a different language is spoken from your native tongue, why not enroll in a language course?

Scheduling your departure

ONCE UPON A TIME, most newlyweds left straight from their reception to go on their honeymoon. There are definite merits to doing this: You've been going at full tilt for months, you're exhausted, you haven't had a quiet conversation with your partner in who knows how long. In short, you need a vacation! The downside to an immediate departure from your reception to your honeymoon is that it takes advance planning – and a lot of it.

You've packed your suitcases *and you're ready to go, but have you got everything you need? Compile a checklist to help you.*

In addition to all your wedding-day duties, you'll need to have packed your bags, gotten someone to watch your house, pets, and plants, and copied your itinerary for a friend or relative. Also make sure to have a set of travel clothes ready to change into, arrange for transportation from the reception, and ask someone to collect and keep your wedding gifts. You'll have to schedule the end of your reception precisely to give you enough time to catch your plane, train, or boat.

Hate the idea of vacationing in a crowded resort? Consider booking your honeymoon for a slower, off-season time – even if it means taking your trip a few months after the wedding.

If this all sounds like too much for you, you can always leave the next day, the next week, the next month – or any time that works for you. The benefits of giving yourself space between the reception and honeymoon are multiple: You can concentrate on getting ready for your wedding day without being distracted by travel matters; you don't have to schedule the wedding and reception rigidly; and you can hang out with your guests. You could even go out with close friends and family after the festivities or meet with them the next day for brunch. Waiting may also be the best choice if you must spend a few months earning enough money to pay for your honeymoon.

INTERNET

www.currencyguide.com/exchange.html

www.exchangerate.com

Two websites well worth visiting if you're taking a foreign honeymoon.

How long should we go for?

YES, MOST OF US would love to lounge for three weeks in some gorgeous locale, but the sad truth is that most of us can't. We either don't have the money or we have jobs to return to, pets to care for, or other obligations. So how long should you take? No one can answer this but you and your partner. I can, however, offer you a few things to consider:

Don't forget your pets! *Can a friend or relative feed them while you're away, or will you need to arrange for someone to look after them?*

Before packing your bags, call the airline to ask about carry-on requirements. Most airlines allow passengers only one or two pieces of carry-on luggage. Bags usually cannot exceed 22" x 14" x 9".

- A three-day honeymoon – providing it doesn't require much travel – is a terrific option for any couple who doesn't have the time do something longer. Besides, it's not the quantity of your time away – it's the quality.
- If your job commitments prevent you from enjoying a weeklong trip, why not take a local mini-vacation each weekend until you feel satisfied? I have friends who did this for six weekends in a row, spending each one in a different place.
- If lack of funds is holding you back from taking more time, ask your travel agent for ideas. A travel professional can often find ways to extend a vacation by a few days at little or no cost to you.
- Want to take a three-week honeymoon but can only afford five days right now? Why not do a shorter trip now and then plan something longer for your one-year anniversary?

Weighing your luggage *prevents any slipups at the airport and also helps you pack sensibly – you want to travel lightly on your honeymoon.*

Time to relax and enjoy

AS STRANGE AS IT SOUNDS, honeymoons can be stressful. First off, it's probably your first big trip after the wedding – if you're traveling soon after your nuptials, you may still be feeling stressed from your big day. Second, it's always a challenge to travel with someone else, even if you adore that person. Third, there are the expectations.

Your honeymoon should be the most romantic trip you've ever taken. It also has to be the most relaxing, the most fun, the most exotic, and the most erotic. All these expectations can set you and your mate up for tension, bickering, and disappointment. To ensure the two of you have the love-soaked trip you've been dreaming of, try the following tips:

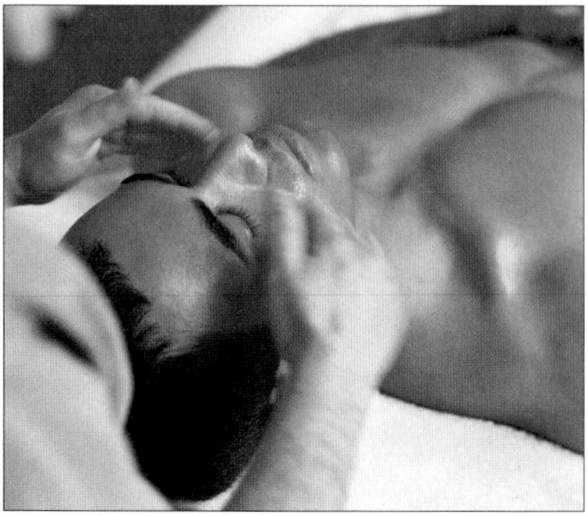

Your honeymoon *is a time to enjoy complete relaxation – relieve any anxiety with a massage.*

- Give yourself a chance to decompress before arriving at your honeymoon destination. You could treat yourself to a professional body massage, a facial, or foot reflexology. Vigorous exercise or journal writing are also time-proven ways to ease tension.
- If your only chance to unwind is on the flight, so be it: Bring some relaxing aromatherapy oil with you (lavender is especially calming and can aid sleeping), some soothing music for your Walkman, some fun treats, and an easy-reading book. Tell your honey that you need an hour or two to calm down – you may want to suggest that he does the same.
- You are two different people with two different minds. It is inevitable that you will have different ideas, opinions, and interests. Instead of seething when your hubby nixes your plan to take a day trip to a nearby rum distillery, calmly ask what his reasons are and then listen to his answer. If he doesn't want to drive a rental car in a foreign country, perhaps you could hire one yourself. Or perhaps he is simply uninterested, in which case maybe you could go without him.

If you're combining a destination wedding with your honeymoon, chances are you'll be vacationing with family and friends. Remember, though, that your new spouse is your main priority. Don't spend all your time with others – you need romantic time to yourselves.

- Don't overschedule your days. Honeymoons are all about relaxing, shaking off the stress of the past months, and enjoying your partner. Don't feel guilty if you want to spend the first few days of your trip in bed – it's your honeymoon!
- Mention any must-do sightseeing to your spouse before leaving on your honeymoon. This way he'll be mentally prepared and will have time to decide if he wants to join you or would rather stay by the pool relaxing with a book.

Either you or your spouse may be changing your name through marriage, but book your honeymoon in the names you were born with. This saves any complications with catching flights, booking into hotels, and so on.

- Learn compromise. Not only is compromise a skill that will help you in your marriage, it can make a honeymoon more pleasant by ensuring neither party feels resentful. An example: If you want to swim in the ocean and he wants to snuggle in bed, perhaps you could go for an early morning dip and reserve the hottest part of the day for lounging in your room.
- Take sensual treats, such as lingerie, scented room spray, candles, and other items that will make your time more fun. After all, it's difficult to be testy with each other when you're enjoying a honeymoon full of romance.

BECOME A HONEYMOON EXPERT

Be prepared *for any honeymoon mishaps.*

How to survive if you're honeymooning abroad:

- **Avoid a sunburn**: Use a water-resistant sunscreen, with an SPF 30 or higher. Reapply it at least every two hours – more often if you get wet or perspire. Don't forget UV-blocking sunglasses and a brimmed hat!
- **Get or renew a passport**: If you don't have a passport, or if your passport is no longer current, visit a passport office a few months before your honeymoon. You may be able to get a passport application at a local post office, town hall, or other municipal authority, which can then be filled out and mailed in; your passport will then be mailed to you.
- **Practice seaside safety**: Taking a tropical vacation? Stay out of the water if you've been drinking, if it's rainy or windy, or if the currents are strong.
- **Stay healthy while vacationing**: In some foreign resorts it's best not to drink the water. Bacteria in it can make you feel ill, so stick to bottled water.

Easing into marriage

YOUR HONEYMOON will give you a taste of what it's like to be a married person. However, a honeymoon is ultimately a vacation and, as such, is a far more comfortable lifestyle than the one waiting for you when you get home. When you return, you'll have thank-you notes to write. You'll also have family members to split your time between, banking accounts to open up, taxes to look into, perhaps some debt to pay off, and, of course, jobs to get back to.

True, single people are also plagued by similar obligations, but as a newlywed you've also got a marriage to build and a spouse to consider. Unfortunately, it's these last two that often suffer in the daily race to get everything done. Fortunately, with conscious effort, you can accomplish what you need to, without ignoring your relationship or your mate:

■ **Socializing with both** *sets of your friends is an important element of married life.*

- If there is anyone you haven't told about your marriage, then do so immediately upon returning from your honeymoon. Likewise, don't forget to introduce your new spouse to friends, acquaintances, and colleagues – you want to show others and your beloved how proud you are of your marriage. (Note: Ask your partner to do the same. I have a couple of friends whose husbands never introduce them to other people. Needless to say, this creates much ill will.)
- Do things as a couple with old friends. Getting married doesn't mean giving up time with your best buddies. Sure you can meet friends at the pub for a drink, or at the theatre for a Sunday matinee – simply include your mate in these plans.

Maintain separate interests as newlyweds. There's no reason to give up those hobbies you enjoyed before marriage. Doing so can create resentment and make you feel trapped.

- On the other hand, it's important to have time alone with your friends. Schedule a girls' night out at least monthly.
- Set boundaries. In-laws can often exert enormous pressure on newlyweds, trying to influence frequency of visits, or how they spend their money or keep house. Discuss with your partner how much meddling you can tolerate, how much time you can spend with each family, and what kinds of comments you find absolutely unacceptable.

- Create shared goals. Working together for a common aim not only strengthens the bonds between you, it helps your relationship move smoothly into the future.
- Celebrate each other's strengths. One of the best gifts you can give your relationship and your partner is to become a cheerleader, someone who celebrates your mate's good qualities.

Respect each other – even in anger. Words like "shut up," put-downs, and sexual slurs have no place in a marriage. You and your partner joined your lives because you found each other to be special.

- Accept your differences. You aren't going to change your husband's mind about some things – that's part and parcel of being in a relationship. Do yourselves a favor and agree to disagree on certain issues if it's going to make life easier.
- Don't let arguments grow into domestic warfare. Cool off and address conflicts as soon as they occur, while they are still small.

Trivia...

John Gottman, Ph.D., author of the much-lauded Why Marriages Succeed or Fail, *(Crown Publishers, 1999), has studied thousands of successful, long-term marriages. Among his findings he discovered that the happiest partners are those who exhibit fondness and admiration for each other, solve all conflicts possible, and create shared goals.*

A simple summary

✓ Your first night as a married couple is special! With the wedding behind you, it's time to enjoy yourselves together.

✓ Adjusting to married life isn't always easy – no matter how much you love your new spouse.

✓ Depression or extreme emotions can be a sign something is wrong. You and your spouse must seek the advice of a counselor in these circumstances.

✓ Almost anywhere can be a honeymoon destination. In fact, the only rule to planning a honeymoon is to choose a location that you both will enjoy.

✓ Honeymoons can be incredibly stressful. Communication and compromise are two ways to keep your vacation a happy one.

✓ Being married is a learned skill, acquired through patience and care. Nurture it and enjoy!

A Simple Glossary

Aerobics A Greek term meaning "with air" or "with oxygen." Aerobic exercise is any activity that uses large muscle groups, generally for 15 minutes or more.

Attendants The people you and your partner choose to help you on your special day and to stand with you at the altar. These include the maid of honor, the best man, bridesmaids, and groomsmen. Child attendants include ring bearers and flower girls.

At-home cards These are preprinted cards or handwritten notes used to inform family and friends of your new address, what name – or names – the two of you will be using after the ceremony, and anything else people should know. At-home cards can either be sent out with your invitations or after you are married.

Ball and chain A derogatory expression that originated in England. It compares the ball and chain that prisoners used to wear with a spouse – most notably, a wife.

Beauty timeline A kind of "to do" list to help you prepare for your wedding. Use one to schedule specific beauty treatments prior to your big day.

Betrothal An old-fashioned word for engagement. It means, literally, to be true or loyal.

Boutonniere Worn by the men in the wedding party, a boutonniere is a small single flower or flower arrangement pinned to the lapel.

Bride's stationery Stationery engraved with the bride's surname or initials that she uses before her wedding. (If she keeps her own surname, she can continue to use this stationery after marriage.) It is used to write thank-you cards to bridesmaids, friends, and relatives. Many partners also have "couple's stationery," which serves the same purpose.

Buffet A popular style of wedding meal, whereby one or more tables are set up with various types of food. Guests choose what they want to eat and carry their own plates back to their tables. Because they require fewer waitstaff, buffet meals are often cheaper than sit-down meals.

Butter cake A moist, rich cake made with a generous amount of butter. A popular choice of wedding cake.

Cake stand A decorative platter – often elevated on a stand or legs – that sits under the wedding cake.

Cake table Used at the reception and reserved solely for displaying the wedding cake.

Cake topper Also known as a figurine, the cake topper is a small statue that sits atop the wedding cake. Made of plastic or porcelain, it is traditionally formed in the image of a bride and groom.

Caterer A person or team of persons who make the food for your reception.

Cocktail hour Most cocktail hours take place between the wedding ceremony and the reception, giving guests something to do while the newlyweds and their wedding party take pictures and relax.

Collar When talking dinner jackets, the collar comes in one of three types: peaked, notched, or shawl.

Color swatch A small piece of fabric, which is used to find exact shade matches.

Columns Visible columns used to support layers of wedding cake. Also known as pillars.

Consummate Used in relation to one's wedding night, "consummate" means to "make complete" through sexual intercourse.

Dance floor As well as being the designated dancing area, the dance floor is also often used for making speeches, giving toasts, cake cutting, bouquet throwing, and garter tossing.

Destination wedding A wedding that takes place in an exotic location, either in the couple's own country or abroad. If your ideal wedding locale is in another country, be sure that you and any guests complete any necessary paperwork well before the ceremony.

Disc jockey Also known as a DJ, this is the person who plays the music during your reception and perhaps even during your wedding. He or she will bring their own equipment, including a microphone, and they may introduce the bridal party, announce the tossing of the bouquet, the cutting of the cake, and any other announcements you request.

Display cake A wedding cake that looks authentic in every way but is actually inedible. Display cakes are used to save time and money.

Elope A dictionary definition of "elope" is to "run away secretly with one's lover with the intention of getting married, usually without familial consent."

Engagement The period between the date a couple decides to get married and the day of the actual wedding ceremony. In many cultures the engagement is a legally binding state.

Engagement announcement A formal public announcement typically placed in a local newspaper. Usually listed no more than a year before the wedding, the engagement announcement is optional.

Estate rentals Luxury homes or mansions that can be rented for wedding ceremonies or receptions.

Favors Optional little party gifts that guests take home with them from your reception. These can be anything from personalized matchbooks or miniature chocolate bars to candles to picture frames.

Flower ring A cake decoration consisting of fresh flowers placed between cake layers.

Groom's cake Smaller than the wedding cake, the groom's cake is traditionally fruitcake or rum cake, though dark chocolate is a modern favorite. Completely optional, the groom's cake is either served alongside the wedding cake or boxed and sent home with guests as a reception favor.

Guest book table For holding the guest book, which is basically a log book in which each guest enters his or her name and any well wishes for the couple. The guest book table usually sits somewhere near the entrance to the reception hall.

Head table The table at which the newlyweds sit, traditionally with their families or attendants.

Honeymoon insurance Offered by some insurance and travel companies, honeymoon insurance offers a set amount of money should something untoward happen during your travels. Depending on the individual insurance plan, this mishap can be anything from lost luggage to stormy weather.

Individual wedding cakes These single serving mini-cakes are a popular option and are served in place of traditional wedding cake.

Joint account A joint account is a shared account – current or savings – in both your name and your spouse's. The two of you pool money to be used on shared expenses.

Jordan almonds Candy-coated almonds that some cultures equate with fertility. Popular reception favors.

Karaoke Taken from the Japanese words "empty" and "orchestra," karaoke is a type of musical entertainment. A person stands in front of an audience and sings along to songs that have been specially recorded with only the tune's instrumental backing track.

Monogram A person's or couple's initials that are stamped, sewn, etched, or drawn onto a material – usually linen – and given as a wedding gift.

Officiant The official – either religious or not – who performs the wedding ceremony. In the case of interfaith ceremonies, two officiants may preside.

Orchestra A group of musicians who play together on various instruments, usually including strings, woodwinds, brass, and percussion. An orchestra is ideal for formal receptions.

Permits Many outdoor and public sites require special permits for wedding or receptions. Check with city officials well in advance to see if your venue has any particular requirements.

Pew cards Also known as "reserved-seat signs," these mark benches or seats set aside for family seating.

Pillars Also known as columns, pillars are placed in between layers of wedding cake. They help create a multiple-tiered effect, with open air between each layer of cake.

Pound cake A luscious, dense cake that gets its name from its original recipe, which called for a pound each of butter, eggs, sugar, and flour.

Proofs In photography speak, proofs are small copies of photographs, made especially for you to examine before deciding whether or not to order the images as regular-sized photos.

Reply cards Small cards that are tucked into your wedding invitations, reply cards are filled in and returned by your guests to let you know whether they are able to attend or not.

Satellite A kind of tiered cake with several separate cakes forming the base and other individual cakes placed above the base layers. A good option for couples needing to feed a large reception.

Separators A cake term. Separators are thin support poles pushed into each layer of cake to support the above layer. They are invisible once the cake has been decorated.

Sheet cake A large, flat cake. Pieces of sheet cake that have the same flavor as the decorated wedding cake are often plated before the ceremony and served to guests. This is cheaper and more efficient than serving all guests pieces of the main cake.

Sit-down meal Exactly as its name suggests – guests are served at their table by waitstaff. Among the most popular reception-meal option.

Site coordinator Also called a site manager, this person is employed by the wedding or reception venue to work with you. With your input, the site coordinator manages the event, helping you decide everything from table placement to how many waitstaff you should have serve guests.

Soloist A vocalist who sings alone during the ceremony, sometimes accompanied by a musical instrument.

Sponge cake This popular choice of wedding cake is light and less rich than a butter- or pound cake.

Stacked A cake term. A wedding cake with multiple layers in which each layer is placed directly on top of the next layer.

Sugaring An ancient form of hair removal used in Israel and the Middle East. Sugaring involves painting the skin with a resinous paste, which is rubbed off, pulling hair away with it.

Sweetheart table A small table for two – the bride and groom – set in the center of the other guest tables at the reception. Preferred by couples who want some "together time" at their reception or who want to avoid the politics involved with seating people at a traditional head table.

Thank-you notes Short, handwritten notes sent out to every person who gives the bride and groom a gift or extends them some sort of kindness. While popular practice is to send these notes out within a year, many etiquette experts insist that they must be mailed within a month of receiving each gift.

Threading An ancient form of hair removal used in Israel and the Middle East. A skilled practitioner uses a length of thread to quickly lasso and pull individual hairs.

Tiered A cake term. A tiered wedding cake is multi-layered, with each layer separated by columns, often several inches in length.

Toast The act of raising a glass (usually of champagne) and drinking in honor of or to the health of a person or thing. The first toast of the reception is typically given by the best man.

Valet A valet parks guests' cars for them and fetches the vehicles when they leave. Similar to valets are parking attendants, who point out parking spaces to guests and help safeguard parked cars.

Vegan A vegan eats no type of animal product, regardless of whether the product was retrieved without killing the animal.

Videographer A relative newcomer to the pantheon of wedding professionals, a videographer tapes your wedding. Usually hired in addition to a photographer.

Vows The most important element of the wedding ceremony. After reciting vows, you are legally considered to be married.

Wedding announcements There are two types of wedding announcements: A couple of lines placed in a local newspaper within a few weeks following the couple's wedding; and formal cards that are sent to people who weren't invited to the wedding but with whom the newlyweds would like to share the news.

Wedding insurance Some insurance companies offer wedding insurance. How it works: You make monthly payments and, in turn, you are protected against vendor cancellations, mishaps, damages – some policies even offer personal liability coverage.

Wedding invitation These are sent out to invite guests to the wedding and/or reception.

Wedding planner A person who specializes in engagement, wedding, and honeymoon help.

Wedding program A chronological outline of the ceremony that allows guests to follow events. If you are including any unusual elements in the ceremony, the program is a great way to explain the significance of them. Most programs also list the members of the wedding party.

Wedding registry A kind of wish list. It is lodged with a particular store and lists the items the bride and groom would like as presents from their guests.

Other Resources

Recommended books

If there is a particular aspect of weddings that you want to delve into further – such as learning how to choose a diamond, writing your own vows, or planning a honeymoon – there are plenty of books out there on the market. Here is a selection:

365 Questions for Couples
Michael J. Beck et al, Adams Media Corporation, 1999

Anti-Bride Guide: Tying the Knot Outside of the Box
Carolyn Gerin and Stephanie Rosenbaum, Chronicle Books, 2001

Bridal Bargains
Alan and Denise Fields, Windsor Peak Press, 1993

Bridezilla: True Tales from Etiquette Hell
Noe Spaemme and Jeanne Hamilton, Salado Press, 2002

Consumer Guide to Diamonds
Joseph Mirsky, Joseph's Jewelry, 2000

Diamond Ring Buying Guide: How to Evaluate, Identify and Select Diamonds and Diamond Jewelry
Renee Newman, International Jewelry Publications, 2002

Engagement and Wedding Rings: The Definitive Buying Guide for People in Love
Antonio C. Bonnano and Antoinette Leonard Matlins, Gemstone Press, 1999

How to Have a Big Wedding on a Small Budget
Diane Warner, Betterway Publications, 1997

How to Have an Elegant Wedding for $5000 (or Less)
Jan Wilson and Beth Wilson Hickman, Prima Publishing, 1999

How to "I Do": Planning the Ultimate Wedding in Six Weekends or Less
Holly Lefevre and Christine Cudanes, Regan Books, 2000.

Let's Elope: The Definitive Guide to Eloping, Destination Weddings, and Other Creative Wedding Options
Lynn Beahan, and Scott Shaw, Bantam Doubleday Dell, 2001

Priceless Weddings for Under $5,000
Kathleen Kennedy, Three Rivers Press, 2000

The Budget Wedding Sourcebook
Madeline Barillo, McGraw-Hill/ Contemporary Books, 2000

The Cake Bible
Rose Levy Beranbaum, Papermac, 1993

The Complete Outdoor Wedding Planner
Sharon Naylor, Prima Publishing, 2001

The Knot Guide to Wedding Vows and Traditions: Readings, Rituals, Music, Dances, Speeches, and Toasts
Carley Roney, Broadway Books, 2000

Wedding-related associations

If you need information on specific issues, there are plenty of specialist organizations that can offer you advice. Here are several you can contact:

American Disc Jockey Association
Representing DJs throughout the United States and Canada.
www.adja.org

Association for Wedding Professionals International
Find trained wedding professionals in whichever part of the world you wish to marry.
www.afwpi.com

Association of Certified Professional Wedding Consultants
A great source for those looking to hire a wedding consultant.
www.acpwc.com

www.coordinatorscorner.com
Read about all the latest wedding trends on this favorite website of bridal consultants.

www.juneweddings.com
Links to a huge selection of U.S. bridal consultants.

www.weddingsbeautiful.com
Information on bridal consultants worldwide, plus advice on how to train as a consultant.

Magazines

It's mind-boggling how many wedding magazines are available today. Here are just a few of them:

The Knot
Fresh, hip, and down-to-earth, *The Knot* lacks the annoying pretension of many "traditional" bridal magazines. A great reference for real people who want to have real weddings.
www.theknot.com

Martha Stewart Weddings
This is a terrific source of ideas and inspiration for do-it-yourselfers.
www.marthastewart.com

Wedding Bells
Everything you need to know about getting married. Published by the people at WeddingChannel.com.
www.weddingbells.com

Weddings on the Web

THE INTERNET IS A GREAT place to browse for wedding information. So, whether you're curious about the origin behind specific wedding traditions, want to know how soon in advance to send out invitations, or are wondering how to deal with meddling family members, here are some sites that can help:

Cold feet

www.theregoesthebride.com

This site offers commiseration and advice for anyone thinking about calling it off. In addition to the many personal being-left-at-the-altar stories, you'll find resources on how to get through this kind of ordeal.

General wedding sites

www.bestweddingsites.com

This site features contests and special deals as well as advice on everything from staying organized to inviting children to your wedding.

www.bridalseek.com

An invaluable wedding and honeymoon search engine.

www.bridalzine.com

A great website that has all the usual engagement, bridal, and honeymoon information, plus terrific articles on subjects such as creating a wedding on a shoestring, and the meaning of specific flowers.

www.bridesmaidaid.com

Lots of advice, including how to throw a shower, help a stressed bride, and what to do with an ugly bridesmaid dress once you're done wearing it.

www.indiebride.com

A fabulous site for the independent-minded bride. Includes more intellectual offerings than the typical wedding site, including essays and discussions on various topics. Highly recommended.

www.ivillage.com/relationships/brides

A wide array of advice on relationships, bridal beauty, planning, and more. Book excerpts, professional advice, and accounts of real-life budget weddings help you save on everything from cakes to gowns to honeymoons.

www.paweddings.com

An advice column for tradition-minded brides.

www-personal.umich.edu/~kzaruba/wedding.html

Information on elopement, destination weddings, theme weddings, alternative weddings, and interfaith weddings, as well as commitment ceremonies, same-sex ceremonies, and more.

www.theknot.com

As well as varied information on wedding issues, this site provides in-depth detail on groom's attire, including photographs of the many styles of suits, tuxedos, and footwear available.

www.weva.com

Learn about wedding videography – and videographers – from the Wedding and Event Videographers Association.

Gowns

www.bridalgown.com
www.discountweddingstore.com
www.egowns.com
www.isaidyes.com

Four great sites that are ideal for those brides interested in finding wedding gowns at a discount.

Health and beauty

www.1st-spot.net/topic_nailcare.html

Learn about nail care, nail products, and nail health on this helpful website to ensure you're fully clued up for your wedding nail care regimen.

www.healthwell.com

This comprehensive site features articles on beauty, nutrition, fitness, and lifestyle issues – information you'll find useful before – and after – your wedding.

www.weddingmakeup.com

This smart site has lots of articles and information on a range of topics, from bridal makeup traditions to treatments and products.

Honeymoon specifics

www.currencyguide.com/exchange.html
www.exchangerate.com

Useful sites if you're honeymooning abroad.

www.embassyworld.com

Planning to go abroad for your honeymoon? Find out what travel documents you require for this destination as well as where the embassies are located and other important need-to-know information.

www.honeymoons.com

Advice for the perfect honeymoon, including tips on choosing the ideal destination and deciding where to stay.

www.mapquest.com

A terrific tool that can be used to find locations throughout the world. Type in your starting point and final destination, and the site creates a detailed map.

Official details

www.changeyourname.co.uk
www.enamechange.com

These two sites offer an abundance of help for those planning on changing their names after getting married.

www.usmarriagelaws.com
www.vitalrec.com/index.html
www.weddingdetails.com

These three sites contain information about where to obtain vital records from each state, territory, and county of the United States.

Religion and beliefs

www.beliefnet.com

This great site has loads of information on the wedding ceremonies of different faiths, as well as practical ways to incorporate elements of two faiths into one wedding.

Rings

www.buyadiamond.net
www.diamondreview.com
www.jewellery247.co.uk

These sites features in-depth research to help you find a reputable jeweler, choose a flattering and practical ring, and learn a little more about the history of rings.

Wedding gifts

www.weddinggazette.com

Great advice on gift registry, gift giving, writing thank-you cards, and other facets of wedding planning.

Wedding planning

www.chefmike.com

All you need to know to cater your own wedding.

www.weddingsonawhim.com

Worth looking at if you have only a short period in which to plan your wedding.

www.wedfrugal.com

If you want to streamline wedding costs, this site is a must.

www.wishuponawedding.com

This site offers planning advice, but what makes it special are tips on staying sane and getting grooms involved.

Index

A

accessories
  bride's, 71
  flowers, 112–15
  groom's, 92
accounts, joint, 57, 63, 209
address, notifying change of, 208
aerobic exercise, 83–4, 100–1
age, legal, 205
aisle, walking down, 243
albums, photo, 174, 177
alcohol, 85
  beverage service, 146–51
  saving money, 62, 147
allergies, 113, 142, 153
almonds, sugared, 142
Ascot ties, 91
attendants, 47–51
  clothes, 103–11
  cocktail party, 224
  flowers, 112–15
  gifts, 134–6
  rehearsal, 240
  showers, 219, 220

B

bachelor parties, 221–3
bachelorette parties, 104, 221, 222
bakers, 157–9
"ball and chain," 236
balloons, hot-air, 196
bar services, 146–8, 171
beauty care, 74–81
beer, 146, 148
bereavement, 228
best man, 47–8
  clothes, 108
  gifts, 135, 136
  receiving line, 248
  toasts, 149–50
betrothal, 15
beverage service, 146–51
"big band" orchestras, 187
birth stones, 16
blood tests, 206
boats, 196
bolo ties, 91
bouquets, 113, 167, 254
boutonnieres, 113
bow ties, 91
"Bridal March," 184, 185
bride
  accessories, 71
  after the wedding, 272–3
  average age, 24
  bachelorette parties, 221, 222
  beauty care, 74–81
  bouquet, 113, 167
  canceling wedding, 230
  "ceremonial feeding," 156, 160
  changing name, 271
  "cold feet," 228–9
  cutting the cake, 156, 253
  expenses, 55
  family disagreements, 232–4
  first dance, 185, 252
  friends, 235–6
  gift from groom, 136
  the kiss, 241
  leaving the reception, 254–5
  legal age, 205
  receiving line, 248–9
  reception gowns, 73
  seating plan, 250
  shoes, 73
  showers, 218–20
  starting married life, 262–3
  surname, 210–13, 271
  the toss, 254
  vows, 241, 242
  walking down the aisle, 243
  wedding gown, 67–73
  wedding transport, 194–7
bridesmaids, 48
  bouquets, 113
  bridesmaids' luncheon, 225
  clothes, 72, 104–6, 109
  gifts, 134–5
  junior bridesmaids, 50, 135
  the toss, 254
brothers, 234
brunches, 61, 140, 225
budgets, 53–65
  attendants' clothes, 109
  average costs, 65
  beauty stylists, 75
  caterers, 144
  debt, 54, 56, 59
  financing wedding, 63–5
  flowers, 169
  honeymoon, 266–7
  how much can you afford?, 57
  photographs, 179
  prioritizing, 58–9
  saving money, 60–2, 63, 145
  wedding consultants, 26
  wedding food, 145
  who pays for what, 54–5

C

cake, 152–9
  cake makers, 157–9
  cake table, 160
  caterers, 145
  "ceremonial feeding," 156, 160
  cutting, 156, 185, 253
  decoration, 154–5
  groom's cake, 156
  options, 155–6
  saving money, 62
  styles, 153
  superstitions, 259
cameras, disposable, 62, 176
canceling wedding, 133, 230–1
candles, 41, 50, 170
cards
  engagement, 118–19
  invitations, 121–5, 127
  reply, 125
  "save the date" cards, 125
  thank-you cards, 133
carriages, 196, 197
cars
  getaway cars, 197, 199, 200, 259
  guest transport, 198
  hiring, 199–201
  leaving reception, 259
  transport to ceremony, 194
cash bars, 62, 147
cash gifts, 130, 133, 254
caterers, 141, 144–5, 217
catholic church, 33
"ceremonial feeding," 156, 160
ceremony, 239–45
  decorations, 168

music, 184–5, 241
order of, 241
photographs after, 244–5
rehearsal, 240
rings, 21
vows, 241, 242
walking down the aisle, 243
certificate of marriage, 205
champagne, 148, 151, 251, 258
chauffeured cars, 194
children
attendants, 48, 50
clothes, 110
entertainment, 191
seating plan, 250
surnames, 211
choirs, 186
churches, 37
city halls, 36
civil ceremonies, 31
clergy, 30, 33
clothes
best man, 108
bride, 67–73
bridesmaids, 104–6, 109
fathers, 109
groom, 87–94
groomsmen, 107
maid of honor, 106
mothers, 111
reception gowns, 73
traveling, 255
trousseau, 38
ushers, 107, 108
wedding rehearsal, 240
wedding transport, 197
clubs, wedding venues, 36
co-ed wedding showers, 219–20
cocktail hour, 248
cocktail party, attendants', 224
"cold feet," 228–9
collars
shirts, 90–1
tuxedo jackets, 89
colors
bridesmaids' dresses, 105
color swatches, 105
makeup, 80
mothers' clothes, 111
superstitions, 111
wedding cake, 157
wedding gowns, 68, 69, 72
columns, tiered cakes, 153
confetti, 254
consultants, wedding, 25–7
consummating union, 258
contracts
beauty stylists, 75
musicians, 189
prenuptial agreements, 207–8
corsages, 113, 115
costs *see* budgets
counseling 204, 229, 262
country clubs, 36
couples counseling, 262
credit cards, 60
crosswyck collars, 90
cuff links, 92
cultural traditions, 32–3
cummerbunds, 92
cutaway morning coats, 90
cutting the cake, 156, 185, 253

D

dancing
dance floor, 171
first dance, 185, 252
music, 185
permits, 186
dates
planning wedding, 35
superstitions, 252
day-after brunch, 225
death
engagement announcements and, 120
postponing weddings, 228
debt, 54, 56, 59, 208
decorations
ceremony space, 168
engagement parties, 217
professional decorators, 167
reception, 170–1
seasonal, 164–6
dental care, 77, 97
deposits, canceling wedding, 231
depression, 263
destination weddings, 34
diamond rings, 16, 19
diet
dietary preferences, 142–3
weight loss, 82, 84, 100
dinner, rehearsal, 127, 224–5
dinner jackets, 89
diseases, blood tests, 206
display cakes, 62
divorce, 234
money conflicts, 57
prenuptial agreements, 207–8
DJs (disc jockeys), 187, 188–9, 190
dresses
bridesmaids, 104–6, 109
maid of honor, 106
wedding, 68–73
drinks
beverage service, 146–51, 171
non-alcoholic, 148, 151
saving money, 62
seasonal, 167

E

elopement, 33–4
emotions, starting married life, 263
engagement, 13–27
announcing, 118–20
canceling wedding, 230
engagement parties, 216–17
length, 14–15
rings, 16–18, 21
short engagements, 15, 43–4
showers, 218–20
stresses, 22–5
engraving, inside wedding rings, 19, 20
entertainment
engagement parties, 217
music, 183–91
non-musical, 191
envelopes, invitations, 125, 126

ethnic weddings, 32
Euro ties, 91
exercise, 83–4, 100–1
expenses *see* budgets
eyebrow shaping, 78

F

fabrics, color swatches, 105
fake diamonds, 19
fall, seasonal decorations, 166
family
- after the wedding, 272
- canceling wedding, 230
- disagreements with, 232–4
- family reunions, 46
- guest list, 45–6
- heirlooms 19, 68–9, 230
- wedding planning, 24–5
- *see also* parents

father of the bride
- clothes, 109
- dancing, 185
- receiving line, 248
- role of, 49
- walking down the aisle, 243

father of the groom
- clothes, 109
- receiving line, 248
- role of, 50

favors, 170
fears, "cold feet," 228–9
fertility symbols, 254
fiancés, 15
finances *see* budgets
fingers, choosing rings to suit, 21
first night, 258–61
florists, 112, 113, 169
flower girls, 48, 167
- clothes, 110
- gifts, 135
- rehearsal, 240

flowers, 112–15
- at reception, 170–1
- bouquets, 113, 167, 254
- cake decorations, 154
- ceremony space, 168
- florists, 112, 113, 169
- seasonal decorations, 164–6

food
- bridal showers, 219
- caterers, 144–5
- engagement parties, 217
- seasonal, 167
- wedding meals, 61, 140–5, 250
- weight loss, 84, 100

four-in-hand ties, 91
friends
- after the wedding, 272
- disagreements with, 235–7

future goals, 56

G

games
- bachelorette parties, 222
- bridal showers, 219

garters, 71
- tossing, 254

gems, engagement rings, 16
genetic diseases, blood tests, 206
getaway cars, 197, 199, 200, 259
gifts, 129–37
- for attendants, 134–6
- canceling wedding, 133, 231
- favors, 170
- gift table, 253
- showers, 218–20
- thank-you cards, 133
- wedding registry, 39, 130–2

goals, after wedding, 56
gowns
- bridesmaids', 72, 104–6, 109
- reception gowns, 73
- wedding gowns, 68–73

gratuities, caterers, 141
greeting guests, 249
groom
- after the wedding, 272–3
- average age, 24
- bachelor parties, 221–3
- canceling wedding, 230
- "ceremonial feeding," 156, 160
- clothes, 87–94
- co-ed wedding showers, 219–20
- "cold feet," 228–9
- cutting the cake, 156, 253
- engagement rings, 17, 18
- expenses, 55
- first dance, 185, 252
- friends, 236–7
- gift from bride, 136
- grooming, 95–9
- groom's cake, 156
- the kiss, 241
- leaving the reception, 254–5
- legal age, 205
- receiving line, 248–9
- seating plan, 250
- shoes, 88
- starting married life, 262–3
- surname, 211–13
- tossing the garter, 254
- vows, 241, 242
- wedding planning, 22–3

groomsmen, 48
- clothes, 107
- gifts, 135–6
- junior groomsmen, 50

guests
- canceling wedding, 231
- cocktail hour, 248
- favors, 170
- guest books, 41
- guest list, 45–6
- hotels, 260
- invitations, 121–7
- receiving line, 248–9
- reception, 248–55
- seating plans, 249–50
- transport, 198
- wedding registry, 130–2

H

hair
- bride's, 75–80, 196
- groom's, 95, 97, 98

hair removal, 78, 96
halls, wedding venues, 36, 44
hands, choosing rings to suit, 21
harp music, 186
hats, 111
headdresses, 71
heirlooms
- rings, 19, 230
- wedding gowns, 68–9

helicopters, wedding transport, 196

hen parties, 221
his-and-her engagement rings, 18
his-and-her wedding rings, 20
hobbies, 272
home, first night at, 260–1
honeymoon, 264–73
canceling wedding, 231
choosing destination, 264–6
costs, 266–7
destination weddings, 34
leaving for, 258–9
length of, 269
planning, 267
safety, 271
stress, 270–1
travel, 267, 268
horse-drawn carriages, 196
horseback transport, 196
hot-air balloons, 196
hotels, 259–60, 267
houses of worship, wedding venues, 37

I

icing, cakes, 154–5
in-laws, disagreements with, 234
interfaith weddings, 33
Internet, buying wedding dresses, 64, 72
invitations, 117, 121–7
rehearsal dinner, 224

J

jackets, groom's, 89–90, 91, 94
jewelry
cuff links, 92
engagement rings, 16–18
studs, 92
wedding rings, 19–21
junior bridesmaids, 50, 135
junior groomsmen, 50
junior ushers, 50

K

karaoke, 189–90
the kiss, 241

L

legal age, 205
licenses, marriage, 205–6
light-jazz combos, 187
limousines, 195
lipstick, 80
liquor, 146, 148
lists
guest list, 45–6
prioritizing spending, 58–9
wedding registry, 39, 130–2
luggage, 259, 268, 269
luncheon, bridesmaids', 225

M

maid of honor, 47
bouquet, 113
bridal shower, 218
dress, 106
gifts, 136
receiving line, 248
toasts, 149–50
makeup
beauty timeline, 76–8
colors, 80
emergency kit, 81
makeup artists, 75
touching up, 81
Mandarin collars, 90
Mandarin jackets, 90
manicures, 76, 96
Mao jackets, 90
maps, for guests, 198
marriage licenses, 205–6
"marriage skills" classes, 204
mascara, 80
massage, 96, 97, 270
matron of honor, 47
mayors, wedding officiants, 31
meals
bridesmaids' luncheon, 225
day-after brunch, 225
reception, 61, 140–5, 250
rehearsal dinner, 127, 224–5
"thank-you parents" meal, 225
Mendelssohn, Felix, 185
ministers, wedding officiants, 30
Moissanite diamonds, 19
money
canceling wedding, 231
joint accounts, 209
prenuptial agreements, 207–8
tax filing, 208
see also budgets
months, wedding date superstitions, 252
morning coats, 90
mosques, 37
mother of the bride
clothes, 111
corsages, 115
disagreements with, 232–3
receiving line, 248
role of, 49
walking down the aisle, 243
mother of the groom
clothes, 111
corsages, 115
dancing, 185
receiving line, 248
role of, 49
mourning *see* death
music, 183–91
at ceremony, 184–5, 241
choices, 186–7
cutting the cake, 253
dancing, 185
karaoke, 189–90
music brokers, 189
musicians, 188–9
at reception, 185, 186
rehearsal, 240
restrictions, 186, 188
saving money, 62

N

nail care 76, 77, 96
names
addressing invitations, 123–5
after marriage, 210–13, 271
nasty-makers, 232–7
neckwear, groom's, 91
Nehru jackets, 90
newspaper announcements, 119–20
nut allergies, 153

O

official details, 203–13
officiants, 30–1

canceling wedding, 231
destination weddings, 34
interfaith weddings, 33
unusual venues, 37
one-upmanship, bride's friends, 235
online auction sites, buying wedding dresses, 64, 72
orchestras, "big band," 187
order of ceremony, 241
organ music, 186
outdoor weddings, 37

P

pages, 50
pants, 94
parents
clothes, 109
disagreements with, 232–4
financial help, 54–5
gifts, 137
roles of, 49–50
seating plan, 250
"thank-you parents" meal, 225
walking down the aisle, 243
parking, guests, 198
parks, as wedding venues, 37
parties
attendants' cocktail party, 224
bachelor parties, 221–3
bachelorette parties, 104, 221, 222
combined his-her parties, 223
engagement parties, 216–17
see also reception
passports, 271
personalizing weddings, 30–4, 242
photographs, 173–7
after the ceremony, 244–5
disposable cameras, 62, 176
how many pictures?, 177
improving your appearance, 175
"in transit" photos, 195
photographers, 179–81
storing, 178
styles, 174–6
pianists, 186
planning, 22–3
choosing venue, 36–7
date and time, 35
guest list, 45–6
honeymoon, 267
short engagements, 43–4
time of wedding, 44
timeline, 38–43
wedding planners, 25–7
poems, 241
pop music, 187
postponing weddings, 228
pre-marital counseling, 204, 229
pregnancy, 205
prenuptial agreements, 207–8
presents *see* gifts
prioritizing spending, 58–9
private cars, 194
private clubs, 36
private homes, wedding venues, 36
processions, 197
proof photographs, 181
proposal, engagement rings, 16
public spaces, as venues, 37

R

receiving line, 248–9
reception, 247–55
cake table, 160
cocktail hour, 248
dancing, 185, 252–3
decorations, 170–1
gift table, 253
guest books, 41
guest list, 45–6
invitations, 127
leaving, 254–5
length of, 248
music, 185, 186
receiving line, 248–9
rituals, 251–4
saving money, 61–2, 145
seating plan, 249–50
wedding meal, 61, 140–5, 250
reception gowns, 73
rehearsal, 240
rehearsal dinner, 127, 224–5
relatives *see* family; parents
religious weddings
cultural traditions, 32–3
interfaith weddings, 33
music, 185
pre-marital counseling, 204
venues, 37
wedding officiants, 30
renting
cars, 194
suits, 92, 94, 107
reply cards, 125
restaurants, 36, 186
rice, throwing, 254
ring bearers, 48
clothes, 110
gifts, 135
rehearsal, 240
rings
canceling wedding, 230
engagement, 16–18, 21
wedding, 19–21, 262
rituals, reception, 251–4
round cakes, 153
rubella, blood tests, 206

S

safety, honeymoon, 271
satellite cakes, 153
"save the date" cards, 125
savings accounts, 63
seasonal decorations, 164–6
seasonal foods and drinks, 167
seating plans, 249–50
servers, wedding meal, 141, 144
sex
bachelor parties, 221–2
wedding night, 258
shaving, 97
sheet cake, 153
shirts, groom's, 90–1, 94
shoes, 109
bride's, 73
groom's, 88
wedding rehearsal, 240
showers, bridal, 218–20

sickle-cell anemia, blood tests, 206
singers, 186
sisters, 233
skincare, 76, 95–6
slimming, 82–5, 100
speeches, toasts, 150
Spencer coats, 90
sponsored weddings, 65
spread collars, 90
spring, seasonal decorations, 165
square cakes, 153
stacked cakes, 153
stag parties *see* bachelor parties
stores
  buying wedding dresses, 73
  wedding registry, 39, 130–2
streetcars, wedding transport, 196
stresses
  engagement, 22–5
  honeymoon, 270–1
  pre-wedding 227–37
string quartets, 187, 188
stroller coats, 89
studs, 92
stylists, beauty, 75
sugared almonds, 142
sugaring, hair removal, 78
suits
  bride's, 69, 71
  fathers', 109
  groom's, 89–90, 92–3
  groomsmen, 107
summer, seasonal decorations, 165
sunburn, 271
superstitions
  colors, 111
  wedding cake, 259
  wedding dates, 252
surnames, 210–13, 271
surprise parties, engagements, 216
suspenders, 92
synagogues, 37
syphilis, blood tests, 206

T

table decorations, 144, 170
tails, tuxedo jackets, 89
tax filing, 208
taxis, guest transport, 198
teeth, dental care, 77, 97
temples, 37
thank-you cards, gifts, 133
"thank-you parents" meal, 225
theme weddings, 31, 191
therapy 204, 229, 262
threading, hair removal, 78
tiaras, 77
tiered cakes, 153
ties, groom's, 91
time of wedding, 44
timeline, 38–43
  bride's beauty care, 74, 76–9
  groom's grooming, 95–8
tipping, 255
tissue, invitations, 126
toasts, 148, 149–51, 251, 258
the toss, 254
traditions, 32–3, 69
train bearers, 50
  clothes, 110
  gifts, 135
  rehearsal, 240
trains, wedding gown, 71
transport, 193–201
  to ceremony, 194–7
  getaway cars, 197, 199, 200, 259
  guests, 198
  hiring, 199–201
  honeymoon, 258–9
travel
  destination weddings, 34
  honeymoon, 267, 268
trolleys, wedding transport, 196
trousseau, 38
tuxedo jackets, 89, 91, 92, 94

U

unusual venues, 37
ushers, 49
  clothes, 107, 108
  gifts, 135
  junior ushers, 50
  rehearsal, 240

V

vacations *see* honeymoon
valet parking, 198
vegan food, 142
vegetarian food, 142, 143
veils, 71
venues
  choosing, 36–7
  decorations, 168–71
  engagement parties, 216–17
  music restrictions, 186, 188
  rehearsal, 240
  saving money, 61–2
  selecting date and time, 35
Very Important People (VIPs), 50
  clothes, 110
  gifts, 135
vests, 92
videotapes, 178, 180–1
vows, 41, 241, 242

W

waistcoats, 92
walking down the aisle, 243
water, drinking, 85, 97
waxing, hair removal, 78, 96
wedding breakfasts, 61, 140
wedding day *see* ceremony; reception
wedding gowns, 67–73
wedding halls, 36, 44
"Wedding March," 185
wedding planners, 25–7
wedding registry, 39, 130–2
wedding rings, 19–21, 262
weight loss, 82–5, 100
wheat, fertility symbols, 254
white-pique shirts, 90
wine, 146, 148
wing collars, 90, 91
winter, seasonal decorations, 164–5

Acknowledgments

Author's acknowledgments
Writing a book is a group effort – even if there is only one author. I couldn't have finished the K.I.S.S. Guide to Planning a Wedding without the following people: my husband Richard Demler (whose proposal a decade ago made me a bride) and our son, L.C. Pedersen, both of whom provided moral support; Pearl Garcia Williams for watching over my family, my home, and me so I could write; my fabulous (and patient) DK team of Angela Wilkes, Kelly Meyer, Julie Oughton, Heather McCarry, Sarah Coltman, Jackie Douglas, Anja Schmidt, Sharon Lucas, and Chuck Lang; Kate Hayward, Aaron Brown, Sharon Rudd, Laura Watson, and the team at Studio Cactus for good cheer and their role in creating this gorgeous book; and to you, dear reader, for your interest.

Packager's acknowledgments
Studio Cactus would like to thank Sue Gordon for proofreading and editorial consultancy, Hilary Bird for the index, and Barry Robson for the dog illustrations.

Picture credits

t = top, b = bottom, c = center, r = right, l = left

Brand X Pictures: 2, 30, 37l, 43, 52, 54, 58, 66, 73, 91, 93, 94, 112b, 143, 149, 172, 177, 178, 179t, 179bl, 182, 192, 199, 200, 210, 246, 248, 256
Corbis: 6/7, 8/9, 12, 14, 17, 20, 28, 34, 40, 47, 48, 70, 86, 89, 90, 96, 102, 108, 110, 116, 138, 154, 158, 160, 162, 166, 168, 169, 179cr, 186, 194, 201, 226, 238, 241, 242, 243, 244t, 244b, 250, 251, 252, 253
Photodisc: 56, 72, 74, 75, 76, 77, 78, 79t, 79b, 82, 83, 84t, 84b, 95, 97t, 98, 99, 100t, 111, 134, 176, 180t, 202, 207t, 211, 212, 254b, 258, 261, 262, 270
Stockbyte: 104, 106, 147, 148, 185, 187, 206, 216, 218b, 236
Studio Cactus: 41

Images are used for illustrative purposes only and do not imply endorsement of any product or service.